Fundraising on eBay®

How to Raise Big Money on the World's Greatest Online Marketplace

Greg Holden

Jill Finlayson

McGraw-Hill/Osborne

New York   Chicago   San Francisco   Lisbon
London   Madrid   Mexico City   Milan   New Delhi
San Juan   Seoul   Singapore   Sydney   Toronto

McGraw-Hill books are available at special quantity discounts to use as premiums and sales promotions, or for use in corporate training programs. For more information, please write to the Director of Special Sales, Professional Publishing, McGraw-Hill, Two Penn Plaza, New York, NY 10121-2298. Or contact your local bookstore.

Fundraising on eBay®: How to Raise Big Money on the World's Greatest Online Marketplace

1234567890 FGR FGR 0198765

ISBN 0-07-226248-6

The sponsoring editor for this book was Marjorie McAneny and the project editor was Janet Walden. The copy editor was Lauren Kennedy, the proofreader was Pam Vevea, and the indexer was Claire Splan. Composition and illustration by International Typesetting & Composition. Cover design by Jeff Weeks.

This book was composed with Adobe® InDesign®

Library of Congress Cataloging-in-Publication Data

Holden, Greg.
  Fundraising on eBay: how to raise big money on the world's greatest online marketplace / by Greg Holden and Jill Finlayson.
      p. cm.
  ISBN 0-07-226248-6
  1. Fund raising. 2. Nonprofit organizations—Finance.
 3. Internet auctions. 4. eBay (Firm) I. Finlayson, Jill. II. Title.
  HV41.2.H62 2005
  658.15'224—dc22
                            2005022761

Contents

PART III   **Leveraging eBay for the Biggest Bang**

CHAPTER 10   **Making Your Charitable Auction a Major Event**   **229**

CHAPTER 11   **Partnerships: Good for Bidders, Good for Partners, Great for Nonprofits**   **269**

Foreword

When eBay emerged as a major new platform for trade in the late 1990s, it was an unexpected boon for many people—packrats were able to find buyers for their now unexpectedly valuable "attic treasures," local mom and pop shops could reach a worldwide audience, and even corporations could find happy buyers for out-of-date, slightly flawed, or overstocked inventories. Moreover, eBay became a social phenomenon—single parents could stay home with their kids while making a living, disabled folks could engage in a community where physical barriers were not a factor, and seniors could supplement their incomes and be respected for their knowledge and experience in a way that might not be possible in the traditional "offline" world.

Today, by any standard, eBay is one of the largest marketplaces in the world. Every day, people find new and creative ways to tap into the opportunities made available by eBay's ubiquitous, efficient, and open and honest trading platform. eBay was founded on the principle that "people are basically good" and that simple golden rule has been borne out transaction by transaction, person by person, millions and millions of times over.

Much as eBay has proven to be a source of new wealth for individuals and companies, eBay also offers tremendous new prospects for nonprofit and other fundraising organizations. With the social sector growing at a pace two to three times the rate of the for-profit sector in much of the world, eBay is uniquely well-suited to helping fundraising organizations find new sources of capital for their causes; initiatives that are often the cornerstones of healthy communities and peaceful societies.

Just as those "attic treasures" and obsolete inventories became unexpected cash-in-hand for individuals and companies, so too can such items turn into valuable new resources for nonprofits and their ilk. Where previously a social sector organization might not have been able to accept a donation of goods or, if accepted, be able to sell these items efficiently, eBay can turn such donations into real money. Furthermore, given that "people are basically good," eBay can also be an innovative platform to ignite contributions from those who might not have otherwise contributed at all. With roughly 75 percent of contributions to charity in the U.S. coming from individuals, the power to more effectively match people to the causes they care about *and* give them a mechanism to help cannot be underestimated!

In *Fundraising on eBay*, authors Jill Finlayson and Greg Holden explore the many ways for fundraising organizations to tap into the treasure trove offered to them via the marketplace and community that is eBay, and these authors are particularly qualified for the task. As an early employee of eBay, Jill brought her talents to bear on advising charitable organizations how they could raise money and connect with others to further their mission. Jill was also an early Governance Committee member of the eBay Foundation and gained an understanding of the concerns and obstacles that confront many fundraising organizations. Greg Holden is one of the world's foremost experts at both using and writing about eBay. His insightful views and clear prose offer the reader helpful and easy-to-understand hints that can be put into practice right away.

Whether your desire is to support a local community center, international relief agency, educational program, or religious institution, this book can help you quickly and effectively leverage the power of eBay to raise money, awareness, and support for your organization. Good luck with your worthy efforts.
(Oh, and it is a lot of fun too!)

Jeff Skoll
First President of eBay and the eBay Foundation
Founder and Chairman, The Skoll Foundation

Acknowledgments

To all the kind and helpful people I have met in the eBay community,
which has changed my life for the better.

Fundraising on eBay enabled me to continue working with a group of professionals I already know and admire, and yet introduced me to a new group as well. In the new category, there's my coauthor, Jill Finlayson, who inspired me with her "Energizer Bunny" enthusiasm, as well as her cohort at M Networks, Paul Berger. In the continuing category, there are Margie McAneny and Agatha Kim at McGraw-Hill, Lynn Haller and Neil Salkind at Studio B, and my own assistant Ann Lindner. I also thank the many eBay sellers and nonprofit representatives who helped in the production of this book, including Tony Cicalese, Thom Karmik, Lu Paletta, Debbie Pope, Patti Sklrda, Marjie Smith, Elana Viner, and David Yaskulka.

—Greg Holden

To my husband Marcos, children Zoë and Maxwell, and my parents for their support.
And to those who inspire me by actively making a difference through their championing
of and participation in nonprofit causes, especially Jeff Skoll, Pierre Omidyar,
Shira Levine, and Karin Stahl, who foster philanthropy at eBay and around
the world through their example and persistence.

Fundraising on eBay would not have been possible without the nonprofits and businesses who shared their eBay experiences and enthusiasm for this project. Their stories will help other nonprofits understand what is involved in undertaking a fundraising auction on eBay, and their tips and insights will save readers immeasurable time and energy. Thanks go to all those who helped, including Ron Antonette, Michael Appleman, Jenny Barnett, Clint Cantwell, Suzanne Coffman, Kristin Cunningham, Julian Ellison, Shayna Englin, Bonnie Frazier, Diana Fryer, Eric Gazin, David Greene, Joan Greene, Laura Iverson, Darren Julien, Jenny Kompolt, Kathleen Langheck, Greg Larson, Clam Lorenz, Scott Merrin, Jay Monahan, Jeff Nortman, Matthew Pye, Cindy Purvance, Tony Rodriguez, Tatiana Shulzycki, Mark Silver, Andy Trilling, Scott Wehrs, Steve Westly, and Irene Wong.

I would like to thank Margie McAneny, Agatha Kim, Janet Walden, and Kate Viotto from McGraw-Hill, and, of course, my coauthor Greg Holden, for their patience, guidance, flexibility, and tolerance as I tried to put everything plus the kitchen sink into this book before, during, and especially after, deadlines. Thanks also to Andrew Finlayson (author, news director, and my brother) who shared tips on working effectively with the news media; Merry Richter, who was a tremendous help particularly with the bonus online reference guide; and Steve Finkel PhD, a longtime friend whose literary contributions have on occasion gone unacknowledged. Finally I would like to thank Paul Berger and David Stern at M Networks for making this opportunity possible and encouraging me in this endeavor.

—*Jill Finlayson*

Introduction

Welcome to the promising new world of fundraising on eBay! Although eBay has been big news for several years now, the idea that individuals and nonprofit institutions can raise money by selling on eBay is still being discovered. Organizations around the world are learning that they can conduct special fundraising events by selling items on the world's most popular auction site, and that they can also improve their financial situation on an ongoing basis by selling on eBay whenever the need arises.

We believe the marketplace is crying out for a book on eBay selling that's geared specifically toward nonprofits. Besides the step-by-step instructions necessary to sell well on eBay, *Fundraising on eBay: How to Raise Big Money on the World's Greatest Online Marketplace* will show you how to make this fundraising effort fit and reflect your nonprofit's unique message and available resources. You'll learn how to integrate this project into your own busy life and those of your colleagues, and how to get your nonprofit leadership and volunteers on board. Equally important, you'll have the chance to leverage eBay fundraising in order to raise awareness for you cause and further your core mission.

This book goes beyond the eBay basics to show you how other nonprofits have used eBay and gives you the tools and ideas to make the most of your fundraising efforts. Each chapter builds upon the previous one so that, by the end, you'll be able to put on an event that fits your organization and goals. Whether you want to sell a handful of items or hold an annual event with a thousand or more separate sales on eBay, this book will provide the creative inspiration and cost-saving tips you need to help make your fundraising project a success.

What You'll Learn

Fundraising on eBay is an inspirational as well as an instructional volume. The inspiration comes in the form of case studies presented throughout the book. The instruction is broken into parts and chapters, and is designed to help you understand the complete process for holding an online auction. Step-by-step instructions walk you through the process of deciding to hold a fundraiser on eBay, choosing merchandise, holding auctions and fixed-price sales, and finalizing transactions. The pros and cons of doing it yourself versus hiring a company to help are discussed, as well as the steps you can take to get the most money and PR out of the event as possible.

Part I, "Mastering the eBay Marketplace: Opportunities for Nonprofits," gives you an overview of eBay's options for fundraisers, and describes different ways in which the proceeds from eBay sales can be designated to charitable causes. In Chapter 1, you'll get an introduction to eBay and its history of philanthropy and charitable fundraisers. In Chapter 2, you'll read inspiring stories about how other nonprofits have been using eBay—from large national charities like UNICEF to celebrities like designer Marc Ecko, and from niche causes like preservation of a national historic landmark to global issues such as providing relief from natural disasters. In Chapter 3, you begin to plan exactly how to hold your fundraising effort, whether it takes the form of a one-time event, conducting ongoing selling, holding an annual fundraising drive, or adding an online auction to "real world" events.

In Part II, "Selling Donated Items," you learn the nuts and bolts of selling on eBay. Listing an item on eBay is inexpensive, but the process of photographing, writing descriptions, and shipping the things you are selling takes time. To make sure you spend that time wisely, Chapter 4 covers what kind of items sell well on eBay so that you can solicit the right types of donations. You'll take a look at what is hot on eBay, and what types of items most households have sitting in closets that you can use to raise money. In Chapter 5, you learn about the different ways to organize your fundraiser, including registering and understanding eBay Giving Works. In Chapter 6, you delve into different options for building your credibility as a seller and for marketing your organization. Chapter 7 leads you step-by-step through the process of putting sales online. Although listing an item for sale on eBay only requires you to fill out a simple online form, there are tricks to listing an item well so that it will sell for a great price. You learn the importance of taking a good photograph and writing good auction titles and clear descriptions. Chapters 8 and 9 investigate ways to be a more effective eBay seller and, by extension, a better eBay fundraiser. You need to know how to get paid, ship the item, and leave feedback. We also give you some ideas of how to build great customer relations and how to keep in touch with those folks long after the auction is over.

In Part III, "Leveraging eBay for the Biggest Bang," you learn how to go from holding a small fundraiser to a larger event on eBay and get the biggest bang for your buck. Chapter 10 explains what needs to happen when you hold a major charity event. First, you learn ways to scale your event and how to coordinate with a real world event. You also investigate auction management tools that make it easier for you to list items for sale in bulk and to automate many aspects of the selling process. Second, if you are now selling very high-price items, or items that will draw a lot of public attention, such as items from high-profile celebrities, you need to take steps to make sure that the bidders and the bid amounts are legitimate. To prevent problems, we show you strategies to prequalify bidders or to verify bids as they come in.

In Chapter 11, you discover how to get companies involved in your event. Your event can help companies achieve their goals of publicity, aiding a good cause, launching new products, or driving traffic to their stores. We examine ways your fundraising efforts might tie in with corporation goals so that both organizations can gain from your nonprofit event. Understanding cause-related marketing is the biggest win-win for companies, nonprofits, and their beneficiaries.

Chapter 12 examines how to market your event. Your efforts will be most successful if you promote them to your constituency rather than relying solely on the eBay marketplace.

Local grassroots efforts, from flyers to local media (radio and newspapers), are very important. Because your sale is held online, however, you also have an opportunity to reach a wider Internet audience of targeted buyers. We show you how you can easily use tools like pay-per-click adwords to show up at the top of the results when someone searches the Internet for what you are selling.

Also included in the book is a glossary of common terms and phrases used in online auctions that will make it easier to understand some of the jargon sellers use on eBay. And as a bonus, we have compiled an online reference guide at both **www.masteringfundraising.com** and **http://books.mcgraw-hill.com/getbook.php?isbn=0072262486** with some sample documents to help you run your fundraising event.

How This Book Works

To keep things fun and help important bits of information catch your attention, we've developed some special elements that will help you get the most out of this book:

- **What We'll Cover in This Chapter**   A list of tasks and topics discussed in this chapter
- **Must Have**   Key take-aways or nuggets of information to remember—even if you forget everything else
- **Warning**   Errors and pitfalls to avoid
- **Moneymaker**   Proven money making ideas or strategies
- **Tip**   Alternative ways of doing things and helpful resources
- **Success**   Tips and case studies of successful nonprofit fundraisers

eBay's site is changing all the time, so don't be surprised if a web page or service doesn't look exactly the same as it does in the book. Often that just means they have added new features or functionality since this book was published, which is usually a good thing. If a web page isn't where the book says it should be, try entering only the site name (such as **www.ebay.com**) or if that doesn't work, try searching for the topic on Google or some other search engine and you will likely find what you are looking for.

Off and Running

We hope you enjoy this book and that it expands your ideas about what fundraising can be. One of the best things about nonprofits is the passion that the organizers and volunteers bring to the table. We believe that fueling that passion with new ideas and new skills will benefit everyone in the long run. If you have other creative ways of using eBay to raise funds, we would love to hear from you. Email fundraisingonebay@gmail.com to share your eBay fundraising experiences and best practices.

Part I

Mastering the eBay Marketplace: Opportunities for Nonprofits

Chapter 1
Why eBay? A Guide for Nonprofits

Since 2000, more than $45 million has been raised for nonprofit organizations from listings sold on eBay.

—Kristin Cunningham, eBay

What We'll Cover in This Chapter:

- Understanding why eBay is a great place for nonprofits

- Following a typical eBay transaction

- Assessing the goals of your fundraising effort

- Joining eBay's giving community

eBay offers nonprofits of all sizes an innovative and efficient way to reach a huge audience and bring needed funds and support to their cause. Whether you represent a city, museum, library, school, church, scout troop, sports team, or other nonprofit organization, eBay can help you raise money to achieve your fundraising mission. How do we know? Many nonprofits are already using eBay. You may have seen the high-profile charity auctions celebrities like Ellen DeGeneres, Oprah Winfrey, and Jay Leno hold. From the Giving Works page on eBay (**http://pages.ebay.com/givingworks/ index.html**, shown in Figure 1-1) you can check out the ongoing auctions by large nonprofits such as the American Red Cross, UNICEF, and the Points of Light Foundation. What you may have missed are the innovative auctions benefiting small nonprofits such as Ratbone Rescues (which helps find homes for abandoned Rat Terriers), St. Mary's School (a Catholic parish school), Atkinson, Nebraska (a small, rural town of 1,200 people), and a myriad of other small nonprofit organizations. All these organizations have found eBay a great way to raise the funds they need.

This chapter addresses three questions you likely have on your mind:

- Why fundraise online?

- Why use eBay?

- Why are nonprofits turning to eBay?

And the logical next question—How can your nonprofit fundraise on eBay?—will be answered by this book. Not only will the answers we provide inspire you, but they will also give you the information you need to be able to convince others in your organization to give it a try. It can be challenging to introduce new ways to fundraise, but if you have some good answers it will be easier for you to evangelize or sell the idea to those in your organization who may be less familiar with eBay than you.

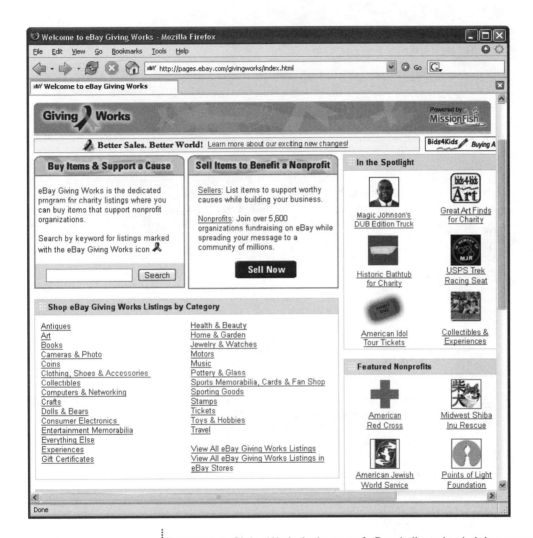

FIGURE 1-1 Giving Works is the part of eBay dedicated to helping nonprofit institutions raise funds.

Why Online Fundraising?

Online giving is the next big thing for nonprofits. Internet donations totaled more than $123 million in 2002, triple the donations from the year before, and this trend continues exponentially as the adoption of the Internet and

The Growth of Online Giving

In the last presidential campaign, "Small contributions nearly tripled between 2000 and 2004, from $46 million to $123 million. This $77 million increase in small contributions accounts for 33 percent of the total increase in money between 2000 and 2004. Another way of putting this is that the Internet may well have been almost as important this year as the increased contribution limit."

—National Campaign Finance Institute, May 25, 2004

"The growing amount of money collected through the Internet has forced many nonprofit leaders to reevaluate their attitude toward online fundraising and its importance to their organizations," says Madeline Stanionis, a fundraising consultant in San Francisco. "People are sitting up and paying attention," she says. "Organizations, especially large organizations, are now putting online fundraising revenue into their budget. Before it was such a small percentage it was gravy, and now it's a line item."

—*The Chronicle of Philanthropy,* June 10, 2004

broadband/high-speed access grows and peoples' comfort level with online transactions increases. According to *The Chronicle of Philanthropy*'s 2004 annual survey of online fundraising, "Online giving to the country's largest charities surged in 2003, as many groups posted double- and triple-digit percentage gains," and smaller organizations are achieving similar increases through online donation processing sites such as Groundspring.org (which saw 167 percent increase in donations Q1 2004 over Q1 2003), Networkforgood. org (whose number of donors doubled to 80,000 in 2003 from 40,000 in 2002), and Justgive.org (which handled $6.4 million in donations in 2003 up from $893,000 the previous year).

Why eBay?

Fundraising events work best when the merchandise being offered appeals to all sections of society. When you're looking to appeal to all of society, eBay is the place to be. eBay works because it's a marketplace that appeals to everyone. When Pierre Omidyar launched the site as AuctionWeb in 1995, it quickly gained acceptance because it gave people around the world a central location to purchase and sell items. By using the Internet, sellers get a worldwide audience for their merchandise. That applies whether sellers are hoping to make a few extra dollars, whether they are running a part- or full-time business on eBay, or whether they are raising funds for a cause.

Today, eBay has become part of the current social fabric; for example, it's featured on David Letterman's Top Ten lists, and woven into *King of the Hill* and many other TV show story lines. By offering items for sale on eBay, you can raise substantially more than if you offer the same items up for auction to those who attend your live event in a school gymnasium or other location. eBay has the potential to turn local, personal causes into global events.

The Size and Scope of the eBay Marketplace

When you solicit donations and recruit volunteers, it pays to know a few things about the power of adding eBay to your fundraising mix. Passing along some facts about the size of the auction marketplace can help build interest and enthusiasm for your event. The eBay marketplace involves $34 billion dollars in annual transactions and more than 135 million users worldwide. To break that down into numbers that are easier to grasp, you are looking at a marketplace where, on average, more than 16,000 power tools sell each week, 258 cash registers sell every day, 43 Coach handbags sell each hour, 1 sports utility vehicle (SUV) sells every 7 minutes, 1 high-definition TV sells every 5 minutes, 1 pair of basketball sneakers sells every 2 minutes, 1 kitchen small appliance sells every minute, and 1 cell phone sells every 20 seconds. It can be hard to comprehend that a car a minute sells on eBay and that more cars are sold on eBay before 9 A.M. than an average dealership sells in a year. But it's true.

What you may be less aware of is that more than 500 charitable organizations have already sold items on eBay and, according to Kristin Cunningham, who runs eBay's Giving Works, "Since 2000, more than $45 million has been raised for nonprofit organizations from listings sold on eBay." Not only are nonprofits selling on eBay themselves, but also eBay in partnership with MissionFish allows anyone to sell and select a nonprofit to receive part or all of the proceeds from the sale of the item(s). In February 2005, eBay added icing to the cake by deciding to donate the eBay selling fees to charity when a seller donates 100 percent of an item's final sale price to a certified nonprofit.

Why Being a Nonprofit Matters

You might ask yourself: Why not have people sell things by themselves and then just donate the cash amount of the proceeds to your charity? There are several reasons. First, if they're like us, they have tons of things that have been sitting in their closets for years but there never seems to be the time to pull them out and either donate or sell them. Having a fundraising event may be just the impetus they need to drag the stuff out. Second, if they do sell the items themselves, they may decide to keep part or all of

eBay Sets a New Standard for Corporate Giving

Before the company even went public, eBay trail blazed a new standard in corporate philanthropy by donating company stock before going public to create a foundation to give back to the community. The foundation was created to extend eBay's goal of empowering people to improve their lives and communities. It was also designed from the beginning to foster employee involvement in philanthropic efforts and, indeed, the first eBay Foundation governance committees were staffed by employees. Today, the Foundation also has matching grant programs that foster employee donations and, more important, foster active volunteer participation in nonprofit efforts grants. Its Champion a Charity program enables eBay employees to recommend nonprofit organizations for Foundation funding.

The eBay Foundation has contributed more than $8 million to nonprofit organizations. The types of organizations the Foundation supports have ranged over the years as the Foundation refines its focus. Overall the focus is on funding organizations that give people the tools or knowledge they needed to make a difference in their communities. Early grant recipients were in the areas of Kids (education, mentoring, esteem), Adults (education, job retraining, volunteerism), and Community (economic revitalization, community improvement). The first grant was given to Friends of Farm Drive, a nonprofit organization dedicated to improving the quality of life for the residents of a San Jose, California, neighborhood facing drug dealing and gang activity issues. The grant helped them establish a summer program targeting "high-risk" youth, ages 14 through 20, and a computer learning center where volunteers offered technical instruction to adults and youth.

Today the eBay Foundation focuses on funding innovative programs primarily in microenterprise development. Examples include Lenders for Community Development, which provides microloan, training, and savings programs for low-income entrepreneurs; One Economy, which supports entrepreneurs looking to start new businesses or grow an existing one; and the Grameen Foundation, which eBay recognized for best practices in microcredit. The eBay Foundation no longer accepts unsolicited funding requests, but rather seeks out nonprofit partners where the Foundation's support can make a significant difference.

eBay Foundation
60 South Market Street, Suite 1000
San Jose, CA 95113-2336
tel 408.278.2200
fax 408.278.0280
http://ebay.com/foundation

Beyond the employee programs and foundation grants, however, the eBay Foundation has special grant-making initiatives that give eBay users the opportunity to suggest nonprofits important to them for Foundation funding. For example, in December 2003, eBay community members were invited to recommend a nonprofit serving homeless families and children for a Foundation grant as part of a Holiday Grant Program. So watch for future initiatives on the eBay Foundation web site (**www.ebay.com/foundation**).

the proceeds. It can be hard to part with cash once it's in your hands. And third, charity auctions often raise more money than "regular" auctions because buyers are willing to pay a bit more for an item if they know it's for a good cause.

eBay's Giving Works partner, MissionFish, conducted an informal study that found what you'd probably intuitively guess: charity items receive, on average, more bids and higher final selling prices than comparable items that are not for charity. Cunningham points out that, "Sellers who donate all or a portion of their sales proceeds to a nonprofit are experiencing, on average, 40 percent higher sales prices and 50 percent higher sell-through rates."And to top it all off, eBay promotes nonprofit auctions listed through MissionFish with a special page on eBay and a charity icon so people can find those items more easily. So let's get out there and start shaking the proverbial trees to make money for your cause.

How Does eBay Work?

If you or your board members have never bought or sold on eBay before, you'll need to understand, and be able to explain, how eBay works. eBay is the world's largest virtual marketplace. In some ways it's like a giant online garage sale. But at this garage sale, people can shop from home and buy new items as well as used things. And the sellers, including individuals, companies, and retailers, can be located anywhere in the world. eBay, once seen only as an online auction site where you had to bid for everything, now allows buyers to purchase items at a fixed price. eBay makes its money by receiving a commission on all sales transactions. This includes a small listing fee when you list the item for sale, optional upgrade and online payment fees, and a final value fee—a small percentage of the final selling price, which you are charged only if the item sells. Generally, these add up to 5–10 percent of the final selling price.

Let's walk through a typical transaction. Jane Seller lists an Excellent Item for sale on eBay from her computer in her home. Joe Buyer searches eBay from the comfort of his lovely home computer (or office computer if no one is looking), and finds the Excellent Item using eBay's keyword search or by browsing categories of items for sale. Upon finding the Excellent Item, Joe Buyer places a bid on the item (or buys the item outright if it's listed with a fixed price). When the listing closes and Joe Buyer is the winning bidder, he sends the payment to Jane Seller. Jane receives the payment and ships the item to Joe. Joe and Jane leave feedback for each other telling other future buyers how the transaction went. Bam! That's it in a nutshell. But it is a very powerful concept because it connects buyers and sellers and provides a marketplace where small and large sellers can compete for buyers on an even playing field. The seller with the best price, product, and service will prevail.

Why Is eBay Good for Nonprofits?

What makes eBay particularly useful for nonprofits? Beyond the general size of the marketplace, one of the main reasons eBay is such a fantastic tool for nonprofits specifically is that an event on eBay can accomplish more than simply raising dollars. A fundraiser on eBay can, and in fact should, achieve several goals with a single fundraising event.

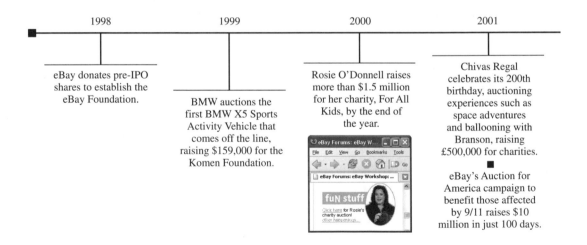

1998	1999	2000	2001
eBay donates pre-IPO shares to establish the eBay Foundation.	BMW auctions the first BMW X5 Sports Activity Vehicle that comes off the line, raising $159,000 for the Komen Foundation.	Rosie O'Donnell raises more than $1.5 million for her charity, For All Kids, by the end of the year.	Chivas Regal celebrates its 200th birthday, auctioning experiences such as space adventures and ballooning with Branson, raising £500,000 for charities.

eBay's Auction for America campaign to benefit those affected by 9/11 raises $10 million in just 100 days.

Highlights of Philanthropy on eBay

The power of the Internet enables individuals and businesses to reach a wide audience and accomplish many goals with a single web site, a communications effort, or a fundraiser. It's a good idea to draw up all of your organization's goals before you start selling. You might find that the way you describe your items and communicate with high bidders can affect more than your bottom line. It can improve your public image as well. The following sections look at some of the goals an eBay fundraising program can achieve.

Raise Funds

Whether it's an urgent one-time capital project or an ongoing need for operating expenses, raising funds is one of the biggest issues for many nonprofits. So why add eBay to your traditional fundraising efforts? The eBay community is caring and has a long history of philanthropy. It's also a powerful and concentrated group of buyers. Selling on eBay allows you to leverage the Internet, in-kind donations, and low start-up costs to go where the people are and where the money is. With the total value of goods and services traded on eBay worldwide reaching more than $34.2 billion in 2004—that's more than $1,085 changing hands per second on eBay—there is no question that nonprofits should get a piece of this action too!

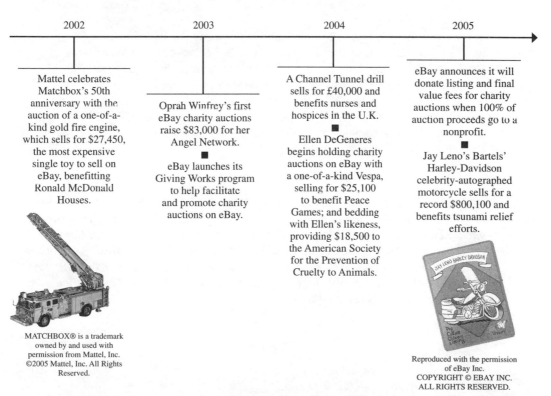

2002 — Mattel celebrates Matchbox's 50th anniversary with the auction of a one-of-a-kind gold fire engine, which sells for $27,450, the most expensive single toy to sell on eBay, benefitting Ronald McDonald Houses.

2003 — Oprah Winfrey's first eBay charity auctions raise $83,000 for her Angel Network.

▪ eBay launches its Giving Works program to help facilitate and promote charity auctions on eBay.

2004 — A Channel Tunnel drill sells for £40,000 and benefits nurses and hospices in the U.K.

▪ Ellen DeGeneres begins holding charity auctions on eBay with a one-of-a-kind Vespa, selling for $25,100 to benefit Peace Games; and bedding with Ellen's likeness, providing $18,500 to the American Society for the Prevention of Cruelty to Animals.

2005 — eBay announces it will donate listing and final value fees for charity auctions when 100% of auction proceeds go to a nonprofit.

▪ Jay Leno's Bartels' Harley-Davidson celebrity-autographed motorcycle sells for a record $800,100 and benefits tsunami relief efforts.

MATCHBOX® is a trademark owned by and used with permission from Mattel, Inc. ©2005 Mattel, Inc. All Rights Reserved.

Reproduced with the permission of eBay Inc. COPYRIGHT © EBAY INC. ALL RIGHTS RESERVED.

eBay Sparks a New Fundraising Craze

People quickly found that they could auction items off and donate the proceeds to charity. Some of the earliest big charity auctions include Bids Help Kids by Entertainment Industry Foundation (EIF), which auctioned off Hollywood memorabilia to benefit a variety of children's charities; the first BMW X5 Sports Activity Vehicle off the factory line, which brought in $159,000 for the Susan G. Komen Breast Cancer Foundation; the Millennium Dress charity auction for ovarian cancer; and the New Langton Arts charity auction for emerging artists. In July 2000, eBay UK hosted an auction of handbags owned by personalities, including Jerry Hall and Margaret Thatcher, whose handbag fetched the enormous sum of £100K, for the charity Breast Cancer Care. eBay promoted these auctions by featuring them on the home page or category pages.

When September 11, 2001 occurred, CEO Meg Whitman took the unprecedented step of mobilizing the company and the community to raise donations for those impacted by the tragic event. Auction for America was born and gave the community an outlet for its grief and a venue to demonstrate its compassion and resolve. It required radical changes to the site and the efforts of many employees to make it happen and happen fast. Within weeks of the disaster, sellers could sell items and have part or all of the proceeds go directly to the charity of their choice, including the American Red Cross and eventually many others. eBay solicited and promoted donations from corporations and celebrities. By the end of the event, eBay had facilitated an outpouring of giving by more than 100,000 people totaling $10 million in just 100 days.

When the tsunami hit in December 2004, eBay once again responded by going beyond providing a simple connection to donors for charities. The company provided a giving page aiding buyers wishing to donate or help out where the proceeds from the items they bought would go to charity. This effort was mirrored at eBay's localized sites around the globe, including eBay Germany, which launched a joint effort with *Deutsche Post* to collect items to be sold on eBay for the relief effort, and eBay.in, eBay's site in India, which committed one month of generated fees to the relief efforts. PayPal, eBay's online payment

note *According the eBay Fact Sheet (12/31/2004), twelve of eBay's categories each generate $1 billion or more in worldwide annualized GMV (gross merchandise value): eBay Motors ($11.1 billion); Consumer Electronics ($3.5 billion); Computers ($3.0 billion); Clothing & Accessories ($2.9 billion); Books/Movies/Music ($2.4 billion); Collectibles ($2.2 billion); Home & Garden ($2.0 billion); Sports ($1.8 billion); Toys ($1.8 billion); Jewelry & Watches ($1.7 billion); Cameras & Photo ($1.3 billion); and Business & Industrial ($1.2 billion).*

solution, reported that PayPal users donated more than $775,000 to UNICEF through a link on its site.

eBay has gone on to support and provide a marketplace for charity auctions from the very small to the very large. From 2001, when eBayers had the opportunity to meet Jack of Jack in the Box restaurant fame at a benefit event for Big Brothers Big Sisters of America and the chance to bid on celebrity donated "little black dresses" in Avon's Little Black Dress Against Breast Cancer to 2004, when Jay Leno, Oprah Winfrey, and Ellen DeGeneres held charity auctions, eBay has played host to a variety of unique charity fundraisers.

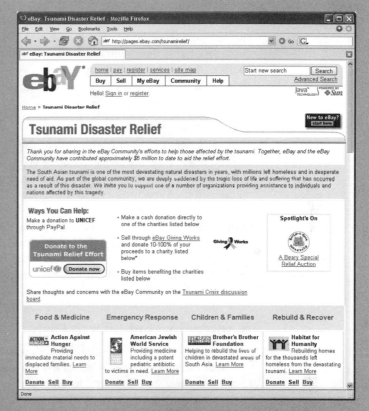

We'll profile a range of nonprofit fundraisers in this book, but take a look at the "Highlights of Philanthropy on eBay" timeline on the previous page spread to see more of the milestone charity efforts that have occurred on eBay.

Increase Awareness

With all those millions of eyes cruising eBay, it should come as no surprise that selling on eBay can be a great way to increase awareness for your cause or mission. You might regard each listing as a poster that lets people know who you are and why you are raising money. On your own page on eBay, you can describe your organization, its goals and accomplishments, link to your web site, and even share best practices so others learn and benefit from your programs. Not only that, if your organization has T-shirts, hats, or other merchandise with your name and logo on them, eBay can be a great place to sell those items as well. The result: You have walking billboards in towns across the country. You can even put your nonprofit's brochure or bumper sticker in the shipping box with your sold auction items so that your buyers can learn about you and spread the word about your cause.

Find New Donors

The more you sell and the more interesting your items are, the more people will find you on eBay and learn about your cause. Every time someone buys an item from you, you have the chance to invite the buyer to join your mailing list and become a future donor. In addition to selling items on eBay, you can also directly "sell" donations. By offering a $50 donation at a fixed price, people can simply buy a donation and pay online instantly. Or you can be more creative and sell what the donation will provide. For example a nonprofit might give bidders the opportunity to buy "school supplies for 50 needy children" for $35. It's another great way to spread the word about what you do and find new donors.

Convert In-kind Gifts to Cash

Any gift or donated item is appreciated, but when you really need cold, hard cash, eBay is the answer. Whether a Cal alumnus bequeaths a large boat to her alma mater, UC Berkeley, in her will or a person in your community walks into your local charity's office to donate used clothes and toys, only some (not all) of these items may be useful to the nonprofit's mission. Some items may even cost nonprofit organizations money to maintain or store. eBay allows you to put these items to good use by converting them to cash. It also helps you provide a receipt for the actual value of the donation. Besides, eBay is perhaps the fastest way to sell these unneeded items so you can start putting dollars toward the things you really need because many items sell at auction in just seven days once you list them on eBay.

Achieve Market Value for Donations

If you auction off items at a black tie ball or other special event, the numbers of bidders and interested buyers is directly limited by the number of people attending the event. By opening your bidding up to a larger community, you're more likely to achieve market prices or better for your goods.

On eBay, only two people need to want an item for bidding to be driven up, and finding the only two people in the world who want that item can happen on eBay. For example, an old wooden San Francisco hotel coat hanger sold for more than $75 because there was a San Francisco collector bidding against a hotel memorabilia collector. For rare or hard to find items, collectors recognize the value of these items and are willing to bid the amount they know is appropriate whereas local buyers may bid less, not knowing the item's true market value. And, remember, just because those squat lamps look ugly to you, it doesn't mean they wouldn't be the perfect kitsch finishing touch to a retro apartment in New York City. The old adage "one person's trash is another person's treasure" is borne out time and time again on eBay.

Generate Positive PR

When Chicago wanted to raise money for an art museum, the city took the opportunity to not only raise money but also to showcase Chicago and what a great city it is. From shining a spotlight on local celebrities to touting the unique restaurants and city events, the items the city sold on eBay became a living advertisement for why you should visit Chicago. Even decommissioned city parking meters and manhole covers painted by local artists became unmatched Chicago memorabilia for devotees of the Windy City, including those Chicagoans who had moved away from their beloved city.

Similarly, eBay offers you the chance to show off what is unique in your organization and to demonstrate what your members can accomplish. You may find you are be able to show off the work of individuals your nonprofit helps, such as by selling donated artwork if you're a modern art museum, or kids' artwork if your programs mentor children. An eBay fundraiser is also a great reason to send out press releases showing the world how members of your organization came together to make the auction possible and how the money raised will be used to make a difference in people's lives. An online auction is also the perfect opportunity to announce a new service or facility, or to publicize a report on your organization's accomplishments.

Involve the Whole Community

Some people cannot afford to part with cash, but everyone has items in their closets that they haven't touched in many years. A 2004 ACNielsen study on unused household items showed that most households have a thousand dollars worth of items that they could part with—from handbags and power tools, to used cell phones and video games they no longer use. Even those who feel they have nothing to donate can participate by helping collect, list, or ship the items. (Children and teenagers are a great, often computer savvy, resource and they may find themselves working side by side with retired senior citizens.) In this way, you're not just asking those who are relatively well off for money but rather allowing everyone to share in the accomplishment.

Educate the Community and Provide Job Skills

Have you ever dreamed of starting your own business? Are there small businesses in your town that have been meaning to start selling online? Did you know some high schools offer entrepreneurship classes for their students? And did you know that as many as 430,000 folks in America make a full time or part-time living selling on eBay? By teaching volunteers how to use eBay, you may be opening up a new career door for them. With selling online job skills, people can start their own companies or supplement

eBay's Giving Community

More than being a collection of buyers, eBay is a community of givers. Both the eBay company and community have a long history of philanthropy. From the creation of the eBay Foundation to the ongoing promotion of charity auctions, eBay has showcased and encouraged philanthropic efforts.

Consider the origins of eBay itself. At its core, the company is about empowering people. When he started eBay, Pierre Omidyar envisioned a marketplace that would leverage the Internet to connect people with common interests and allow individuals to run their own businesses and compete on an even playing field against other businesses regardless of their size. It did more than that. From the early days, eBay enabled a variety of people to create their own jobs, flex around child-care demands, stop receiving welfare and disability assistance, and start making their own living selling on eBay.

One of the reasons for eBay's success is its trust in the community and its belief that people are basically good. The strength and compassion of the community was demonstrated from the start. Did you know that the first customer support representatives were hired from people in the community who were already on the chat boards helping others use the site out of the goodness of their hearts? This personality typified what would become known as being *eBaysian*. The term suggests both a sense of fair play, equality, and community spirit.

Another example of this spirit is one of the earliest chat boards that sprang up on eBay, the Giving Board:

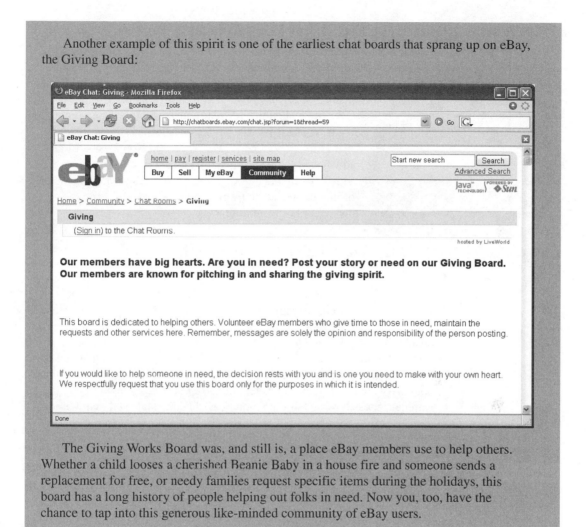

The Giving Works Board was, and still is, a place eBay members use to help others. Whether a child looses a cherished Beanie Baby in a house fire and someone sends a replacement for free, or needy families request specific items during the holidays, this board has a long history of people helping out folks in need. Now you, too, have the chance to tap into this generous like-minded community of eBay users.

their income through online selling. This can have a lasting economic impact on both the individuals and their communities, especially in small rural towns or economically challenged areas where job opportunities may be limited. In some small towns, it could be the difference between people staying in their hometowns and people having to leave to find better jobs or bigger locations for their businesses.

Leverage the Global Marketplace

Another reality and challenge those in fundraising face is asking the same people over and over for donations. By selling online, you invite people outside your community or donor base to send dollars to your town or organization. If you think about bake sales or local offline auctions, it's really just the same money changing hands, whereas having buyers from around the world truly brings in "new money." For Atkinson, Nebraska, a rural town of just 1,200 people, this meant bringing in more than $12,000—in a matter of a few short weeks—and the majority of that money came from people who live far from the townspeople's front doorsteps.

Liquidate Old Equipment, Clear Unneeded Inventory

Does your organization have furniture or equipment it no longer wants because they've been replaced by newer items or are no longer needed? Do you have logo merchandise that's gathering dust? What do you need to get rid of? One small town needed to sell a fire truck! The state of California found a warehouse full of boxes that had been untouched for years; Governor Arnold Schwarzenegger realized that not only were these items unneeded, but also that simply maintaining the warehouse was costing the state money. He had the state sell many of the items on eBay, then got rid of the warehouse, too. As you can see, such "found money" is also a great way to get rid of clutter, free up space in crowded offices, and discover a potential source of cost savings.

Further Your Mission

Why not use this fundraising effort to further your organizations primary objectives? If you're a town, why not work with the Main Street retailers to promote their stores and drive foot traffic to their businesses by making their stores drop off points for donations? Or perhaps you could showcase a few of the high-end items from your auction in their stores? How about promoting their stores by having them donate and auction off some of the exciting new items they carry? If you're a museum, why not auction off a year membership or private tour? This way you gain new members and promote visiting the museum.

Have Fun and Be Creative

Books and written instructions can't convey the experience of selling something on eBay. The fact is, selling on eBay can be a lot of fun. There is nothing like watching the price zoom up in the final seconds of an auction or receiving questions from a collector across the globe. There is the unexpected surprise when something that you couldn't make someone buy for $0.50 at a flea market soars past $50.00 dollars on eBay. But perhaps the most fun can come from being creative and coming up with surprising and amusing things to sell. Why just auction off antiques when you can auction off the chance to lead the town parade, cut the ribbon at the opening ceremony for a new library, turn on the holiday tree lights, take a tour of the museum with the curator, go on a special backstage tour at a theater, or hold a birthday party at a zoo? An auction on eBay is still a local event, albeit on a global platform, so part of the fun is coming up with local experiences and items that will get your community buzzing and bidding.

What Are Your Goals?

Here's a handy recap of the previous sections. Check all that apply:

- ❏ Raise funds

- ❏ Increase awareness

- ❏ Find new donors

- ❏ Convert in-kind gifts to cash

- ❏ Achieve market value for donations

- ❏ Generate positive PR

- ❏ Involve whole community

- ❏ Educate community and provide job skills

- ❏ Bring in cash from outside your donor base

- ❏ Clearance of unused equipment or inventory

- ❏ Further your nonprofit mission

- ❏ Have fun and be creative

must have

This chapter has introduced you to the eBay community and its philanthropic origins. In the next chapter, we will take a closer look at the ways nonprofits have been using eBay. Case studies are often the easiest way to understand what is possible. After that, we'll show you how your nonprofit can get started. But for now, the key things to remember are

- eBay has a history of giving, and the community is generous and empathetic.

- Nonprofits should tap into the eBay marketplace because it is so very large, and both online giving and buying are increasing exponentially each year.

- Charity auctions bring in as much as 40 percent more, on average, than comparable noncharity items.

- Using eBay for fundraising allows nonprofits to achieve multiple goals. Rather than only raising dollars, nonprofits may, at the same time, be able to increase awareness for their cause, find new donors, and more.

- eBay allows nonprofits to tap a global marketplace and bring in dollars from outside their membership or community.

Chapter 2
eBay Fundraising Success Stories

We have absolutely developed relationships with new donors through our eBay auctions.

—Andy Trilling, Starlight
Starbright Children's Foundation

What We'll Cover in This Chapter:

- Encouraging donations from eBay sellers

- Improving public awareness by holding a one-time event

- Raising funds by having members do the selling

- Scheduling regular fundraising events for your organization

- Pulling together a one-of-a-kind celebrity auction event

Everyone learns by example. Nonprofit organizations can learn from success stories just as much as entrepreneurs who are hoping to create their own successful online businesses can. Think about it: How did you determine your current fundraising strategies? Chances are you got on the phone and consulted with other nonprofits, or you heard about successful live auctions, casino nights, or dinner dances other groups held, and then decided to conduct your own similar events.

eBay is a well-developed marketplace that has now been around for more than a decade. Its organization is robust enough that there's no single way to use it. You can pick the approach that's best for your resources and your goals. In this chapter we describe how a number of nonprofit groups have used eBay. Along with detailing issues and strategies that apply to many different organizations, we provide examples of the types of nonprofits that have used eBay successfully for their giving campaigns. Hopefully, you'll find an example that matches your own situation and that you can use to design your own eBay fundraising effort.

note *The number of nonprofit organizations that hold annual or semiannual fundraisers on eBay is too long to mention. You can read some of their stories in the Success Stories area of the Giving Works site (**http://givingworks.ebay.com/success**) and in the Case Studies area on the MissionFish site (**www.missionfish.org/ForNonProfits/fornonprofits .jsp**). And although this chapter focuses solely on success stories, you'll also find success stories throughout succeeding chapters that illustrate how best to handle specific tasks related to selling on eBay.*

Soliciting Donations from the Community: The National Multiple Sclerosis Society

Setting up a fundraising event is a potentially time-consuming and complex undertaking. Wouldn't it be nice if you were simply able to tell donors what you do and what you need and put out a call for donations? Wouldn't it be great if individuals took it upon themselves to answer your call and simply donate to you, at any time of the year?

This scenario might sound too good to be true. But it's a reality for the National Multiple Sclerosis Society. When we spoke to the society's director of special events in Chicago, Debbie Pope, she had just received an e-mail message from eBay the day before.

"We got a message saying that someone had completed a sale of some coins on eBay and that some of the proceeds had been donated to us," she said excitedly. As it turned out, an eBay member who participated in the National MS Society's annual fundraising walk along the Chicago lakefront had put several items up for sale on the auction site, including the jewelry shown in Figure 2-1.

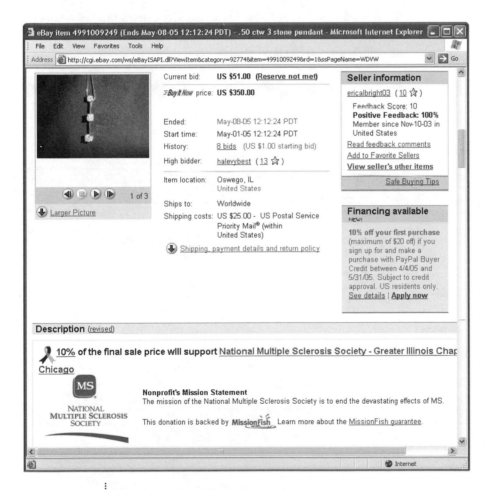

FIGURE 2-1 The National MS Society is always happily surprised to receive a donation like this from sellers.

Since the National MS Society had been consumed with planning for its annual walk, the eBay donations came as an unexpected bonus. It's the kind of fundraising a nonprofit with limited resources can conduct all year around, with very little overhead and virtually no staff time required. To enable the National MS Society to receive donations through eBay, the society only had to follow a few simple steps:

1. It registered with eBay's charitable arm, MissionFish (a process we describe in Chapter 5). This added their organization to MissionFish's directory of certified nonprofit organizations that can receive donations from eBay sales.

2. It contributed its organization's logo and wrote a brief description. MissionFish included both on a page it created for the National MS Society (see Figure 2-2).

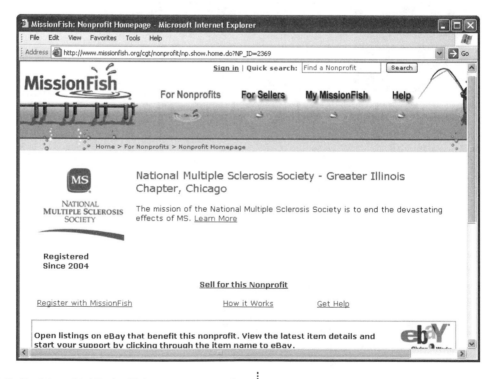

FIGURE 2-2 Register with MissionFish so you can receive donations from eBay sellers.

3. It created a page soliciting donations to eBay that appears on the web sites of each of the state chapters of the Society; the Maryland chapter's page (**www.nationalmssociety.org/MDM/donation/campaign.asp?d=1523**) is shown in Figure 2-3. (The page refers to Giving Works, the name of the system used to create sales listings and make donations through MissionFish.)

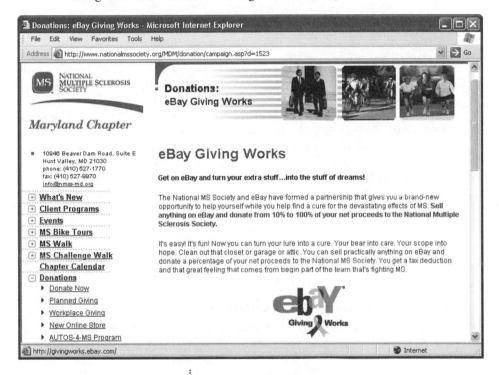

FIGURE 2-3 You can solicit donations from your organization's own web site as well as on eBay.

note *You don't need to register with MissionFish in order to receive donations from sellers on eBay. If you aren't included in the MissionFish directory, sellers can still donate to you, as long as you send them a letter of permission that's displayed along with the auction description. But signing up with MissionFish makes you an "official" nonprofit on the site—and besides, registration is free.*

The Chicago branch of the National MS Society sees eBay as one of the new technology tools the organization can use to help increase donations to traditional fundraising events. But perhaps the biggest benefit is that eBay gives sellers the power to choose the amount they want to donate and pick the most convenient times for their donations. Since anything that sells on eBay is often a surprise, the percent that's earmarked as a donation seems like not much of a sacrifice. It's a convenient and painless alternative for people who may be experiencing donation "burnout." "It's much easier to give people the ability to make a contribution themselves than having someone ask them for money," says Pope.

$$$ moneymaker

Whenever someone donates a percentage of an eBay sale to the Chicago branch of the National Multiple Sclerosis Society, Debbie Pope calls or e-mails the individual to thank them for his or her efforts. In the course of the conversation, she finds out what prompted the donation. It may be that the person heard about the MS walk or another fundraising project. Such information can help the organization encourage the same kind of generosity on the part of other sellers. At the next MS walk, for instance, the organization might post signs encouraging participants to sell on eBay as a way of boosting the amount they're able to donate.

One-Time Event Equals Big Publicity: Illinois Institute of Technology

Thom Karmik already knows a thing or two about selling on eBay. "I collect baseball memorabilia," he explains. "I have bought and sold things on eBay for six or seven years now. It's a great place to sell anything."

When Karmik, executive director of marketing and communications at the Illinois Institute of Technology (IIT), ran into a dilemma in the workplace, he decided to extend eBay's reach and help out his employer. The university was looking to increase the positive attention it gets in the news media. The campus, which is located just south of downtown Chicago, has several unique architectural features. Anything that will make the public aware of its architectural heritage will put it before the eyes of prospective students and alumni donors.

ILLINOIS INSTITUTE
OF TECHNOLOGY
Transforming Lives. Inventing the Future.

Main Building, Suite 503
3300 S. Federal Street
Chicago, IL 60616

312.567.5057
Cell 773.552.1712

Thom Karmik
Director
Communications & Marketing

karmik@iit.edu

Crown Hall, a building on the IIT campus that was designed by the famed twentieth-century architect Mies van der Rohe, has been designated a National Historic Landmark. When the university scheduled a major restoration to coincide with the building's 50th anniversary, it decided to generate some publicity. It planned to attract some major celebrities to a "Smash Bash" where the highest bidder would break one of the building's plate glass windows.

"Crown Hall is well-known in the architectural world; we don't have to do a lot to promote it among architects," explains Karmik. "The challenge was to generate some mass appeal and tell the public what Crown Hall has to do with modernist architecture. We want to expose modern architecture and Mies to a wider audience."

The problem: It's difficult to get celebrities in the same place at the same time. Due to scheduling problems, Karmik came to the conclusion that his original idea wasn't going to work. He says, "We had a date and time set for the 'Smash Bash,' and we were trying to get celebrities to fit into that small window. So the challenge became twofold: finding a way to create a buzz about what we were doing, and then getting publicity a full month before the event happened."

Karmik had observed the success of the Great Chicago Fire Sale, a successful fundraising event held on eBay in late 2004 (and described in Chapter 6). "Having seen some other successful auctions on eBay, and considering that this was a one-shot deal, I thought eBay was the way to go. It gave us the opportunity to promote the event nationally, and to promote it so it was of interest beyond the subject matter. That is the key for nonprofits who are trying to promote something that is narrowly focused."

The sale was held April 15–22, 2005. A total of 55 bidders competed for the right to smash one of the building's 10-foot plate glass windows. The high bid, $2,705, was posted just as the sale ended. The winning bidder turned out to be Dirk Lohan, a Chicago architect and the grandson of Ludwig Mies van der Rohe himself. He's shown here wielding the sledgehammer with his son Carsten.

As Karmik discovered, the novelty of holding a fundraising event on eBay gets the general news media interested. "We were on every TV station in town, in the daily papers, on radio stations, and even got coverage in the *The New York Times* and the *The Washington Post*. We had a tremendous payback for something that didn't generate huge amounts of money—generally speaking, it's nice to have a $2,700 donation—but that was secondary; the primary thing was to promote this historic event to a general audience." Karmik was able to create a list of all the news stories related to the sale (see Figure 2-4); the report notes that about 200 web sites posted his original press release, including those of the *Los Angeles Times*, Yahoo! News, Google News, and CBS MarketWatch.

FIGURE 2-4 If you're able to sell something unusual on eBay, you'll get lots of attention for it.

Events and special "experiences" that you sell on eBay are easy to deliver (you don't have to worry about packing and shipping, after all). Because only one item was for auction, Karmik was able to do the project himself. He urges other nonprofits to plan at least several weeks in advance.

He also advises nonprofit sellers not to be discouraged if they don't attract bids as soon as the sale goes online. "When the sale went online, I was afraid, and I remember thinking, 'What if we only get two bids? I was very heartened; the sale went online at 9 A.M., and by noon we had seven or eight bids already. I knew then it would work. Eventually, the auction web page had 6,500 page views, which was amazing. For nonprofits, I think eBay is a tremendous way to promote what you're doing, have a little fun, and get some earned media attention, all at the same time."

> note *The IIT fundraiser was not held through MissionFish, but was conducted as a conventional eBay sale. Many eBay sellers make donations to nonprofits on their own, without working through the "official" eBay fundraising organization. For the sale, Karmik created a unique User ID (**the_mies_van_der_rohe_society**) and set up the seller's account so that the Mies van der Rohe Society would receive the sales revenue. By not working through MissionFish, however, the Society did have to pay eBay's insertion fee and Final Value Fee. If it had registered with MissionFish and specified that it was donating 100 percent of the sales revenue to the Society itself, eBay would have donated back its fees.*

eBay-Only Fundraising: The Disabled Online Users Association

Can a nonprofit organization depend on eBay for all of its funding? Can its members turn to the auction site for a good portion of their individual livelihoods? A group called the Disabled Online Users Association (DOUA) is proof that eBay is an important resource not just for nonprofits but also for those in need.

"We do all of our fundraising on eBay," says the DOUA's founder, Marjie Smith. "Our fundraising User ID is **funds4doua**. If you go to the About Me page for that username, it explains everything there."

As the page (see Figure 2-5) explains, the DOUA raises funds to help its members, who are disabled individuals, sell on eBay. In order to help disabled people find independence, the group gives them five items to list on the auction site. New members also receive telephone and e-mail support from an assigned mentor.

"If you do a search for the keyword 'DOUA' on eBay, you'll pull up every auction that's being held by one of the group's members," Smith says. (Members are required to include "DOUA" in the title to make their sales easier to find.) "The bulk of our funds come from people in the eBay community. In 2004, the Professional eBay Seller's Alliance (PESA) raised $15,000 at a convention for us."

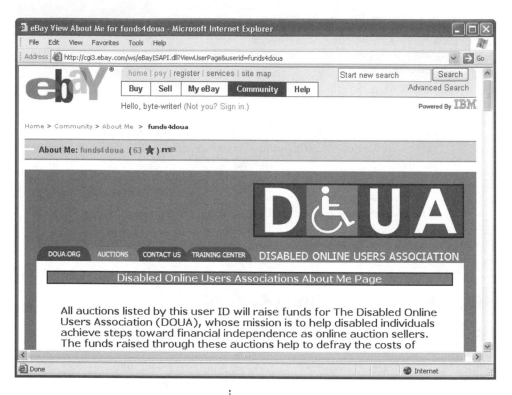

FIGURE 2-5 The DOUA depends on eBay for all of its fundraising needs.

The DOUA's About Me page (**http://cgi3.ebay.com/ws/eBayISAPI .dll?ViewUserPage&userid=funds4doua**) mentions another way nonprofits can raise funds online. The page encourages interested parties to donate directly using eBay's PayPal payment service. If your group has a seller's account set up with PayPal (and you should if you intend to sell on eBay), you can instruct others to send you money via PayPal, too. It's easy to set up a seller's account; find out more on the service's web site: **www.paypal.com**.

Smith knew there was a need for the DOUA because she felt the need herself. A member of the Marines who served in Vietnam, Smith was confined to a wheelchair due to complications after surgery. She says, "When I first started selling on eBay, with the use of one hand and one leg, I needed some special help. In the early days of eBay, there were no third-party auction management services, and no one on the site openly declared themselves as disabled. For the first five years I didn't let anyone know I was disabled. When I decided to do so, I got a lot of support. It just snowballed from there."

Since it was launched in October 2003, the DOUA has grown to include 1,025 members from around the United States and countries such as Canada, Austria, and Germany. "Who knew there would be such a need for this?" Smith says. "The disabled are very underserved in most communities. Because our community is eBay, we can work together, even though we're located all over the world. My executive assistant is a volunteer who lives in Ohio; the executive director lives in Maryland. Other volunteers live overseas. They help new people through the training center and instant message and the phone. We not only have online tutorials but our web site (**www.doua.org**) is a place where anyone can come and ask questions. We provide a lot of encouragement and support and handholding. We've found that all you have to do is open your mouth and ask; the worst you'll hear is 'no'."

Fundraising as a Regular Activity: The Child Welfare League of America

All nonprofits realize that fundraising isn't a one-time event. In fact, fundraising events tend to occur on a yearly basis. For the Child Welfare League of America (CWLA), fundraising on eBay has taken the form of an ongoing event—an effort that can help boost the group's bottom-line every six months.

"eBay has been a really good thing for us, not just for fundraising, but for making contacts," says Elana Viner of the CWLA. The group's first eBay fundraiser was held in April 2004, in conjunction with Child Abuse Prevention Month and the Children's Memorial Flag Campaign. The results of that sale and two subsequent efforts are shown in Table 2-1.

Viner points out that the April sales didn't do as well as the November event, Adoption Awareness, because spring is such a busy month for the CWLA. And, since she is the only staff person available to work full-time on the events, it's difficult to sell more than 20 to 30 items at a time. The sales have been successful enough that the CWLA has held two conference calls with the staff of eBay's MissionFish in an effort to train local chapters around the country on how

Date of Sale	April 2004	November 2004	April 2005
Associated event	Child Abuse Prevention/ Children's Memorial Flag	Adoption Awareness	Child Abuse Prevention/ Children's Memorial Flag
Total number of items listed	51	97	38
Total number of items sold	32 (62 percent of items listed)	75 (sold 77 percent of items listed)	27 (sold 71 percent of items listed)
Total revenue	$866.91	$4,544.55	$2,669.79
Average final bid	$27.00	$60.72	$98.88

TABLE 2-1   CWLA eBay Charity Auctions

to hold their own eBay sales events. But the biggest benefit has not been monetary, Viner emphasizes.

"I regard this as friendraising as much as fundraising," she says. "The revenue generated through our eBay auction program is not huge. But the relationships we have cultivated along the way, in addition to the public awareness we have been able to raise regarding children's issues, have made all the difference in the world."

The CWLA has cultivated personal relationships by completing transactions not through the mail or PayPal, but by telephone. Having a CWLA staff person talk to each successful bidder has brought great results, Viner says.

"Since we have a small staff team it is really effective for us to get on the phone and say, 'Would you like more information about who we are and what we do?' Sometimes, we get more donations at the end of those phone calls. After we explained how we help children one person said, 'You know what? Charge my credit card for $45 rather than $30.' Other donors sign up for e-newsletters and legislative alerts. The majority, however, aren't interested since they are regular eBay users who bought something they were looking for and who aren't interested in engaging with the charity. That's fine. But we've also had people who bid specifically because we are a charity."

Like other eBay sellers, the CWLA has discovered that the charity component helps generate more attention for their sales. "Once, we auctioned off a vacation package to the Broadmoor Hotel in Colorado. One man said he actually had made a reservation at the hotel before he noticed the sale on eBay. He thought, 'I'd rather give the same amount of money to a charity.' Plus he was able to play two rounds of golf for free, since that was part of the package. Selling on eBay has been great PR for us. We have had our name and our cause literally exposed to an audience of 130 million people."

> note *The CWLA uses its web site (**www.cwla.org**) to solicit donations for its eBay sales. Interested individuals are encouraged to donate such things as Lunch with a Leader, Behind the Scenes, and other unique experiences; airline tickets; tickets to college and professional sporting events (box seats or sets of multiple tickets sell best); donations from restaurants, salons, bookstores, cafes, or florists; spa/salon visits; art; jewelry; watches; and electronics. All of these are tried-and-true sellers on eBay; see Chapter 4 for more on what you should try to solicit for your own fundraiser.*

The eBay Celebrity Connection

eBay has always been a popular venue with celebrities who want to contribute to a cause. Television talk show host Rosie O'Donnell (whose organization For All Kids has the User ID **4allkids**) was among the first celebrities to embrace eBay. Singer Jimmy Buffett (whose fan club uses the User ID **the-virtual-parrot-head-club**), *Tonight Show* host Jay Leno, and comedian and talk show host Ellen DeGeneres (User ID **ellen-degeneres-show**, whose About Me page is shown here) have all taken advantage of eBay's capability to bring together a worldwide audience to help a cause.

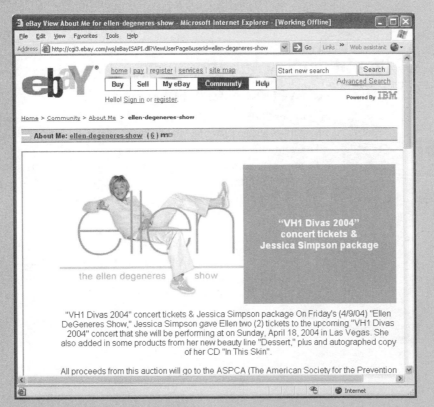

(continued)

When Oprah Winfrey held her first online charity auction, the response was tremendous. She sold the Ralph Lauren traditional leather club chairs that were used on the *Oprah Winfrey Show* set from 1996 through 1998. She shared some of the history of the chairs, including a list of a few of the famous behinds that spent time in those chairs (John F. Kennedy Jr., Halle Berry, Michael Jordan, Jim Carrey, and Tom Hanks); the chairs eventually sold for $64,000 and benefited Oprah's Angel Network.

Often times, celebrity-signed items end up carefully framed or locked up behind glass, but that would have been tough to do with the chairs. Interestingly, the chairs went on to help raise even more money for charity: The buyer, founder of Thrillionaires Ruth Ann Harnisch, who planned to have the chairs tour public libraries and schools, was approached by Liz Toole, a mom and volunteer at Redcliff Middle School. Liz thought the chairs would be a great centerpiece for the Literacy Week celebration at her kids' school, especially since Oprah promotes reading through her Oprah's Book Club. The chairs did indeed prove to be a great magnet, drawing people to the week's events and making their fundraising efforts more successful as well. And, of course, everybody got a chance to sit in the chairs and imagine what it would be like to be on Oprah's show. (For more on high-profile celebrity auctions and eBay, see Chapter 10.)

Combine eBay Auctions with Live Events: Marc Ecko

marc eckō
enterprises

Marc Eckō Enterprises
40 West 23rd St.
New York, NY 10010
Tel. 917.262.3002
email: info@eckō.com
www.marceckōenterprises.com

In summer 2005, fashion designer Marc Ecko undertook a unique eBay fundraiser, "Style & Sound: A Case for a Cause." What made the event unique was not the fact that it was on eBay—which is becoming a common venue for fundraisers—but that it was on eBay Live Auctions. Live Auctions is a part of eBay, but it conducts sales the "old-fashioned" way. Following a week of prebidding, the sale is held on a single day, and items are offered one after another in rapid succession. Ecko planned to auction custom Apple iPod cases designed by many of the hottest fashion designers. Before the event, we asked Clint Cantwell, director of corporate communications for Marc Ecko Enterprises, to discuss the process involved in organizing a celebrity auction on eBay.

Q. What kind of audience are you hoping to attract on eBay?

A. The power of eBay is its ability to draw a mix of individuals to a particular sale. Take our auction as an example: Custom iPod cases created by several of today's hottest fashion designers, each featuring a new iPod and a playlist created by the designer's celebrity partner. A very real potential exists to attract bidders who are simply looking for an iPod at a reasonable price (thus, the reason for setting minimum bids at a low level); individuals looking for a truly unique iPod case; a collector of anything by Marc Ecko, Donna Karan, or any one of the designers; a fan of P. Diddy, Jessica Alba, Cindi Lauper, or another celebrity partner; and so forth. It's an audience that auction houses had no idea how to access five years ago, and today it has enhanced their business exponentially.

Q. You have partnered up with LiveAuctioneers, an online auction facilitator that conducts the sale on eBay for you. How did you choose them, and how important is it to pick the right seller for a celebrity auction?

A. In the end, we chose LiveAuctioneers because of their experience in developing and executing similar charitable sales, and the amount of back end support they provide. Given the sheer amount of effort involved in putting such a sale together, from securing designers to generating media coverage for the event, it is a comfort to hand a major portion of the sale over to someone, knowing that the catalog, banner ads, buyers premiums, etc. will be handled in a professional manner.

Q. Is there a central location where merchandise will be collected and shipping will take place?

A. We have compiled all of the designer cases at our offices, created descriptions of each, and photographed them for the eBay Live Auctions "catalog." Once complete, LiveAuctioneers will work with eBay to format the information properly and bring the sale live. Once the auction is complete, we will ship items to winning bidders.

Q. How long will the sale last?

A. The sale is occurring in two stages, presale and live bidding. The appeal of eBay Live Auctions is the ability to allow remote bidders an opportunity to participate real time in a physical auction. Additionally, putting the items online 10 or 15 days prior to the live sale allows us to get the process started, hopefully raising the asking price to a nice level before the auctioneer even takes the stage the evening of our event. That evening, our celebrity auctioneer will introduce each lot and will open the floor for bidding. While various people attend the gala bid, LiveAuctioneers will manage real-time bids coming in through the eBay platform, ensuring that these bids are recognized on the floor. With only 15 items featured, the sale should take no more than 45 minutes to complete.

Q. Who will benefit from your auction event?

A. "Style & Sound: A Case for a Cause" is actually a multifaceted fundraising initiative developed by Marc Ecko and the CFDA (Council of Fashion Designers of America) in support of Fashion Targets Breast Cancer. In addition to the live and online auction, we are hosting a star-studded benefit gala, are introducing a Fashion Targets Breast Cancer iPod case to be sold through major retailers this summer (with net proceeds going directly to the organization), and are offering an exclusive single by the Black Eyed Peas for sale on the iTunes site.

Building Your Small Business Through Charity: Laura Iverson Gallery

Sure, charity auctions are good for nonprofits, but are they good for business? Laura Iverson found the answer to this question and saw her

business boom in return. Laura is an artist who began selling her oil paintings on eBay in August 2002 (User ID **iversongallery**). She only sells online, preferring the eBay marketplace with its low overhead and minimal time commitment to the cost and effort of showing her work. Iverson found that her vivid landscapes and floral paintings did well on eBay, but she still wanted to find a way to incorporate philanthropy into her business.

In January, 2004, Iverson heard about the new Giving Works program that eBay was launching and thought this might be a way to build donations into her sales. She put some paintings up and immediately noticed that those paintings with a portion of the proceeds going to charity received three times as many *hits*, or page views, than similar paintings not listed through Giving Works. In February, all of the charity pieces sold while none of the noncharity paintings did. By March, she switched the majority of her listings over to Giving Works and earned PowerSeller status that same month.

So convinced that the giving aspects of her listings were having a significant impact on both the number of bids and final selling prices, Iverson started chatting on the art boards with fellow women artists using eBay. In May, they formed the group Worldwide Women Artists (search eBay listings for the acronym WWAO to see all the works by these artists) and by their one-year anniversary, WWAO had 100 members. Many of the WWAO members list a portion of their art on eBay through Giving Works and have been able to create "events" for specific nonprofits.

Whereas the WWAO initially chose nonprofits they had a particular passion for (Iverson's personal cause is the Seva Foundation in Berkeley, California), they now schedule events and are frequently contacted by nonprofits wishing to partner with them. To select nonprofits to work with, Iverson says, "We look for organizations that will help promote the event and drive new bidders to eBay to check out the art category." For example, Iverson was impressed by Michael Appleman from Burn Survivors Throughout the World, Inc. Not only did Appleman contact them, but he also immediately added the event onto the nonprofit home page and e-mailed its membership to promote the event.

Nonprofit partner promotion efforts help raise the maximum dollars for the cause and help increase awareness for those artists representing themselves on eBay. The WWAO experiences demonstrate that sellers and companies don't have to forgo all profits to help a nonprofit cause. Rather, the charity element can help them gain new customers, and, yes, sell more and make more money while helping a good cause. Creating events with specific starting and ending dates also helps promote the artists on the Giving Works page. Iverson says, "We try to ensure visibility on eBay with proactive marketing. Any time we can put together an event that eBay is willing to promote, we definitely see a spike in activity."

By giving a portion of the proceeds from the sale of her artwork, Iverson has increased her business while raising more than $5,000 for 25 different nonprofits. The real win in her mind, though, has been the improvement in her mental outlook and attitude. "It helps you think less about yourself and more about others," Iverson says, "and it has also helped my motivation and productivity. It is one thing to finish a work for yourself, but when others in a nonprofit are counting on me to deliver artwork for their event, I make sure it happens."

The Iverson Gallery
Original Art by California Artists
www.iversongallery.com
(408) 260-2391
Laura Milnor Iverson   laura@iversongallery.com
Artist

eBay's Spotlight on a Cause

eBay often conducts its own fundraising activities. For example, it has supported Breast Cancer Awareness Month in October as part of its Spotlight on a Cause campaign. Spotlight on a Cause, now in its fifth year, enables eBay community members, nonprofit organizations, and corporations to use the eBay marketplace to raise money for breast cancer research. Since 2000, more than $400,000 has been raised through items sold through eBay in support of Breast Cancer Awareness Month. Go to **/www.ebay.com/ spotlightonacause** to bid on hundreds of items donated by celebrities and notables, nonprofit organizations, national companies, and eBay community members, all of which will be sold to benefit various breast cancer charities.

Using a Trading Assistant: The Country School

What started out as an effort to help his son's school turned into a vocation for Mark Silver. Silver had discovered eBay in 1996 and began by selling salt and pepper shakers and cookie jars. He started to grow his online business and expanded onto Amazon.com, taking a leap of faith and agreeing to sell 100 items a week for six weeks. This leap not only brought him added success on Amazon.com, but gave him a reason to learn how to "bulk list" on eBay. Until that time, he had been listing each item individually, so learning how to use the software to list hundreds of items at a time was a great way to take his eBay selling to the next level.

With his new-found efficiency and speed, Silver began to sell for other people. His reputation was now established on eBay and his years of experience helped his items sell for top dollar. It was at this point that Silver decided to propose using eBay as a new fundraising tool for The Country School. The fundraising committee was initially reluctant to give it a try, but Silver persisted, and in 2001, he helped the school solicit items from the school families for its first-ever eBay fundraiser.

The school, which is conveniently located close to Universal Studios in Los Angeles, California, has some families in "show biz." Thus, it was able to obtain some unique items beyond the "normal" household contributions. Signed scripts and a prop or two from a TV show helped the fundraiser deliver $10,000 in the first year. This was incremental to the school's other regular fundraising efforts.

It was clear to Silver that his son's school was not the only one facing funding issues, so he put together a presentation for schools and went out to pitch his fundraising ideas to local and private schools in his area. When eBay created the Trading Assistant program, Silver was one of the first to join (Figure 2-6). He created a formal program whereby he would help schools register their own User IDs on eBay, but then handle the operations, from photography to managing the auctions, to shipping for a low fee of just 20 percent (or 15 percent for nonprofits), which was about half of 30–40 percent the typical auction "drop shops" were charging.

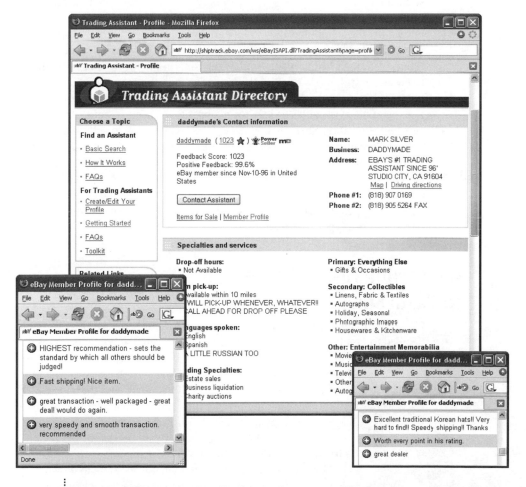

FIGURE 2-6 When you hire a Trading Assistant, you gain not only an experienced seller, but also a person whose reputation will help you earn top dollar for your donations.

Be sure to review the feedback for a Trading Assistant before hiring this person since he or she will represent your organization to the public.

According to Silver, one of the main things schools have discovered is that "Autographed items did much better on eBay than they had done in silent auctions in prior years. At one event, a school sold two signed helmets from the movie *Ladder 49*, one at their live silent auction and one online. The signed helmet by itself sold for $1,000 on eBay, whereas the signed helmet complete with a full gift basket and poster, sold for just $150 in their silent auction." Further, he says, "Not only that, but the dollars raised on eBay almost all came from outside the school community, which took the burden off the school families to buy all the items."

To market his services, Silver relies primarily on word-of-mouth referrals, though he has also found advertising in the local "money mailer" to be successful, too. Additionally, he works with the school partners to get information into school newsletters and local articles. Silver continues to expand his skills and services for nonprofits. As well as being an eBay certified Education Specialist who can teach others how to sell on eBay, he recently became a Dealer Assistant by completing a training program and becoming authorized to sell vehicles on eBay. "Selling cars for charity is a great way to increase proceeds, even if just a portion of the proceeds go to charity," Silver points out. "I felt it was important to become certified to sell cars so that I could help nonprofits leverage all their resources and get the most for those types of donations."

Converting In-Kind Items to Cash: State of California

California made a big splash when Governor Arnold Schwarzenegger decided to empty a government warehouse by selling the contents on eBay. Not only did the state get rid of the contents but it got rid of the warehouse as well, saving the ongoing tax dollars that were being spent on rent. This one-time event was all well and good, but the state had another ongoing problem. According to unclaimed property laws, money and items left in bank accounts, telephone accounts, traveler's checks, and safe deposit boxes are all turned over to the state after a certain amount of time.

Cash is easy to deal with, but what is the state to do with items found in abandoned safe deposit boxes? Unclaimed items often include jewelry, foreign currency, coins, silver spoons, and watches. But there are many other things found in the boxes,

such as collectibles like comic books and vintage
baseball cards. Not all of the unusual items
have been pleasant, either. Some safe deposit
boxes have turned out to house dental gold,
food, and even a dead bird. Some of the more
amazing finds have included an 1847 half cent
in uncirculated condition, which went for
$3,200; and a Cartier emerald and diamond
bracelet, which was sold for $21,000 at
auction. "Another interesting item found was
an autograph book dating to before the [American]
Civil War with autographs from the President, Vice President, Secretary
of War, and Cabinet, Senate, and Supreme Court members," according to
California State Controller Steve Westly.

tip *In California, you can go online to see if there are any unclaimed funds or items for
you by visiting **www.sco.ca.gov** and clicking on the Search for Unclaimed Property
link. This is rather enjoyable, as you search for family and friends who might have funds
they are unaware of, from bank accounts that were set up when they were children, to the
$20 dollar rebate from college telephone accounts. If you find funds that you think might
be yours, the site shows you how to make a claim for this found money.*

Because of the storage cost, and according to Section 1563 of the Code
of Civil Procedures, the state is "required to sell the items to the highest
bidder at a public auction." But those in the State Controller's Office began
to wonder if the benefits of online auctions could help them secure better
value for the items, and in 2002 sought legislation changing the law to allow
the Controller to use online sales if it was cost effective to do so.

In May and June of 2003, with the new law in place, the State Controller's
Office began a pilot study using eBay and Yahoo! online auctions. According
to Westly, "We found that using online auctions to dispose of unclaimed
merchandise resulted in significantly higher proceeds." In fact, the pilot
study demonstrated that online gross sales averaged 137 percent above the
items' appraised value! Some of the reasons for this success include not being
constrained to a single physical auction venue and leveraging the Internet to
open bidding to a much larger audience, and for a longer period of time, such
as ten days instead of a just one.

The government is not traditionally known for embracing new
technology. How, then, did the State Controller's Office build support for
this unprecedented endeavor? "The pilot program was very important," says
Westly. "It demonstrated the value of using online auctions." Not only that,

State of California
Steve Westly, State Controller

State of California Unclaimed Property Program
www.sco.ca.gov

(916) 445-2636

300 Capitol Mall, Suite 1850
Sacramento, CA 95814

but it also was important to broach the topic of the learning curve involved in adopting a new technology. As Westly explains, "The government does not want to be on the bleeding edge of new technology, but when there is a technology proven to be efficient and valuable in the private sector, the government needs to embrace it."

That may be easier said than done, but Westly says, "Just do it. There will always be organizational resistance to change. Innovation takes experimentation before it is embraced." Here are three key steps to successful adoption for cities and states considering online auctions:

- **Build a consensus** Use a test or pilot program to show people what can be done.

- **Lead the way** Make the decision and commit to the program. Let your team know "We're going to do it because it is what our customers expect and demand."

- **Do the metrics** Accountability is essential, so make sure that you can "show me the money" by analyzing your auction results.

Under the guidance of the State Controller's Office, the state experimentation on eBay (User ID **ucpauction**) sold more than 2,200 items, raising in excess of $783,000. At the present time, the State Controller's Office has contracted with Lone Star Auctioneers, a company that provides its own online auction technology, which is customized for government contracts as well as real-world auctions. Even with a commission of 17.5 percent to a third-party company, the state is coming out far ahead of where it was before it adopted online auctions (see Figure 2-7).

If your city or state is looking to put together a contract and request for proposals from companies that may be able to implement an online auction program for you, Westly suggests the following:

- States/organizations should research how their particular item types would fare with an online auction vs. a live auction to achieve maximum proceeds. Westly says, "It is our experience that some items do well in an online auction and others fare much better in a traditional live auction. For example, collectible and esoteric items generally do better online because online bidders often buy items that are nostalgic and meaningful to them personally, but would be undesirable to live auction bidders."

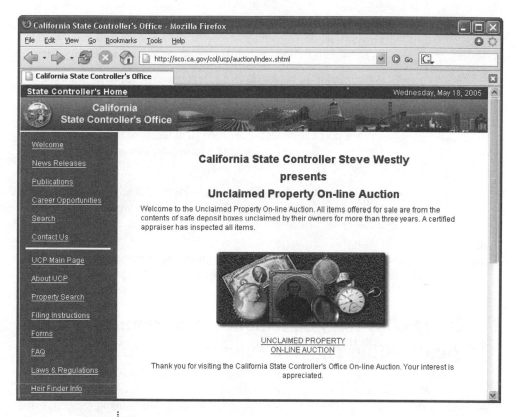

FIGURE 2-7 Cities and states, such as California, have found online auctions to be a great way to handle unclaimed or confiscated property.

- The contract should ensure a qualified independent appraiser, who has experience in online marketing, an extensive background on the types of the items to be auctioned, is familiar with historical periods, has valuation training, and who, at a minimum, meets Federal guidelines for appraisers as provided in the Uniform Standards of Professional Appraisal Practice (USPAP) guidelines, is involved.

note *Always make an effort to ensure that the items are accurately described. The state of California is very careful about fraud and forgery. Every item is inspected by a certified appraiser before it's put up for auction. For example, one safe deposit box included counterfeit designer belt buckles. In another state, a forgery of a Salem witch death warrant was found.*

- Sufficient staffing should include dedicated IT staff, customer service support (pre and post sales), accounting reconciliation staff, a contractual liaison, and customer relations staff for all inquiries.

- A budget for all hardware and software costs, appraisal fees, dues, and subscriptions.

- Equipment should include software/hardware, digital cameras, any support equipment, dedicated work areas with scanners and lighting, credit-card processing equipment, invoices, shipping boxes of various sizes, and bubble wrap.

- You should have the ability to ship with major carriers: USPS (United States Postal Service), UPS (United Parcel Service), FedEx ground/ express, and Brinks.

note *See Chapter 4 for information on other ways cities like Atkinson, Nebraska, and Chicago, Illinois, have used eBay for fundraising.*

Using eBay to Complement Your Existing Fundraising: The U.S. Fund for UNICEF

United States Fund for UNICEF
333 East 38th Street
New York, New York 10016

Telephone   212 686 5522
Facsimile   212 779 1679

www.unicefusa.org

For every child
Health, Education, Equality, Protection
ADVANCE HUMANITY

unicef

The U.S. Fund for UNICEF was not looking for eBay when eBay found it. Tatiana Shulzycki, who is responsible for eBay auctions at the U.S. Fund for UNICEF, describes eBay as a "community with a conscience." She explains it was the grassroots upswelling of support and desire to help by hundreds of eBay sellers that led eBay to create a special page to facilitate giving to the U.S. Fund for UNICEF and other relief agencies after the December 2004 Indian Ocean tsunami. The caring eBay community raised an estimated $250,000 in 2005 alone for the U.S. Fund for UNICEF.

The great part for the U.S. Fund for UNICEF was that these critical dollars came in with very little expense on the organization's part. It also demonstrates how tapping into the caring eBay community can be easily added as a complementary channel of giving. Says Shulzycki, "In the past, donations of in-kind items were hard to handle in an efficient manner. Many items had to be turned down. Now we have a way to use those items and translate them into aid. By simply asking the donor to sell the item on eBay on our behalf, we can benefit from the gift with minimal administrative overhead. Cash contributions allow the U.S. Fund for UNICEF to procure exactly what is needed at the best rates, get the supplies to their destination quickly and efficiently, and does not necessitate additional transportation costs and customs requirements."

Equally important to the U.S. Fund for UNICEF, eBay is a trusted venue. "It is a nicely secured, safe environment," says Shulzycki. "We feel comfortable referring people there because the accounting is in place and the process is worry-free." Through the outreach on the U.S. Fund for UNICEF's site and the eBay Giving Works page, the organization has had more than 1,200 unique individuals sell items on its behalf.

When the U.S. Fund for UNICEF has been fortunate enough to be selected as the recipient of the proceeds from a larger celebrity auction, the group makes an effort to promote the auction to their existing donors. The organization links to the event from its web site and supports the PR efforts. Some high profile donation highlights include golfer VJ Singh's Buick (the PGA matched the sales donation!), *Teen People* magazine "behind the scenes" with Ashley Simpson, *Harper's Bazaar* magazine's auction of designer and celebrity bags (see Chapter 11 for more details), Sirius Satellite Radio's guest visit with Bam Margéra, and a tennis racket signed by Andre Agassi.

During major giving efforts, such as the drive for dollars to aid the December 2004 tsunami victims, the U.S. Fund for UNICEF has also used a third-party company to set up and manage its eBay store. The unique aspect to its store was that it also "sold" donations. People could donate $25 or $50 or more just by clicking "Buy It Now" and purchasing the donation.

To make the donation more concrete and memorable, the U.S. Fund for UNICEF showed what the donation would provide (see Figure 2-8). For example, one donation people could purchase was the School in a Box. This incredible item included almost everything a local person would need to establish a makeshift classroom anywhere for up to 80 children, thereby ensuring the continuation of childrens' education in the first 72 hours of an emergency. The School in a Box contained supplies from exercise books and pencils to blackboard paint that turns wood or metal surfaces into an instant chalk board.

Selling a donation like this clearly communicates how the U.S. Fund for UNICEF is specifically solving a problem for needy children. Making its cause tangible provides people with a compelling reason to make a donation and increases their awareness of the issues facing some people around the globe.

FIGURE 2-8 U.S. Fund for UNICEF's About Me page made donating more compelling by showing what the buyer's donation would achieve.

"This is just beginning," Shulzycki explains. "eBay is a great new marketplace that will continue to play a bigger role in fundraising. It is a great way to reach more people and share the mission of your organization."

Partnering for Proceeds: Starlight Starbright Children's Foundation

The catalyst for the Starlight Starbright Children's Foundation to use eBay came from *Wired* magazine. *Wired* was interested in the use of technology to advance prosocial causes. Starlight Starbright was looking for ways to diversify its fundraising and engage new supporters in their mission to improve the lives of seriously ill children and their families through the use of technology and entertainment-based programs. Together, *Wired* and Starlight Starbright partnered in an online auction fundraiser (The WIRED Auction, shown in Figure 2-9), featuring the latest cutting-edge gadgets and gear, as well as memorabilia, luxury getaways, and much more.

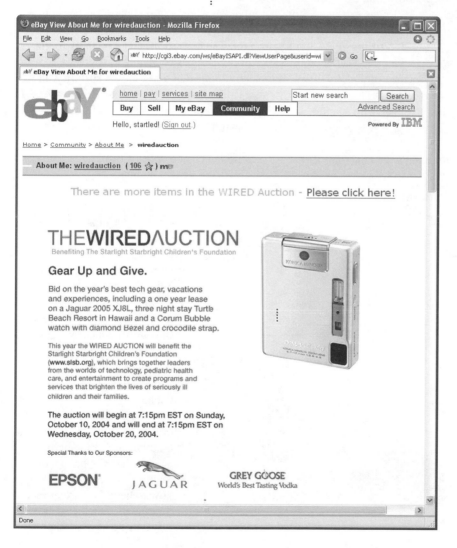

FIGURE 2-9 *Wired* magazine runs an annual fundraiser for the benefit of the Starlight Starbright Children's Foundation.

Wired has proven to be a very successful partner for the Starlight Starbright Children's Foundation. It promotes the event each fall with a special section in the magazine the month before the auction showcasing the most desirable items that will be for sale. The event culminates in a live event where attendees can bid online at one of dozens of computer kiosks (in addition to the millions online who can bid). Not only is Starlight Starbright the sole beneficiary of all proceeds, but it also leverages the tie-in with *Wired*'s mission to sell donations to Connect-a-Kid, a campaign that connects children with life-threatening illnesses to each other. For a $100 donation, Starlight Starbright can provide a child with the connection to the network.

"It was extremely important that we were both on board for the right reasons, and that we were committed to being a good charity partner," said Andy Trilling of Starlight Starbright. The organization is now in its fourth consecutive year and the caliber of items it has been able to solicit and secure continues to grow. It looks for items that don't have a specific value, including Hollywood experiences (for example, a set visit to the show *Angel*, together with a signed "stake" prop, brought in $16,400, see Figure 2-10) and the newest technology, which both helps magazine sponsors showcase new products, and appeals to *Wired*'s "early adopter" reader audience.

It is not just about the items Starlight Starbright sells, but about the relationships it creates with the item donors. "It is important to engage your donors and develop a relationship with them" says Trilling. "Be thoughtful and realistic about your request. In your introductory meeting, it can be helpful to present the donor with a menu of items that they can consider donating."

The idea behind partnering or co-venturing is, of course, that the sum of the parts is greater than the parts alone. Trilling suggests discussing how to help the partner meet their goals, whether that be positioning or reaching an

FIGURE 2-10 The Starlight Starbright Children's Foundation looks for donations that provide a unique experience or have a celebrity component, such as this signed prop from the TV show *Angel*.

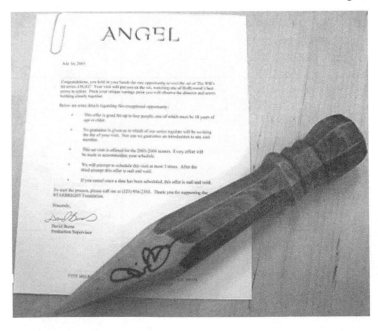

audience, in order to help new ideas to come forward. For example, Nikon donated five digital cameras for the online charity auctions to draw attention to its Pride and Joy Baby Photo $25,000 scholarship contest. "It was great to be able to put the two together to leverage a new product with broad exposure," says Trilling. As good stewards of the relationship, Trilling makes sure Starlight Starbright follows up with donors after the event because it helps quantify the relationship for them, so that they're more inclined to participate again with you in the future.

"People support people," Trilling emphasizes. One of the reasons Starlight Starbright has been successful at cultivating donors is that in addition to donating items for the auctions, the organization tries to engage the partners directly with the programs and children. As Trilling says, "When our supporters know more about our efforts, and that their gift is meaningful, they are more interested in exploring additional ways to help. Many of our partners have expanded their donations to be integrated directly into our programmatic services—with the bottom line that it all benefits the kids and families we serve."

Not content with just the annual event, the Starlight Starbright Children's Foundation carries out ongoing auctions themselves. As one of the nonprofit pioneers using eBay, it has learned to do everything on its own because that was the only way that was available in the beginning. Whether the nonprofit is selling donated items or printer cartridges it can no longer use because the printer broke (by the way, those sold for $119!), it finds eBay to be a great outlet. "This way," Trilling points out, "nothing is wasted." It continues to do its own listings, descriptions, and fulfillment; and from experience, the Foundation offers these tips for those just starting out:

- **Create an informative About Me page**   The simple template is fine for new organizations starting out, but you may want to customize it further as you go on. Says Trilling, "We used it as a catalyst for staff development and encouraged them to learn how to use HTML."

- **Create a "vanity URL"**   This means, if possible, create an URL that is both easy to type and remember for people, and one that the media can use to promote the event, such as www.yournonprofit .org/auctions.

- **Create a "button"**   You can provide other web sites with a graphic with a link to your auction. The key here—you really need to create multiple ways to get people to your auctions.

- **Build a relationship with eBay Giving Works**   Send an e-mail to let Giving Works know about your event, and be proactive by providing this arm of eBay with the graphics it can use to promote your event. This makes it easier for eBay to help you out.

- **Save time by setting up a place to take pictures** A clean environment with good lighting and backdrop will expedite the time it takes to photograph items.

- **Get your item descriptions done ahead of time** Make sure your titles are crisp and attractive. Use the subtitle to point out the proceeds benefit your cause. But overall, Trilling advocates, "Say what you'll deliver and deliver what you say. It is important to do it right the first time. You will be rewarded with positive feedback—we make it a priority to maintain our 100% positive approval rating."

Trilling's parting words: build a friendship with your auction donors and buyers by providing a personal note and more information about your cause after the sale. You never know who might turn into a major donor for your cause. "We have absolutely developed relationships with new donors through our eBay auctions," Trilling explains. "For example, donor and Dallas Mavericks owner Mark Cuban has become an ongoing supporter after donating an item for auction and seeing the impact his donation had; and the person who won his item was invited to attend a real-world fundraiser and ended up becoming one of the sponsors for the event!"

Auction Management Service Maximizes Celebrity Events: The First Amendment Project

When a nonprofit comes up with a major charity auction and wants to ensure that everything goes smoothly, it often turns to an auction management company for help. Large companies like Levi's, British Airways, and the Grammys, and smaller organizations like the American Kennel Club Canine Health Foundation and *Guitar Player Magazine* have taken advantage of the expertise that companies like Kompolt Online Auction Agency and AuctionCause can provide. Why? Ask Executive Director David Greene of the First Amendment Project:

"As a nonprofit, you hate to give up a penny of funds raised," Greene says, "but the more high profile and complicated our auction became—bidding for the right to have a celebrated author include your name in his or her next book—the more we realized we needed help. We ultimately came to the conclusion that we would net more funds if we hired a service to administer the auction rather than doing it ourselves."

The First Amendment Project, a nonprofit advocacy organization dedicated to protecting and promoting freedom of information, expression, and petition, was in dire need of funds. Greene invited board members and supporters to throw out some innovative fundraising ideas. Author Neil Gaiman, who had auctioned items on eBay himself to benefit the Comic Book Legal Defense Fund, came up with the idea of an author auctioning off the opportunity to name a character in their next book after the winning bidder. Pulitzer prize–winning author Michael Chabon took the lead in reaching out to the author community. They were so successful that the goal of eight participating authors was far surpassed—16 authors agreed to participate.

FIRST AMENDMENT PROJECT

A Nonprofit, Civil Liberties Organization

1736 Franklin St. 9th Floor
Oakland, California 94612
www.thefirstamendment.org
Tel: (510) 208-7744
Fax: (510)208-4562
fap@thefirstamendment.org

With so many well-known authors, the opportunity to garner significant media attention grew. Greene thought about running the auctions himself initially, but realizing the potential of the auctions and seeing the administrative tasks mount, he called the auction management companies listed on the eBay site and chose AuctionCause. "I was most comfortable with Eric Gazin, and he was very excited about our auction," Greene recalled. "I was thrilled by the way he conceptualized the publicity and took on the creative design and organizational responsibilities."

AuctionCause and other auction management services bring a number of key ingredients to the table: eBay expertise, efficient event management, professional creative design, and marketing. What this translates to is more dollars raised. One of the major benefits of working with a company with eBay experience is that they understand how communicative the eBay community is and the necessity of writing complete descriptions to minimize the number of questions. Especially with a high profile auction, if you are not thorough in your descriptions, you could easily find hundreds of questions in your e-mail inbox the day after your auctions go live. Knowing what information is important to bidders can take time to learn, so using an auction management company can be a great help.

Says Greene, "AuctionCause helped us write descriptions that were very specific. For example, rather than just saying that your name will be mentioned in a book, we worked out with the authors exactly how the name would appear and the type of character. Now bidders will know if they bid on appearing in the next Neil Gaiman book, they will find their name on tombstone, and if they choose to bid on Andrew Sean Greer's auction, they will find they "own" a soda fountain. Peter Straub makes it clear in his listing that bidders 'should be advised that the fictional person who winds up bearing his or her name may be of dubious moral character'." This clarification not only helped bidders but addressed and allayed concerns the authors had as well. AuctionCause also worked to ensure that the legal i's were dotted by incorporating text in the listing clarifying the conditions of the auction, such as the winner must have the legal right to use the name in the book, and so forth.

Knowing what to include in a listing is one way an auction management company helps streamline the auction process, but the design of the listings and the About Me page on eBay can play a critical role as well. "We were really pleased with the design AuctionCause created for us," Greene says. "With high profile authors comes a high level of scrutiny as well. People will be inclined to bid more if they see the auctions are professionally presented." (See Figure 2-11.)

As part of the auction management, AuctionCause provides the customer support for the auctions. How the auction runs reflects on the nonprofit organization, so it is important that the company you work with represents your organization well. When a buyer loves the product

FIGURE 2-11 Because of the scope and high profile nature of the event, the First Amendment Project hired AuctionCause, an auction management company, to create their About Me page and run their auctions.

or experience, and they like the way the auction has been handled, not only will they compliment you, but they will take a closer look at your organization and may well take an interest in your cause. This helps your nonprofit message go beyond your pool of existing supporters and typical prospects to reach a much broader audience of prospective donors that you would have no other cost-effective way of reaching.

The bottom line is that an auction management company can help you make your auction a reality. "Speed to market" is a popular phrase in the corporate world, but it is important for nonprofits as well. With the assistance of an auction management company, you will be able to mobilize and market your eBay charity auction much faster, which means the dollars are in your bank account sooner. Says Greene, "Our auctions start next week. We would never have been anywhere near this far by now without AuctionCause."

must have

In this chapter we provided some examples of different types of fundraising events that nonprofits and individuals have conducted on eBay. You learned about some best practices associated with each approach, including:

- When you aren't able to hold your own fundraising event, you can solicit donations from eBay sellers, who can direct a percentage of their sales to your cause.

- If you register with eBay's charitable arm MissionFish, you can add your group to the directory and have eBay donate back its fees if you sell on your own behalf.

- If you have an unusual experience or exceptionally newsworthy item or experience to sell, you can offer it on eBay and gain positive media attention for your organization.

- If you gather a group of sellers to sell regularly on your behalf, you might be able to meet all of your fundraising needs on eBay.

- Your group can schedule regular fundraising events on eBay as a way to boost your bottom-line on a periodic basis.

- Charity auctions can help your organization find and cultivate new donors.

- Celebrity auctions require a high level of coordination, and you're well advised to hire an experienced Trading Assistant or auction management company to sell on your behalf.

Chapter 3
Planning Your eBay Fundraising Event

It's very important to develop a sense of community among your volunteers and staff. My belief is that when you are doing something in the charity realm, it's not just about the money.

—Joan Greene, Joan Greene
Design Group, Inc.

What We'll Cover in This Chapter:

- Building support for your eBay fundraiser

- Setting goals and time parameters for your fundraiser

- Identifying the type of auction event that's right for you

- Understanding the costs and processes involved in selling on eBay

- Deciding who will do the work

- Starting the planning process far enough in advance

Planning is the key to any fundraising effort, whether you're hoping to attract "virtual visitors" to your items for sale on eBay or bring real, live attendees to a dinner dance in a rented hall. As you might expect, an eBay fundraiser is easier to arrange than a traditional live auction or other event. You don't have to rent the hall, contract with a caterer, or provide entertainment. However, if you haven't sold on eBay before, you should expect to encounter some steps that are unique to selling via an online auction. These include setting up a seller's account, finding a payment service, taking digital photos and posting them online, and finding packing material, to name a few.

But like any fundraiser, an eBay sales campaign can be broken down into a series of easily followed steps. Fundraising on eBay is something you can do regardless of whether you have sold on eBay or not, and whether you have a hundred volunteers or a handful of volunteers available. This chapter describes the pieces you need to put together your event and make it happen smoothly.

note *This chapter focuses primarily on step-by-step planning for nonprofits that intend to do direct selling on eBay (selling directly on eBay to benefit their own groups), rather than community selling (having community members sell on eBay and donate sales revenues to a cause). We discuss the community selling option in Chapter 5.*

Step 1: Build Support

You already know *you* want to hold a fundraiser. Now you need to get the important members of your immediate community to decide they want to undertake an online auction fundraiser. It's essential to get your board members, staff people, or townspeople on board. Make every effort to instill them with enthusiasm by sharing the size and benefits of the eBay marketplace along with the success stories we describe in Chapter 2 and throughout this book. Be prepared to hear and answer some commonly asked questions from your colleagues and constituents:

● **Q: What's the advantage of holding a fundraiser on eBay rather than a brick-and-mortar facility?**

A: An eBay fundraiser enables you to attract potential bidders from around the world rather than from just your local area. With more people competing for merchandise, you're likely to attract higher bids. Equally important, rather than tapping the same people over and over for donations, much of this money comes in from people outside your traditional fundraising reach. You may need to find a storage area and a source of computers that are connected to the Internet, but with an online auction you save substantially on overhead by not having to rent a facility, cater, and hire entertainment.

● **Q: Does it require more work than a "live" fundraiser?**

A: Yes and no. In some ways eBay auctions are easier than traditional fundraising because you have the option of eliminating the "real world event" component. In other ways, it's exactly the same—you have to solicit donations, sell them, and receive payment. eBay initially requires extra work because of the learning curve the first time you use it and the additional tasks involved in selling online, including photographing items and shipping items to buyers.

● **Q: What kinds of things sell well on eBay?**

A: This is the good news, most anything can be sold on eBay and everybody can contribute items for the sale. In general, items that routinely sell well on eBay include new and brand name items, collectible items, and common household items such as purses, cell phones, and electronics. But you're not limited to items; experiences can be extremely popular on eBay and raise big dollars. (See Chapter 4 for more on this subject.)

● **Q: What does it cost to sell on eBay?**

A: Generally, you can assume selling on eBay will cost about 10 percent of the item's selling price if you do it yourself, and up to 40 percent of the selling price if you hire a professional service to run the auction for you. (Note that if you donate 100 percent of proceeds, fees could be as low as just the credit card fees of 2.9 percent.) Compare this expense to the cost of running a real-world event. Offsetting these expenses is also the additional value the eBay platform provides in terms of PR benefits and access to a larger audience, which often results in finding new donors and receiving, on average, 20–40 percent greater prices for the charity items.

● **Q: How much can we raise?**

A: The amount of money you can raise depends primarily on two things: the total number of items you sell and the average selling price of the items you sell. It's probably reasonable to target an average selling price of $20 per item unless you're looking at selling fewer but higher-priced items such as cars, celebrity items, and experiences. A small organization or town could, as rural Atkinson, Nebraska, did, collect 1,000 donated "everyday" items and raise around $12,000, whereas larger organizations with access to higher-ticket items and experiences could, as the city of Chicago did, raise $250,000 in the same amount of time and with fewer items. See the following sidebar for other factors that will affect your success.

Factors Determining the Success of Your Fundraiser

Another early step is to assess your potential by determining whether your fundraiser has the potential to be a success. The key factors are

● **Volunteers**   How many people do you have available? How many do you need? Two is a bare minimum; anywhere between 10 and 100 is better. You'll need to designate who will perform critical tasks, such as soliciting donations, photographing merchandise, preparing sales descriptions, and handling packing and shipping.

● **Organization**   Do you have support and structure? You'll need top-down organization support to get the resources that you need, and bottom-up support to ensure grassroots community participation. With many staff and volunteers involved, you'll need to be organized, maintain a schedule, establish your own processes, and have clear roles and responsibilities. Ideally, you'll have people in your organization or volunteer ranks with some expertise in computers, the Internet, marketing, and public relations that you can tap for troubleshooting and support in this endeavor.

● **Donations**   Do you know what auction items to go after? It takes time and money to list items for sale on eBay. You need to make sure you solicit items that bidders are likely to want. Before collecting donations and listing items for sale, understand what sells well and what doesn't by doing research of the sort described in Chapter 4 so that you get the right stuff.

● **eBay experience**   Do you or your volunteers already sell on eBay? If you already know what makes a good description, you're a step ahead. Having people who have sold on eBay before will enable you to begin selling sooner and make it easier to train volunteers. Experienced sellers can help you avoid common mistakes and answer questions if things don't go the way you expect.

- **PR expertise** Does your nonprofit group already have a public relations staff and are those staff able to work on your eBay fundraiser? Some high profile events like the Great Chicago Fire Sale or the Mies van der Rohe window destruction we describe in Chapter 2 (and shown here) benefit from conventional press releases and media contacts. But marketing eBay sales can also involve link exchanges, keywords, ad word purchases, and other online marketing approaches that your PR staff may be less familiar with. (See Chapter 12 for advice on marketing your eBay sales.)

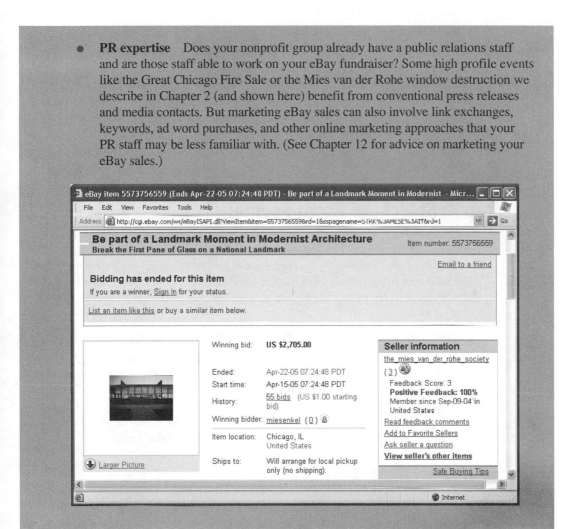

Step 2: Define Your Goals

The immediate goal you need to accomplish with your eBay fundraising effort is probably clear to you from the beginning: "We need to raise money to build a new playground," "We need to make up that budget shortfall," or something similar. You probably have a number figure in mind, too: "We need to raise $5,000," for instance. Although you know what the immediate need is for your fundraiser, there's a difference between that immediate need and the objectives you want to accomplish in the long run.

In Chapter 1, we discussed goals you might have in addition to raising funds. Choose and prioritize these objectives; they'll affect your decisions about the type of event you choose and your timing. For example, if in addition to raising funds your secondary goal is to increase awareness, then it makes sense to solicit items with media or celebrity interest and tie the event with the announcement of a new service or program. Conversely, if you have in-kind gifts and donations that you need to convert to cash or you just want to sell unused inventory, the timing and public relations elements will be less important.

Step 3: Select the Event Format

When you bring eBay into the fundraising mix, you gain a whole new set of options for reaching out to donors. Some organizations might choose to hold a fundraising event on eBay as a one-time event, while others may see it as an annual event or ongoing fundraising to boost your bottom line. Still others might see it as a way to add new life to a familiar fundraising occasion.

Combining eBay with Conventional Fundraisers

Many organizations tackle a variety of fundraising activities, both on the Web and in the "offline" world. For many institutions that have been raising money for years, eBay sales provide an additional incentive for people to give to your cause. It makes sense to use multiple approaches to reach different groups of potential donors. But to get the most out of this integrated approach, you need to follow some common-sense practices.

Segment Your Audience

eBay doesn't necessarily have to compete with your preexisting sources of income, or with events you've already scheduled. For many groups, eBay sales can be something different and exciting—a supplement to your usual campaign and a way to bring in younger, tech-savvy donors. Even if you're planning to hold a live auction, a dinner, a Monte Carlo night, or other traditional event, eBay can supplement your efforts in situations like these:

- *Do you have tangible goods that can't be transported easily?* Items such as furniture might be difficult to bring to a live event. Photograph them and describe them on eBay.

- *Do you have items that appeal to a nationwide audience?* A plate decorated with the handprints of your daughter and her classmates will appeal only to parents of those children. A Princess Diana collector's plate will have wider appeal and you are likely to attract more money for it on eBay.

- *Is a segment of your target audience more easily reached online than offline?* Busy young professionals might be reluctant to give up a free evening to attend a fundraising function. But you might be able to get them to buy on eBay from the comfort of their own homes, on their own schedules. Target them by selling electronics, current fashion, and other up-to-date items on eBay, while keeping other donations such as vacation trips and restaurant discounts for your traditional event.

success

As this was being written, Menlo School, which enrolls grades 6 through 12 in Atherton, California, was planning its annual fundraising event. A luncheon and fashion show was scheduled to be followed by dinner, a live auction, and dancing. Along with this traditional approach, the school was holding an auction on eBay. In this way, the school could reach a variety of different audiences. Menlo School's organizers asked parents and other benefactors to drop off items with the auction selling service AuctionDrop, as shown here. This popular chain has numerous drop off locations via its partner UPS Stores around the country.

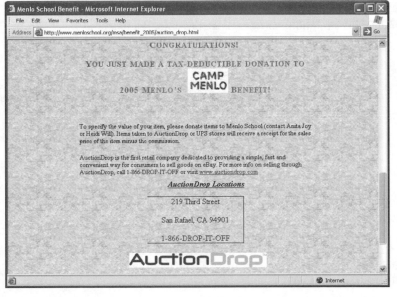

(continued)

> Those providing merchandise to the Menlo School were asked to only donate items with an estimated value of at least $75 that weighed less than 25 pounds. Consider doing the same with your own sale; items that are low in value might not be worth the effort required to photograph, describe, pack, and ship them. Items that are too heavy would be difficult to carry, pack, and ship. You might not settle on a minimum value as high as $75, but a more realistic $50 or $25.

Present a Consistent Message

When you use more than one venue for fundraising, you need to make sure you don't put forth more than one message. This can be a challenge, when different sets of volunteers are working on your dinner, on your evening show, on a mailing, and on your eBay sales.

Make sure each of those teams of volunteers communicates the same information. It isn't just about including a standard statement such as "All proceeds go to …" in your printed material or your eBay sales descriptions. It's about *branding* your institution. A brand is more than a name, a slogan, or a logo; it's a total relationship between an organization and the people who contribute to it, either with their money, their time, or their energy. To brand your cause and your institution, you need to convey simple concepts in the most straightforward language possible. For example:

- Your institution makes peoples' lives better. You might express this through a phrase such as: "We're all about people."

- You are continuing a long tradition of service: "Celebrating 100 Years of Education."

- You do something no one else does: "Fighting Back Against Drunk Drivers in Minnesota."

An integrated approach to fundraising gives you an ideal way to brand yourself and spread your core message. Use every communication tool at your disposal to convey your mission statement. Your task is to strike up a one-to-one relationship with your donors by attracting, retaining, and upgrading them over time. The Web is the perfect place to do it, and including a standard phrase or message in an eBay auction description can play an important role in your campaign.

The term *integrated fundraising* refers to the use of multiple channels to solicit support. Online sales for a nonprofit or charitable cause are unlikely to completely replace traditional fundraising. To maximize support, combine eBay sales with other techniques such as direct mail or phone solicitations—or even with other forms of online fundraising such as e-mail announcements and web site advertisements.

Running an Online-Only (Stand-Alone) Fundraiser

One of the best things about staging sales on eBay is the low overhead: you don't have to rent space, acquire furnishings, prepare food, or buy other tangible supplies, so the decision as to whether to hold or cancel a sale is an easy one. If you decide to add a few eBay sales at the last minute to supplement your dinner dance, you can do so in a matter of a few weeks; you can also cancel your eBay sales if you have second thoughts. And you can conduct an online only auction with far fewer volunteers than a combined event with a real-world component would require.

A bonus for online-auction-only events is that everyone can participate regardless of geographic location. For example, if your members are situated all over the country, eBay gives them a perfect way to donate and make contributions. A group of several members can work together in a single location to gather merchandise and make it available online; they can then notify their membership, who can visit the sale's web site on eBay and place bids. Or, members around the country or around the world can hold individual sales and donate all or part of the proceeds to the cause of their choice.

One-Time Event

Some "organizations" are only organized on a one-time basis. A tornado brings together citizens who want to help their neighbors; a community center needs a new furnace; the family of a child disabled by an accident needs help constructing wheelchair ramps and customizing a van. In such situations, the group that needs to raise funds exists only for the purpose of creating a single event.

Many eBay fundraisers are held for a specific purpose. Tsunami Relief auctions were held by several nonprofits specifically to benefit the victims of the December 2004 tsunami that affected many countries on the Indian Ocean, for instance. Such events don't require ongoing fundraising efforts but rather a one-time major infusion. In these cases, because you're only planning to hold your event a single time, you might well consider hiring a company that can help you with registering on eBay and creating sales listings. This will simplify the process and allow you to get your auctions up in a timely manner.

Annual Event

Your goal might be to hold a fundraiser each year on eBay. If that's the case, it's to your advantage to get a system in place. Find a set of computers you can use each year, set aside time for an ongoing donation effort, name fundraising directors who, hopefully, will be able to work on the project on a yearly basis, and set up and keep track of processes so you don't have to reinvent the wheel each year.

For the past several years, the Child Welfare League of America (**www .cwla.org**) has held a weeklong fundraiser on eBay to benefit abused and neglected children. The event (which is publicized on the group's About Me page shown in Figure 3-1) is held in April in conjunction with National

FIGURE 3-1 Many nonprofits hold annual fundraisers on eBay.

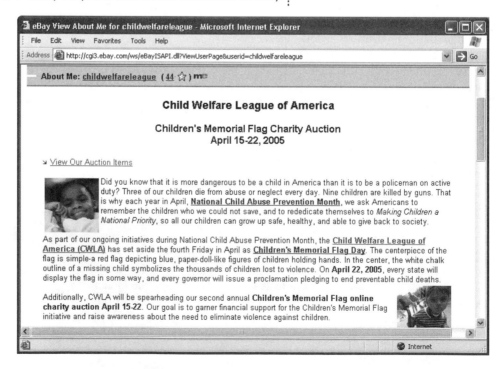

Child Abuse Prevention Month. Since they hold the event annually, the Child Welfare League of America decided to put out an online training guide, which they can use each year and any affiliate groups can refer to so they know what they need to expect when they hold their own fundraisers.

Ongoing Fundraising

You can use eBay for fundraising without having an organized event. You may choose to have a continuous presence on eBay, selling a number of items each week. The Points of Light Foundation, for example, in addition to holding occasional "big" events on eBay, is continually selling in-kind donations they receive. If you plan to sell on an ongoing basis, it makes sense to make an investment in auction management software and training for staff to ensure you sell on eBay efficiently.

Nonprofits can also benefit from others' ongoing selling on eBay. Once a nonprofit is registered on MissionFish, the organization that powers eBay's Giving Works program, individuals selling on eBay can allocate part or all of the sales proceeds to the nonprofit of their choice. The National Multiple Sclerosis Society (see Chapter 2), for example, encourages eBay sellers to donate some of their sales revenue to its organization on an ongoing basis. Promoting this activity is a great way to raise extra money without having to stage a special event, and to gain revenue from eBay sales year-round while your other special events are taking place. (Find out more in the section "Encourage Others to Sell on Your Behalf" in Chapter 5.)

Step 4: Determine Timing

It's clear that, for eBay auctions that are part of a larger fundraising program, the dates are predefined by that larger, offline event. But one of the advantages of stand-alone eBay auctions is that they aren't dependent on the weather or school schedules. Since you can choose when the event occurs, you can try to find the time for your organization that will optimize the dollars raised. You'll need to take a number of factors into consideration when selecting the dates for your event: PR/organization purposes, seasonal peaks for eBay, staff and volunteer availability, and necessary lead time.

warning *Timing is everything if you're planning to donate part of your eBay sales to a charity and take a tax deduction. For individuals selling to benefit a nonprofit, it's important to complete the sales before December 31 if you want to be able to claim the deduction for that year. But on eBay, the period between Christmas and New Year's Day is dead as far as sales are concerned; the best time to conduct sales is between Halloween and Christmas. Such nuances can make a difference. For instance, if you donate $1,000 and you're in the 28 percent tax bracket, you're able to deduct $280. But keep in mind that only those who itemize can deduct gifts to charity.*

Optimal Timing for PR

Time your event to maximize publicity by using the eBay event to draw attention to your cause and garner more public relations by having it coincide with related news stories or national awareness occasions such as Earth Day or Breast Cancer Awareness Month. Specific to your nonprofit, you may be able to coordinate the event with award ceremonies, new program announcements, new facility openings, and so forth.

Optimal Timing for Staffing

Making sure fundraising efforts don't occur too frequently is important in order to avoid donor fatigue. You also want to make sure that your buyers and volunteers are around and available. During summer months, your key staff may be vacationing. December may be a great time to sell on eBay but if your volunteers are tapped out with holiday and personal demands, it may be difficult to get the support you need.

Optimal eBay Timing

Since you presumably want to attract the widest audience possible—an audience of shoppers who will bid enthusiastically on your merchandise and who don't necessarily know about your group or your fundraiser until they read one of your auction descriptions—you should also pick a date that's good for sales on eBay. The busiest time of year on eBay is between November 1 and December 15, as shoppers flood the Internet looking for holiday gifts. The slowest time is late summer, when vacations keep people away from their computers.

Traditional fundraisers and other events tend to take place in March through May, and this is also a good time to hold an event on eBay. However, the end of the year peak, with sales starting to pick up in

September after school has started, is still a better bet. Like the city of Chicago, which held its online fundraiser in early December 2004, you might consider holding your event during the pre-Christmas rush if possible. You'll probably attract even more shoppers than you would at any other time of year.

> tip   *Just because you hold your eBay event during a particular time of year, that doesn't mean the merchandise you sell needs to be tied to that time of year. Even though the Great Chicago Fire Sale took place in December, for instance, the city auctioned off the chance to dye the Chicago River green for St. Patrick's Day and to turn on a lakefront attraction called Buckingham Fountain at the end of April.*

What's the best time of week for an eBay sale? Here, you also have freedom. Rather than being limited to Fridays and Saturdays (the traditional days for real-world fundraisers), try to end your sales at the time when most bidders are likely to be present: on Saturdays and Sundays. If you choose the popular seven-day auction format, start the sale on the preceding Saturday or Sunday; if you want to pay eBay's 10-cent-per-sale surcharge and would rather choose the ten-day format, start your sales on the preceding Wednesday or Thursday so they'll finish on a weekend. You could even choose the five-day format and start your listings on Monday or Tuesday and they'll still finish up on the weekend. For commodity-type items, this can be a fine choice since most of the bidding comes at the start and end of the auction anyway. But generally it's best to utilize the full seven days to give bidders time to find your items.

> tip   *All eBay sales don't end on a weekend. There's nothing wrong with ending your sales on a weeknight. You might, however, avoid ending sales during business hours on a weekday—unless you're offering office supplies or other merchandise that might appeal to business sellers.*

Optimal Lead Time

The dinner dances, luncheons, and fashion shows that serve as the occasions for fundraisers are held after as many as five months of planning. Do you need that much time for an eBay fundraiser? If you're holding your eBay sales in conjunction with a live auction, bingo night, or other event, the answer is yes.

On the other hand, if you're only planning an eBay event, much of the advance time is needed to solicit donations and do marketing. The actual sale can take a week; the completion of the sale another week. To be safe, you should ideally try to give yourself at least three months to plan and execute your eBay fundraiser. Table 3-1 gives you a rough schedule you might want to follow for a 12-week fundraiser.

Time	Tasks
Weeks 1–3	Set goals; appoint officers; decide on dates; register on eBay; tap volunteers
Weeks 4–6	Create an About Me page or eBay Store if necessary; publicize your event; locate storage/warehouse facility; locate computers to use
Weeks 7–8	Continue publicity; gather donations and photograph items
Weeks 9–10	Prepare sales descriptions and get your sales online
Weeks 10–11	Actually hold your sale
Week 12	Ship items; do accounting; report on income; and evaluate your level of success

TABLE 3-1   eBay Fundraising Timetable

tip *If you need to obtain the approval of governing boards, or if you're looking to obtain sponsorship for your fundraiser, be sure to earmark even more time. The committees that decide whether to sponsor your event usually meet once a month, and it might take one to two months before your request for sponsorship gets on the agenda.*

Step 5: Assess Your Resources

In order to know what resources you'll need, it's important to have an overview of the eBay selling process. Once you know what tasks are required, you can determine whether you can do it all yourself, or if you'll need volunteers or professional assistance to achieve the type of event you'd like to conduct. Take stock of the personnel, time, and equipment you have available. For each of these steps, you have the option to do it yourself or to outsource the tasks for a fee. Your decision to outsource part or most of the work will depend on the resources you have available, how elaborate you would like to make the event, whether you already have the items you wish to sell, and how "high profile" your auction items are.

Understand What You Will Need to Do Up Front

The tasks for an individual and an organization selling on eBay are the same. Here is a brief overview of the key steps (details will follow in subsequent chapters):

- **Register with eBay and MissionFish**   This includes both setting up accounts and setting selling preferences, as well as signing up for PayPal or other online payment solutions that allow you receive credit card and debit card payments.

- **Obtain inventory/donations**   This involves both soliciting and collecting donations from individuals and companies. It can include flyers, newsletter articles, solicitation letters, and recruiting unique experiences and items, as well as physically collecting items through drop points, events, or pick up.

- **Create event branding**   This can be as simple as naming your event and creating your personal page on eBay to as advanced as having graphic artists and web designers create a logo and selling templates.

- **Photograph items**   Most items sold on eBay will need at least one photograph, and, in many cases, two to three images are very helpful.

- **List items for sale**   This can be filling out the simple Sell Your Item form on eBay with a description of the item, or for a large number of items, it could involve using software to expedite the listing process.

- **Market auctions**   The scope of your efforts can range from publicizing the event to your constituency through e-mail, newsletters, and press releases, to leveraging online marketing opportunities.

- **Manage auctions**   The bulk of the work here is answering e-mails from the eBay bidders. If your descriptions are complete and clear, this will be less burdensome; but there will always be questions and replies need to be timely.

- **Complete sales**   At the conclusion of the auction, the seller invoices the buyer, receives payment, ships the item, and leaves feedback for the buyer. Of these, carefully packing and shipping the items can take the most time.

You might consider holding your fundraiser in summer, when school computer labs either aren't being used at all, or are experiencing lighter use than usual. High school students are likely to be available in summer, too. But keep in mind that summer is, in general, one of the slowest times on eBay because many potential buyers are traveling.

Assemble Your Tools

One of the wonderful things about eBay is the ease with which individuals and organizations can conduct sales. You don't need the latest and greatest computer, the largest monitor, or the fastest Internet connection speed. As long as you have the bare-bones essentials listed here, you can sell with the biggest of big-time sellers:

- **Internet connection**   While it's great to have a fast Digital Subscriber Line (DSL) or cable modem connection, the important thing is that your connection is reliable. You need to be able to get your e-mail up to several times a day and respond to it as quickly as possible.

- **Computer and monitor**   Computers are becoming more powerful all the time, and it's more affordable than ever to obtain a machine with a gigabyte or more of memory (Random Access Memory, or RAM) and a super-fast Pentium or Celeron processor. The important thing is that you have enough memory space to operate a web browser, an e-mail application, and a graphics application for editing digital images. It helps to have spreadsheet software like Excel as well. If you have a group of volunteers working on your fundraiser, you'll need multiple computers—either a bank of machines in a computer lab, or individual computers and laptops located in volunteers' homes.

When you're selecting computers, consider how much access you'll have to them. (Will you be able to use them late into the evening, when the auctions are closing?) Are there school firewalls that could impede your access to eBay? Can you designate computers for listing and a computer for bidding to avoid the appearance that you're bidding up your own items? Resolve these questions well in advance of your auction date.

- **Digital camera**   You need to capture digital images of your items. As described in Chapter 7, you can use a flatbed scanner to obtain images in the form of digital files or have a photo lab return photos you have taken with a conventional film camera on a computer disk, but the easiest way to take digital images of your sales merchandise is with a digital camera.

- **Storage space**   Whether you sell out of a home office or out of a business, you need space where your merchandise can be photographed, stored, and shipped out.

- **Packing materials**   You'll need clean boxes, insulating material such as bubble wrap or newspaper to prevent damage, and packing tape. The USPS and other shipping companies make their shipping boxes and envelopes available at no cost. A measuring tape and digital postal scale will help you describe items and calculate postage costs.

eBay, of course, is a convenient and economical place to buy computers, digital cameras, postal scales, and other necessary equipment. You can also find extra memory for your computer as well as photography accessories such as a tripod, batteries, and auxiliary lights.

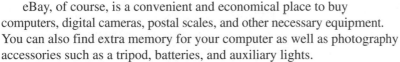

Centralizing Computers

When you decide to conduct your eBay fundraiser yourself, people are only one part of the equation. Finding computers that your volunteers can access is another important consideration. You need computers not only to prepare sales descriptions, but also to perform the other tasks that go with an online event, such as:

- **Training**   You need to show volunteers how to check listings, respond to e-mail, and (optionally) calculate shipping fees online.

- **Bidding**   Your volunteers will probably be interested in placing bids after they get a look at the merchandise that's been donated.

- **Answering questions**   Bidders will ask questions about the items you have up for auction. Someone has to monitor the e-mail account that has been set up for your sales, respond to questions, and sometimes update the item description with more information.

- **Revising descriptions**   Often, the questions you're asked need to be shared with other bidders, if only to prevent a flood of similar questions. eBay doesn't let sellers delete or edit their original descriptions, but they're free to add new information if they wish.

The ideal situation is to gain access to a computer lab in the public library or in a school. It also works well if one of your volunteers has access to a set of computers in the office that can be loaned for the fundraiser. That way, volunteers can do their work in a central location. Not only can you have more than one person working at once, but also volunteers can then help each other if questions arise.

Arrange for Technical Support

Your volunteers may be generous, but you can't expect them necessarily to be computer experts as well. If a computer crashes, an Internet connection goes down, or something else doesn't work correctly, you need to have some support staff on call so your volunteers can get their problems solved quickly. You might also provide them with instruction sheets, pamphlets—or copies of this book. But there's no substitute for human assistance, especially when technical glitches occur.

Find the Key Staff People You Need

How many volunteers do you need? That depends on the type of sale you plan to hold. Here are some suggestions:

- **The do-it-yourself option**   If you want to donate to a charity you're interested in and you don't work for a nonprofit yourself, you can do the donating by yourself through Giving Works. If you work for a nonprofit and you have a single item to sell, such as dinner with the president of a company or principal, you can do it yourself, as long as you have a minimum of two to three weeks to handle the publicity as well as the creation of the sales description.

- **Multiple-item sale on eBay**   Many nonprofits sell anywhere from a dozen to a thousand items on eBay over a period of one or two weeks. Don't expect to be able to handle such an event yourself. You'll need, ideally, a team of two to five people to list the sales online in advance. You'll need an event coordinator, and two or three people to receive items and to handle packing and shipping: a total of six to a dozen volunteers is a minimum amount.

- **High-profile event**   If your nonprofit is well-known and you hope to raise tens or even thousands of dollars, hire a trading assistant or auction management company. Hiring an experienced professional enables you to focus on soliciting donations and working with the local media; the trading assistant can get multiple sales online in a hurry to ensure that your sale proceeds on time. (For more information, see "Hire a Trading Assistant" later in this chapter.)

Step 6: Create Your Team

After you've assessed your resources and have a sense what staffing will work best for your event, you need to actually line up your team. Finding the people to help you carry out the event takes some time. Here are details to consider as you recruit volunteers and/or hire professional selling assistance to do some or all of the auction tasks.

Find Home-Grown Help

If you're on a budget, the most cost-effective way to hold an eBay fundraiser is to find volunteers in your own community. Working with volunteers toward a common goal can be a rewarding experience. When everyone shows up on time and follows through on his or her commitments, fundraisers can go smoothly. But be prepared for volunteers to fall sick or be called away by other obligations. You can avoid encountering "speed bumps" on your road to fundraising success by following the advice presented in the upcoming sections.

Make Sure You Have Enough Volunteers

One of the most common problems with holding a large-scale fundraising event is a lack of helping hands. Consider the timing of your auction and, if possible, try to schedule it when folks are available (not too close to holidays or tax time, for example). When you're planning, try to get more people than you need at first. There isn't a hard-and-fast rule for how many people you need. Be aware, though, that you'll need people to handle the following tasks:

- Handling publicity, such as putting up (and taking down) flyers around town

- Receiving donations, cleaning them if needed, and evaluating whether or not they should be sold online

- Describing and photographing items

- Packing and shipping sold items

- Answering questions from prospective bidders

You'll need at least one person for each task, but two or three people are better in case someone becomes unavailable. Where do you find volunteers? Think of the following resources:

- **High school students**   If you hold your event in the summer, you'll have access to plenty of young people who can help you out and who have time on their hands. Savvy high schoolers can handle tasks such as hauling, packing, and transporting items to the shipper. They're often quite adept with computers, which is an obvious bonus.

- **Retired people**   Even if they don't work on the computer, older folks can answer questions, help with packing and shipping, provide food and refreshment for other volunteers, and the like. And eBay is easy to use, so there may be some retirees eager to learn how.

- **Stay-at-home moms or dads**   People who work at home or care for their children have ready access to their computers and the Internet. They're also able to gather items from around the house to donate to your cause. If they have a digital camera and have used eBay, so much the better.

Find an eBay-Savvy Volunteer

You may be tasked with organizing a fundraising event and selling on eBay. But that doesn't mean you're necessarily an expert on the subject. You don't have to be an expert as long as you're able to locate someone who has at least a moderate amount of experience selling on eBay, and who's willing to help. In every small town or in practically any group of people, you're likely to find someone who has bought and sold on eBay. When you begin to recruit volunteers, put out a call like this:

> "If you know how to sell on eBay and want to help with our fundraiser, we want to hear from you!"

If you're looking for a quick course on how to prepare sales descriptions on eBay, follow the instructions in Chapter 7. Even if you know how to sell on eBay, having other experienced sellers there to help you is invaluable. They can help train your other volunteers, for one thing. Many newcomers (known on the Web as "newbies") can learn, but many find selling on eBay more intimidating than they thought. Though they're eager to help, it's possible newbies aren't terribly good with computers, don't have a good Internet connection, or won't be able to handle other problems that come up.

It's possible to conduct an eBay fundraiser with as few as one or two volunteers, as long as you space out the number of sales you create over a period of time so the workload is manageable. For instance, rather than trying to get 250 sales online in a single day, create 25 sales a day for ten days. PowerSellers, sellers who are used to selling on eBay and who make use of bulk listing software, can easily get 20 or 30 sales online in a day. In the beginning, especially if your volunteers lack eBay experience, you should shoot for a more modest goal of perhaps 6 to 10 item listings per person. You can create your item sales listings in advance of when you want the sale to start, as long as you specify a time in the Start time section (see Figure 3-2).

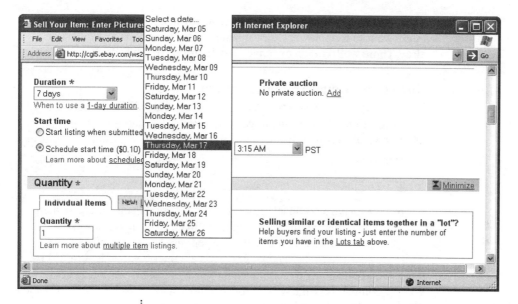

FIGURE 3-2 You can get item descriptions online gradually and schedule them all to begin at your desired time.

The Start Time options appear in Page 3 of the Sell Your Item form, the form that eBay provides for getting sales descriptions and photos online. (See Chapter 7 for instructions on how to use the form.) The point is that the more people—and computers—you have, the easier it will be to get all your items listed for sale online.

Hire a Trading Assistant

If you feel you have more items to list for sale online in a shorter period of time than your volunteers can handle or if you feel you need assistance selling valuable items, consider hiring a trading assistant, trading post, or auction management company to do some or *all* of the work for you. In these cases, it will cost you a percentage of the money raised, but could save you tremendous time, potentially deliver higher bids, and help ensure a smooth running event.

> **note** *The term* trading assistant, *in this case, is being used generically to refer to anyone who sells merchandise on eBay on consignment for someone else. Anyone can be a trading assistant; however, individuals who have the formal Trading Assistant designation are ones who have met eBay's requirements and who are included in eBay's database of such sellers.*

If you have a high-profile organization or just a lot of items to sell, you might want to hire one of the companies that sell on behalf of others on eBay. Three well-known examples are described in the following sections.

Hire an Individual Trading Assistant

You find Trading Assistants (TAs), who have been certified by eBay to sell on behalf of others, by doing a search of eBay's TA database (**http://pages .ebay.com/tahub/index.html**). As of this writing, the requirements for being a TA are

- You have sold at least 4 items in the previous 30 days.

- You have a feedback score of 50 or higher. Feedback is a system in which eBay members leave comments (positive, negative, or neutral) that describe their experience with each other in a transaction. The feedback score is a numeric value determined by adding up positive comments (which count for +1 point), negative comments (which count for –1 point), and neutral comments (which count for 0).

- At least 97 percent of your feedback is positive.

- Your eBay account is in good standing.

A good trading assistant will present your nonprofit organization with a game plan of how he or she is going to market the goods. You need to know how your items will be priced, how they'll be advertised, what their fees are, and how you're required to pay them. Be sure to thoroughly discuss how they'll photograph items, write item descriptions, answer questions, collect funds, and ship items for you. TAs on eBay are able to specify their own terms of sale, and many restrict their activities to particular categories of merchandise that they're already familiar with. They might charge 10–15 percent of the purchase price, or a flat 25 percent of the highest bid. Others charge $1 per listing plus 4–5 percent of the final sales price; you should search the database yourself and ask one or more candidates questions before you settle on one that's right for you.

Some advantages of working with a TA include:

- **They're local**   If you're lucky, you can find someone who lives in your geographic area, or perhaps even your own town. You can meet the seller in person and transport your merchandise to the TA yourself, rather than having to ship it. In some cases, the TA will pick up your merchandise from you.

- **They speak different languages** If you do an advanced search of the TA database as we describe in the upcoming sidebar, you can find one who speaks Spanish, for example.

- **Some specialize in selling for charitable causes** You can narrow your search to TAs who sell for charity and who have experience working with MissionFish and nonprofits.

It's a good idea to look through several TA listings to see what kinds of merchandise the seller specializes in. If you tend to get donations of toys and children's items, for instance, it makes sense to find someone who has a lot of experience in that area. Also take a look at the TA's current sales by clicking on the User ID to view the TA's profile, then clicking the Items for Sale link.

Use a Trading Post "Drop-Off" Store

eBay has become successful by providing shoppers with an alternative to brick-and-mortar wholesale outlets, antique malls, and discount stores of all kinds. It might seem surprising, then, to think of heading to a brick-and-mortar store in your neighborhood in order to sell on eBay. But many nonprofits are turning to drop-off stores—brick-and-mortar storefronts where employees photograph and list items on eBay for their owners—for just that purpose.

Finding a Trading Assistant to Help You

eBay TAs are located around the United States and in many other parts of the world. Hopefully, you'll be lucky enough to find several in your geographic area that specialize in nonprofit fundraising. Some TAs discount their standard percentage charge for nonprofits so it's worth asking about it. Follow these steps to locate a TA:

1. Go to the Trading Assistant Program home page (**http://pages.ebay.com/tahub/ index.html**) and open the Trading Assistant Directory.

2. Click Advanced Search in the Find a Trading Assistant form.

3. When the Find a Trading Assistant: Advanced Search page appears, fill in the Zip Code box.

4. Scroll down to the section heading Show only Trading Assistants with the following specialties: and check the box next to Charity auctions.

5. Click Search Directory.

(continued)

Scan the list of results to see who's available in your area. For example, in a search on Chicago, less than 20 trading assistants were located in the zip code used. As a result, eBay automatically enlarged the geographic area being searched, and sorted the results by feedback number rather than zip code. In this case, the trading assistants at the top of the list weren't necessarily the ones closest to the area within the zip code. Clicking the ZIP Code heading in the list of search results shown in the following illustration focused the search to present the TAs in zip code order, and scrolling down the list located the ones closest to the zip code used.

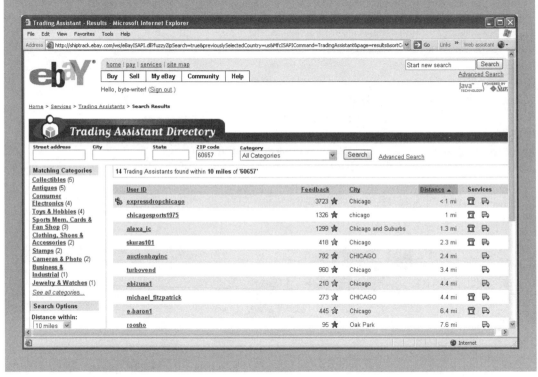

AuctionDrop (**www.auctiondrop.com**) is the biggest and most prominent drop-off site. With its partnership with UPS (they now have locations around the country), you stand a good chance of finding a store near you. And with a feedback level of more than 20,000 at this writing, AuctionDrop qualifies as one of eBay's most successful PowerSellers. But they are by no means the only game in town. You might be able to save a few dollars, and have a good experience, using a smaller outlet in your local area. A store called ExpressDrop (**www.expressdrop.com**, shown in Figure 3-3) is located just a few blocks from the home of one of this book's authors, and it has built up a feedback level of more than 3,000 in the year or so since it's been open.

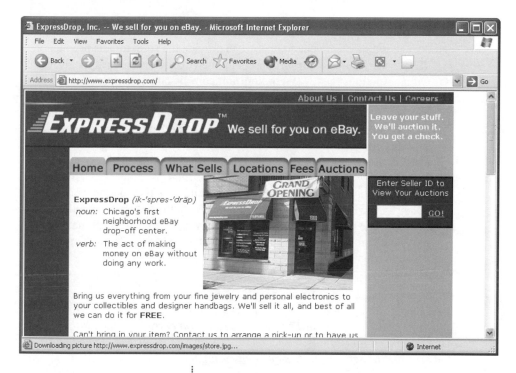

FIGURE 3-3 You might consider hiring a local eBay drop-off store to manage your fundraiser.

Some advantages of working with a trading post include:

- They have a physical location that you can use as the drop spot for all donations.

- They use proven practices, especially the larger chains, and high-quality photography.

- They have an established reputation on eBay and relationships with shippers to keep shipping costs down, which can make items more appealing.

- They may discount fees for nonprofits (though unfortunately the fees may be high to start with—up to 40 percent).

Hire a Complete Auction Management Company

An auction management company can provide the soup to nuts production of your charity auction, from concept through execution and analysis. Kompolt Online Auction Agency (**www.kompolt.com**) is one of the premier online auction management companies specializing in high-profile and nonprofit fundraising events for both charities and brand-name companies conducting cause-related marketing. One advantage of using Kompolt is that you gain visibility for your brand as well: Kompolt is a promotional agency that uses auction management as a way to increase visibility for a company. It's worked with such high-profile clients as the U.S. Fund for UNICEF, British Airways, the Starlight Starbright Children's Foundation, and the *Today Show*. Kompolt also has experience with the bidder prequalification process—the process that ensures the bids you receive are legitimate and not "joke" bids. Prequalification can reduce the chances that bidders will back out after the sale and refuse to pay.

> **tip** *For different occasions, nonprofits may find it best to sell themselves, easiest to have people sell and send them the proceeds, or most compelling to recruit donations themselves and have a third party sell for them on eBay for a fee. Rather than relying on inexperienced individuals selling on eBay, using an experienced person or business can expedite the selling process and deliver higher final values.*

Other advantages of working with an auction management company may include assistance with:

- Soliciting auction item donations

- Developing custom creative pieces and branding for the auction campaign

- Marketing and public relations, including press releases

- Internet marketing

- All auction management and customer support

For more information on auction management companies see Chapter 10, which discusses major charity auctions.

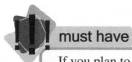

If you plan to hold a fundraiser in the coming year, the time to start planning is now. Because eBay is easy to use and learn, but can be difficult to master, it's important for nonprofits to understand what's involved in selling on the world's most popular auction marketplace. This way, they can decide how to best use their resources and volunteer staff. eBay is not the answer to every organization's total fundraising needs, but it can be a valuable tool.

In this chapter, you explored the different steps involved in planning a fundraiser on eBay. Not all of the steps apply to every situation, and the sequence of steps differs depending on the group and its goals. The planning steps you need to do include:

- Before you do anything, get the important officers in your group on board with your eBay fundraising project. Make an effort to instill them with enthusiasm, and tell them that a fundraiser has public relations, as well as monetary, benefits.

- Whether your eBay fundraiser is a one-time or ongoing event, be conscious of the public relations value of holding such a sale. Use the event to spread the word about your group, along with trying to raise much-needed funds.

- Combining eBay auctions with a real-world event adds a new flair to traditional events and extends the reach and participation possible beyond the geographic locale.

- A single person can hold a small-scale event, but for large events where dozens of separate items are sold and the goal is to raise tens of thousands of dollars, make sure you have sufficient staff to solicit donations, prepare sale descriptions, and handle packing and shipping tasks.

- Allow enough time for planning so that the event can be a success.

Part II
Selling Donated Items

Chapter 4
Deciding What to Sell

We thought, if it [an old Remington shotgun shell case] brings in $10, it'll be great. It brought $350.

—Patti Skrdla, Atkinson,
Nebraska

What We'll Cover in This Chapter:

- Gathering donated items that will sell on eBay

- Researching completed sales for suggestions of what to sell

- Looking at your own existing items with an eye toward sales

- Connecting with people who are sympathetic with your goals

- Focusing on high-value, high-demand merchandise

- Considering shipping requirements before you sell

- Including one-of-a-kind experiences in your sales mix

- Selling your leftover items rather than discarding them

As you've already learned, making the decision to sponsor an eBay sales event can be an important first step for effective fundraising. You can use such an event to attract donors as well as to raise funds. The best way to connect with potential bidders and buyers, and to make your work pay off for your chosen cause, is to find the right things to sell. eBay enables you to go past traditional events such as rummage sales, car washes, or bake sales. You're freed from the need to organize a cocktail party or an auction held in a brick-and-mortar location. With eBay, you suddenly gain the ability to reach people in all corners of the world. What's even better is that these people don't have to get all dressed up and find their way to a location where you're in charge of feeding and entertaining them. If you find the right sales items, you can reach a wider audience for your cause than you ever thought possible.

But an eBay fundraiser presents another kind of challenge: even though millions of items go up for sale every day on eBay, the fact is that many of those sales are destined to end without a successful purchase. So, although you can't always predict what's going to sell on eBay, it's important to realize that research can help make your efforts more efficient. Doing some homework in advance to learn what sells, how to put lots together, how to price items, and what items are hot on eBay will help your nonprofit sell more efficiently on eBay. Understanding what eBay shoppers want can provide the range of items you can sell from commonplace merchandise to extraordinary experiences.

It's liberating to realize that conventional fundraising wisdom doesn't always apply online. Things that are offbeat and odd and that would never lead to success in a conventional auction can sell like hotcakes at a nonprofit event held before eBay's worldwide audience. Sometimes, coming up with winning inventory is a matter of taking a new look at items you already have on hand. And when it comes to soliciting merchandise and donated events, you can tell potential donors that selling on eBay is a great way to publicize their organizations, especially if the donated item proves especially newsworthy. In this chapter, we'll describe what you, as the nonprofit auction organizer, can tell your donors and volunteers to get them thinking along the right lines when deciding what to put up for sale.

Research What Sells on eBay

Every nonprofit dreams of attracting new donors to its cause. eBay makes that possible: Your auction merchandise is made available to millions of people who surf the world's most popular auction site, whether they're specifically intending to donate to you or not. How do you reach the millions who are browsing eBay for general merchandise from both for-profit and nonprofit sellers? You do what every good seller does—you conduct some simple research and determine what sells on eBay. You scour your own attic and storage areas to see if you have any items that fit the bill; you encourage your volunteers to do the same. You discard the things that aren't likely to sell, and focus on the ones that will make money (to save your own time and effort, not to mention eBay's Insertion Fee, the fee charged when you create a listing for sale). In the sections that follow, we explain the qualities to look for more specifically and address how to do your own research so you can get the maximum result for your fundraising efforts.

Look for High-Value Collectibles

It's often difficult to predict what will sell well on eBay. Much of this chapter, in fact, is devoted to suggestions about how you can plan to gather merchandise that bidders will find attractive. Planning is useful, and you should do as much research as you have time to do. (It's especially important to take shipping and packing into consideration, as we explain in the section "Before You Sell, Plan How to Ship," later in this chapter.)

But the fact is that you can't always tell what people are going to find desirable. Those old lamps from the 1950s that are sitting in a corner of your basement gathering dust might seem positively ugly to you. But to someone in Manhattan who's redesigning an apartment in 1950s style, they might be just the design element needed to give that space a cool retro look.

Patti Skrdla, a volunteer who prepared many of the sales listings for the Atkinson, Nebraska, fundraiser that raised $12,000 for the town in 2004, was surprised by many of the items that ended up attracting the highest prices.

"All of the vintage and retro stuff sold like crazy, but the highest price came for a little old Remington shotgun shell case. We thought, if it brings $10, it'll be great. It brought $350. Old vintage lamps sold like hotcakes for $75 or $80. One lady brought in an Aladdin San Francisco Bay lunch box. She hadn't been able to sell it for $10; it brought more than $100."

On the other hand, Skrdla says they received donations of many items that would never sell on eBay: old used pillows, "garage sale" quality clothing, and the like. They had to accept all the donations, but the volunteers who prepared the sales descriptions (some of whom are shown in this photo) exercised their own discretion and picked the items that would actually be listed online.

You're likely to find that, in general, the types of items that attract bidders and buyers on eBay are ones that:

- Are either new, like new, or in excellent condition

- Have recognizable brand names

- Are of high quality

In general, electronics items, toys, jewelry, and collectibles sell well on eBay. But generalizations only go so far. The moral? Use your common sense. Anything that you might consider a vintage or antique item might sell on eBay, especially if it has a recognizable brand name, place name, or famous person's name attached to it.

Research Completed Sales

You don't have to look far to discover the kinds of things that attract bidders on eBay. The best place to look for the most up-to-date sales statistics is eBay itself. Before you start trying to sell—ideally, before you and your fellow volunteers begin to gather merchandise and solicit donations—do a little homework. Know which kinds of sales attract lots of bids and which turn out to be duds. While it's often useful for for-profit businesses to focus on a particular type of merchandise, for nonprofits, it doesn't pay to be choosy. Often, you simply have to take what donors are willing to give. Before you put the sales online, however, it's always a good idea to verify that there's a market of buyers for the kinds of merchandise you want to put up for auction. The sections that follow provide you with some tips for doing the research.

> *tip* *The eBay Community area is one of the best places to research just about anything you need to know with regard to the auction site. Scan the message boards to get an idea of the kinds of problems sellers tend to confront, so you can watch out for them yourself.*

Searching on eBay Itself

Whether you're planning to look through your own living quarters, ask your relatives for heirlooms they want to donate, or instruct your volunteers on what to list on eBay, it pays to be efficient. You can easily spend hours cleaning, photographing, and listing merchandise only to see it fail to attract bids. If that happens, you're not only losing time, but you're also losing a small amount of money. eBay charges an Insertion Fee—a fee for listing an item for sale—and you're required to pay that fee whether the item sells or not. For an individual sale, the fee isn't large. But if you list a dozen or more items that don't sell, the Insertion Fees can eat into the profit you make on other sales. The Insertion Fee depends on the starting bid of the item. The fees that were current at this writing are shown in Table 4-1.

Starting Price	Insertion Fee
$0.01 to $0.99	$0.25
$1.00 to $9.99	$0.35
$10.00 to $24.99	$0.60
$25.00 to $49.99	$1.20
$50.00 to $199.99	$2.40
$200.00 to $499.99	$3.60
$500.00 and up	$4.80

TABLE 4-1 eBay Insertion Fees

note *eBay's fees change periodically; you can find the latest fees at **http://pages.ebay .com/help/sell/fees.html**. When you're planning your fundraising event, it's a good idea to calculate the fees you can expect to pay to the auction site and subtract them from your projected profits.*

By searching through eBay's completed sales, you can compare the kinds of merchandise you have to sell with similar items that have been put up for sale recently. It's hardly a scientific or comprehensive survey because, after all, eBay's database of completed sales only provides you with sales that have completed in the last ten days or so. But a quick search of completed sales can give you a good idea of which items tend to attract bids and which don't.

Conducting an Advanced Search   If you've bought or sold on eBay before, you're probably familiar with eBay's Search: Find Items feature. From any eBay page, enter a term in the box that contains the "placeholder" phrase **Start new search** and then click the Search button that appears in the upper right-hand corner of the page. Then, in order to search through sales that have already ended, you must access the Advanced Search page. Follow these steps:

1. Either click Advanced Search at the top of any eBay page or, if you're on the Basic Search page, click the Advanced Search link at the bottom of the form.

2. When the advanced version of the Search: Find Items page appears, click the Completed listings only box to search for Completed Items (see Figure 4-1).

3. Type your search terms in the box labeled Enter keyword or item number.

4. Scroll through the rest of the options on the page to focus your search even further; for instance, you can filter words out of your search results by entering those words in the box labeled Exclude these words. Other options on the page let you search by geographic area, price range, or specific sellers.

5. When you're done entering search options, click the Search button at the bottom of the form.

Optionally, you can limit your search to only items that have been listed through Giving Works by nonprofits like you. You do this by checking the box next to eBay Giving Works Items for Charity. At the time this was

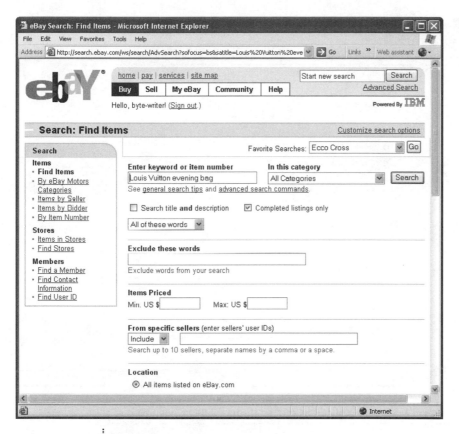

FIGURE 4-1 Search through completed sales on eBay to discover which items attract bids—and which turn out to be duds.

written, the box was highlighted near the bottom of the Search: Find Items form (see Figure 4-2). By the time you read this, the filter may no longer be considered "new" and might be in a different location.

warning *Keep in mind that when you list items on eBay, even if they're part of a fundraiser, those items will be available to everyone who shops on eBay, whether they're interested in making a donation or not. That's the advantage of holding a fundraiser on eBay; you cast the widest net possible and make your sales available to a potential customer base of millions. If you're primarily interested in evaluating the monetary value of a piece of merchandise, you don't need to limit your search to only items that are offered through Giving Works.*

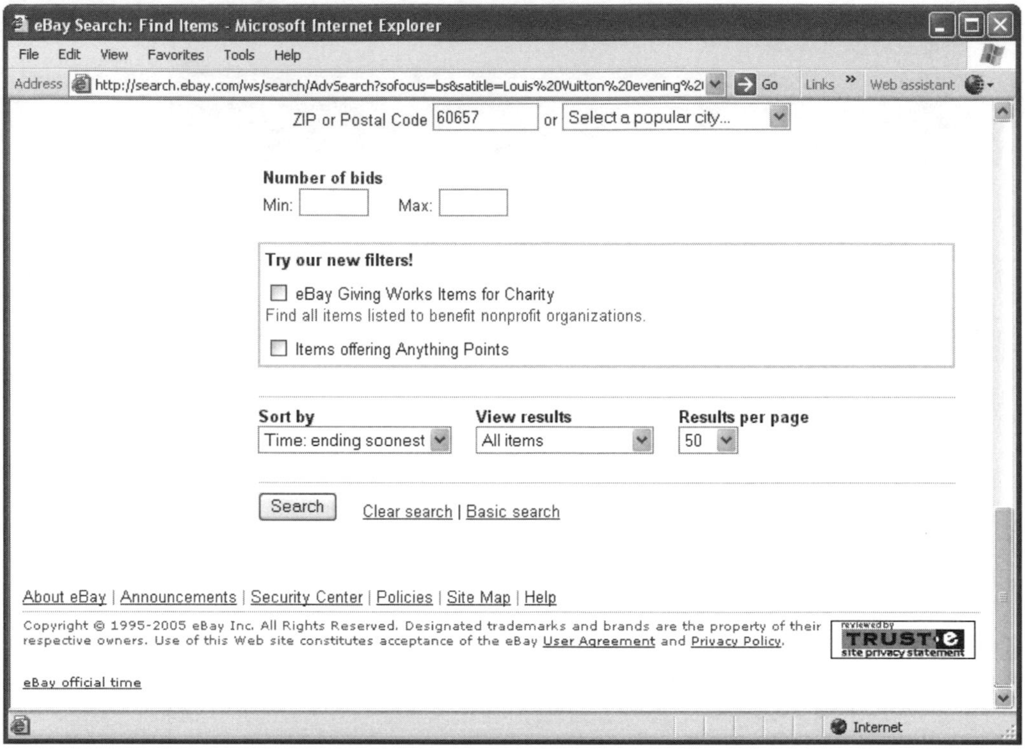

FIGURE 4-2 You can limit a search to only items offered through eBay Giving Works.

When you do conduct your sale, make note of what has sold recently in the item's category of interest, what the final sales prices were, and how many people are selling similar items. Suppose someone has donated the following items: A DVD player, a set of 1998 Encyclopedia Britannica books, a Blue Bear Beanie Baby, and a Davenport Princess Diana collector's plate. Our search of the completed transactions for these items in February 2005 yielded the data shown in Table 4-2.

tip   *It's a good idea to calculate eBay's Insertion Fees and Final Value Fees, as well as PayPal seller's fees, to get a realistic idea of how much you can expect to make from any particular item on the auction site. Such calculations can help you determine whether or not an item is worth listing in the first place. Fee Finder, a program from HammerTap (www.hammertap.com/FeeFinder.html) calculates the fees automatically for you.*

Item	Bids	Starting Price	Final Price	Insertion Fee	Final Value Fee	Profit/ Loss
Sony 5-Disc DVD Player	10	$13.75	$32.50	$0.60	$2.20	$29.70
1941 set of Encyclopedia Britannica books	0	$0.99	n/a	$0.25	n/a	–$0.25
Blue Bear Beanie Baby	0	$9.49	n/a	$0.35	n/a	–$0.35
Davenport Limited Edition Princess Diana collector's plate	14	$9.99	$20.84	$0.60	$1.09	$19.15

TABLE 4-2 Results of Completed Transactions

The dollar amounts in Table 4-2 might not apply precisely for nonprofit auctions on eBay. If 100 percent of the proceeds go to a nonprofit, for instance, eBay donates the Final Value Fee to that group. And the preceding calculations don't take into account the fees MissionFish charges. But the point is that you need to evaluate what you have to sell and make an effort to sell only items that you are reasonably certain will attract a profit. Ideally, the profit should be in the $25 to $50 range. Items like Beanie Babies are out of fashion and don't sell on eBay the way they did in the 1990s; items like a set of encyclopedia books are expensive to ship and have been replaced by CD-ROM versions. Don't waste your time and money trying to sell such things on eBay.

> **tip** *If you're not currently viewing a page on eBay and you want to do a search, you can connect directly to the Search: Find Items page at **http://search.ebay.com**. The form on this page gives you a variety of options for filtering sales by time, price, distance, and category. And you can use the link provided under the search option boxes to connect directly to the Advanced Search page.*

Turn to eBay's Seller Central   If you need to provide your volunteers with written instructions about the kinds of items that sell well on eBay, visit Seller Central. The main Seller Central page (**http://pages.ebay.com/ sellercentral**, shown in Figure 4-3) contains links that lead you to detailed and up-to-date statistics on what's "hot" in many eBay categories.

It can take some fishing around to find the data you want, however. Look for sales reports that list the most popular items sold on the auction site. They contain tips on what constitutes a good sales item.

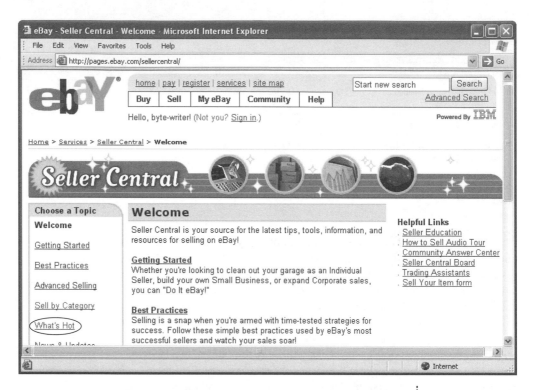

FIGURE 4-3 Visit Seller Central for detailed lists of "hot" items in many categories.

Uncover Lists of eBay's "Hot Items"

For instance, suppose you have received a donation of exercise equipment—weights, stationery bicycles, and treadmills—from the local fitness center. Such items can be heavy and costly to ship, and difficult to pack besides. You naturally want to know if it's worthwhile to list such items for sale. eBay's Seller Central area puts out a number of publications for buyers and sellers in especially popular areas, including the Sporting Goods and Memorabilia category. First, see whether exercise equipment is among eBay's current list of "hot items." Follow these steps:

1. Under Choose a Topic on the Seller Central page, click What's Hot.

2. When the What's Hot page appears, click Hot Items by Category.

3. A detailed report of "Hot Categories" for the current month appears. Read through the introduction to get an overview of how the categories and subcategories are rated: they're defined as Super Hot, Very Hot, and Hot.

4. Scroll down to the page on which your category of interest appears. (For this example, you would consult the Sporting Goods and Memorabilia category).

5. Find the category, or categories, that matches the item you have for sale. In this example, you discover that exercise and fitness equipment, such as cardiovascular equipment and weights, are listed in the Very Hot category, so these are good items to sell.

Once you have an idea of the items that are considered Super Hot in a particular month, you can get more specific brand names and tips from Seller Central. Return to the home page (**http://pages.ebay.com/sellercentral**) and follow these steps:

1. Click Category Tips.

2. Scroll down to the category of interest (in this case, Sporting Goods and Fan Shop) and click In Demand.

3. When the In Demand page appears for your selected category, scroll down to the section that contains the items you're researching and make note of the brand names. For instance, in this example, Bowflex, Nordic Track, and Nautilus appear.

Such statistics are especially helpful if you want to provide donors with a list of items they might give to your fundraising effort. If you have plenty of clothing and toys and are looking for more electronics and sports-related equipment, you can scan the In Demand lists to provide suggestions.

note *You can also use eBay's advanced Search: Find Items page to do a search for completed transactions involving specific types of exercise equipment. Such a search gives you more specific information than one of the general reports on Seller Central. See the "Conducting an Advanced Search" section, earlier in this chapter, for more.*

Searching Outside of eBay

The Search: Find Items page is only the most obvious way to find items being sold on eBay. A search on Google (**www.google.com**) and other search services will turn up items being offered in a seller's eBay Store. One of the best services for searching eBay completed transactions, however, is outside eBay—it's on a site called Andale (**www.andale.com**). Here's how to use it:

1. Go to the Andale Price Finder page (**http://cms.andale.com/research/price-finder.html**).

2. Enter a keyword or phrase in the Research Item box.

3. Click Search.

That's all there is to it. In a few seconds a page appears with a chart illustrating the average price for the item and examples of completed auctions conducted over the previous month (Figure 4-4). Another great pricing resource specifically for antique and collectible items is Price Miner (**www.priceminer.com**) which, for an affordable $9.95 per month, works in a similar way summarizing data of actual prices paid online.

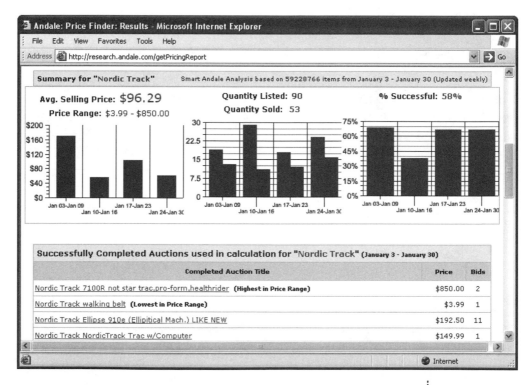

FIGURE 4-4 Andale's Price Finder searches a wider range of completed transactions than eBay's Advanced Search utility.

note *Many eBay-related software products contain their own tools for searching eBay sales listings. EZ sniper, a product by Abercrombie Software (**www.ezsniper.com**), contains its own search tool called EZ search.*

Focus on High-Value Merchandise, Nonprofit Trading Assistant Advises

Lu Paletta, owner of Bid-n-Pack (**www.bid-n-pack.com**) and an eBay Trading Assistant who helps nonprofit organizations, advises her clients to focus on high-quality, high-value merchandise to ensure a profit.

If you don't think you'll get a good return on your merchandise—for instance, at least $25—don't put it up for sale on eBay. That's one of several pieces of advice from Paletta, who's helped several church groups, schools, and other nonprofits raise funds on the auction site.

Paletta's second piece of advice: forget about selling stuffed animals, including Beanie Babies. "Unless you have a very rare one, it's not worth it," she says. "Books don't go for very much, either. Sporting goods memorabilia will sell if it has a certificate of authenticity." She points out that high-priced brand-name items of all types also attract bids, as well as jewelry and consumer electronics components.

Paletta urges nonprofits to do research before putting something up for sale—or having a Trading Assistant sell it. She also advocates not to sell something if there are already lots of other auctions online for the same item. "Let's say you're selling NASCAR telephones. You do a search, and you see that there are 50 other people out there offering that. Your telephone can get lost among all the other sales."

Subtitles are especially important: Look for eBay promotions when subtitles only cost a penny. Even if they don't, subtitles worth the investment. You can add a phrase such as "Proceeds go to the [*fill in the blank*] Foundation" in the subtitle. When you write the main auction description, be sure to put the same notice there, too, so people clearly understand that the item is being offered as part of a fundraiser.

"When you do a school auction, obviously the person has to be there," Paletta adds. "With eBay, you don't have to be here. Be sure to send out flyers to everyone who might be interested, telling them how long the auctions will run, describing the items, and urging people go to eBay."

Don't be reluctant to sell some "crazy stuff" that you might not think would sell, she advises. "Some of the crazy stuff you might sell as general merchandise can work, too. One set of items was a bath set designed as a cowboy boot, a cowboy hat soap dish, and shower curtain hooks that looked like stars. We thought it might sell for $5; someone in Manitoba, Canada, paid $37 for it."

Look Close to Home

You don't always have to cast a wide net to find collectibles and other merchandise that will attract bids. Begin by looking around your own home or the space in which your organization does business. Often, you discover desirable merchandise sitting right under your nose. The trick is to look at those items in a new way. Suggestions for the criteria you need to look for are presented in the sections that follow.

Find a New Purpose for Unneeded Items

Nonprofit institutions that serve the public frequently have display items that are taking up storage space and can be used in a fundraising effort. For instance, the Museum of American Heritage mounted an exhibition on the evolution of technology that featured early typewriters. In the course of the exhibit, a number of typewriters were gathered, but not all of them were actually exhibited. The leftovers could not be kept because there was very little storage space available. Occasions like these can be opportunities. For example, the museum could sell the excess typewriters on eBay as a way of publicizing the exhibit itself, allowing them to clear out the unneeded items while giving bidders the chance to "own a piece of history."

An eBay fundraising event can help promote an institution's current activities. In the case of the

When Searching for Merchandise, Think Locally

Sometimes, things that can help you raise valuable funds are literally sitting in your storage area gathering dust. An article in the *The Washington Post* (**www.washingtonpost.com/ wp-dyn/articles/A30409-2004Dec27.html**) reported on an eBay fundraising effort conducted by a local theater troupe in late 2004. Arena Stage auctioned off a silk kimono used in the production of the musical *M. Butterfly* on eBay for $637.76. It also unloaded two hand-carved thrones from *Camelot*, attracting $152.50 for the pair—and attracting valuable publicity at the same time.

Staffers at Signature Theatre in Arlington, Virginia, took notice and followed suit, unpacking the body-parts grinder from its production of Stephen Sondheim's *Sweeney Todd* and the Grand Central sign from its production of Sondheim's *Company*. The *Sweeney Todd* props weren't the first Sondheim-related items to be sold on eBay: in February 2003, Sondheim himself auctioned his 1985 Jaguar automobile to benefit the group Young Playwrights Inc.

typewriter exhibit, the museum could have sold the typewriters at the same time the new exhibit opened. Each sales description could have mentioned the current exhibit. The sale could, in this way, help the museum raise money and market the museum's activities to a wider audience at the same time. Even if you don't make a large profit through your online fundraiser, you can ensure that the event will generate goodwill and a positive "buzz" about your organization.

Appeal to Your Core Constituency

When you regard your eBay fundraising effort as a part of your overall effort to market and publicize your business, the question of what to sell becomes clearer. You need to sell merchandise or events that will appeal to the people who share the same concerns as your institution.

Weimaraner Rescue of North Texas offers T-shirts for sale in its eBay Store (**http://stores.ebay.com/WEIMARANER-RESCUE-NORTH-TEXAS**) that are guaranteed to appeal to those who love the dogs the rescue center helps. The shirts bear photos of the dogs. Such items are on sale for long periods of time, whether the center is conducting a fundraising event or not. That's the advantage of having an eBay Store: It gives you the ability to appeal to your core constituency by offering merchandise that connects with their concerns and by presenting another opportunity to raise funds for your organization.

Look for the Four Most Important Attributes

Certain qualities are almost guaranteed to elicit bids and purchases on eBay. If an item has one or more of those attributes, your chances of success increase. When you're soliciting donations or looking around your own facilities for items that can be "repurposed," make sure you focus on objects that:

- *Have a recognizable brand name*. Most eBay shoppers search for merchandise by entering one or more keywords in a search box. Items that have well-known brand names are more likely to be found than "no-name" objects because they'll turn up in keyword searches.

- *Are in good condition*. A few collectibles will sell well even though they're clearly the worse for wear: a baseball that is waterlogged and scuffed because it was hit by Barry Bonds into San Francisco Bay will still be in demand, for instance. But for most everyday items, the better the condition, the higher the level of interest. That's because, with millions of items going up for sale every day on eBay, collectors and other shoppers are able to pick and choose. If they don't win one auction, they know they're likely to see a similar item appear on eBay sooner or later that's possibly in better condition.

- *Are cross-collectible.* Items that traditionally fetch the highest bids at auction are those that appeal to many different collectors or shoppers and that fit into more than one category. An antique bank adorned with two monkeys that was examined on the PBS television program *Antiques Roadshow* was worth thousands of dollars because it not only appealed to the many collectors of American toys but it also appealed to those who collect animal (or even monkey-related) objects. If an item fits into two or more categories, it's twice as likely to turn up in a keyword search on eBay.

- *Are related to a celebrity or other famous figure.* Merchandise doesn't necessarily have to be autographed to be of value on eBay. Autographs can be difficult to authenticate unless they are being sold by a well-known and highly respected institution. But photos, booklets, keychains, watches, books, records, and other items that bear a famous person's name or face generally do well in eBay sales.

tip *Look around your area for small companies that might be willing to make bulk donations. They might be happy to unload their discontinued, excess, and seasonal inventories as a tax write-off.*

When you're soliciting donations, also consider the time of year when the sale takes place. If you hold a fundraiser in the late fall, you'll do well if you focus on holiday and gift items. Even if you schedule your fundraising event for summer, which is traditionally the "slow season" on eBay, you're more likely to attract bidders if you can offer back to school items as well as camping and outdoor equipment.

note *When accepting donations, there are two schools of thought about giving receipts. Some organizations, such as Good Will, give a receipt acknowledging the items received but leave it up to the donor to attach a value to the donation. Others prefer to give a receipt to the donor once the item has sold, for the "market value" the item actually achieved.*

Typically, nonprofits do not give buyers a receipt when they purchase an item because the buyers have received value. But if the price paid for the item exceeds its retail value, the difference could be considered a donation. You can see how determining that difference could become time consuming and why many consider the price an items sells for to be the fair market value. We are not tax experts, so ask your tax advisor for tips and best practices for your organization. For more discussion on receipts, see Chapter 8.

Before You Sell, Plan How to Ship

One of the things that makes fundraisers so enjoyable is the fact that businesses and individuals often donate unusual, noteworthy, or one-of-a-kind things. Events like lunch with the mayor or a behind-the-scenes tour of the local museum are easy to "deliver." But tangible objects that are heavy and bulky can cause problems when it comes time to ship them.

According to Joan Greene, who organized the successful Great Chicago Fire Sale on eBay in late 2004, "experience packages," such as the chance to dye the Chicago River bright green on St. Patrick's Day, were easier to handle than tangible items, especially when it came to shipping. Offbeat items like Chicago parking meters and manhole covers sold on eBay, but they turned out to be difficult to pack and expensive to ship. If you don't plan ahead and provide an estimate of shipping costs in your sales description, you can end up in a dispute with a buyer.

Be sure to accurately estimate the weight of what you're going to sell before you sell it. If an item weighs hundreds of pounds, traditional shippers like United Parcel Service (UPS) and the United States Postal Service (USPS) may not handle it. You might have to pay extra to a freight shipper in order to successfully complete the transaction. An accurate scale— something you can find economically on eBay itself—is essential for any eBay sale, whether it's a fundraiser or a for-profit affair.

Be sure to make eBay's Shipping Calculator available to your shoppers. The calculator is an option included in eBay's Sell Your Item form, which is the form the auction site provides for preparing sales descriptions. When you specify in the course of filling out the form that you want to use buyer-calculated shipping rates, eBay provides a calculator in the body of the auction description (like the one shown here). The potential buyer can enter his or her location in the calculator and it calculates the shipping cost.

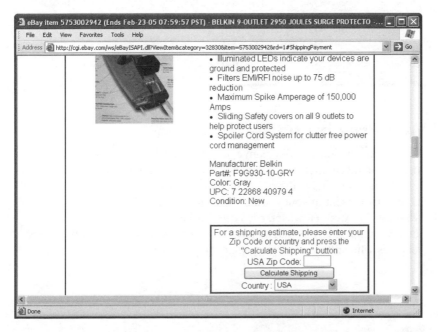

Alternatively, you can add an actual shipping rate to your auction description. But be sure to take into account the total weight of the item after it's packed, however. If you're selling something lightweight, such as an antique postcard, shipping is easy to estimate. Many sellers simply choose U.S. Priority Mail service and specify $6 or $7 for shipping. But if you're selling something bulky that needs to be packed in a box filled with packing material, don't forget that some packing material (particularly paper) is heavy. The item itself might weigh 5 pounds on a scale but be sure to add a pound for the box and packing material just to be on the safe side. Because shipping differs depending on the destination, it can be difficult to provide a single flat rate that covers all potential buyers. Some sellers go through the effort of providing an elaborate table that lists all the possible shipping costs, such as the one shown here. To find out more about packing, shipping, and other steps involved in completing transactions, see Chapter 8.

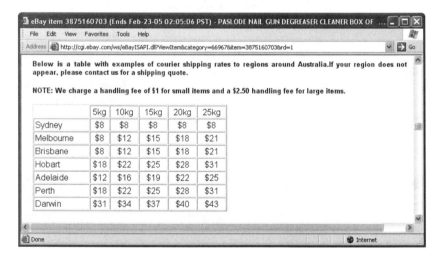

Let Your Creative Juices Flow!

Fundraisers are known for creative, one-of-a-kind offerings such as events and personalized gifts. Tours, lunches, and parties are guaranteed to appeal to individuals who live in your immediate geographic area: after all, they have to be present in your town or come to your facility in order to "collect" what they've won. However, such offerings can also appeal to out-of-towners who want to donate to a cause; if they win, they can let friends or relatives who still reside in your area enjoy the actual event.

Offer One-of-a-Kind Experiences

Everyone likes to get something unique. Nonprofits that are experiencing "donor fatigue" due to frequent fundraising events can energize their constituents by offering one-of-a-kind special events such as these:

- A chance to ride in a vintage car in your town parade

- Lunch with your mayor, school's principal, company's president, or another noteworthy individual in your organization

- The chance to have a holiday named after them

- The ability to throw a party in the local museum

- A ride in a vintage car to dinner, a birthday party, or any special occasion (not just a parade)

- A group of local schoolchildren's artwork on a plate, pottery, painting, etc.

The event doesn't even have to be a "real" one. During 2004 presidential campaign, the DraftWesleyClark.com web site offered a "virtual" dinner with Wesley Clark. Instead of getting to meet the candidate face-to-face, the prize was a group of items being sold on eBay: Four army MREs (meals ready to eat); four "Draft Wesley Clark" mugs; and four Clark bars for dessert. The winner paid $1,025 for the "virtual" prize.

eBay can still prove valuable in helping to publicize such events, even if the events primarily appeal to a local, rather than a nationwide, audience. The same potential donors who live in your area will be scanning your sales on eBay to read detailed descriptions of them and to check on the current high bids. Be sure to use the auction site not only for offering tangible merchandise, but also for offering intangible experiences and services as well.

> **tip**   *Consult with your group's board members, who may be able to offer their own tangible assets or their expertise in your fundraising effort. Some board members may be willing to have lunch with auction winners on their boats, for instance; others might be able to donate their professional services, even if only for an hour or an individual consultation.*

Focus on High-Profile Items

When it comes to auctioning off donated services or special events, keywords and recognizable names play an important a role, just as they do with durable goods. It's easier to advertise your more imaginative offerings when one of the following applies:

- The event or service has a historical component

- It is connected to a celebrity or noteworthy individual

- It is unusual and offbeat and might appeal to the local news media

Accordingly, the sale of property that is in a prime location, collectible automobiles or boats, and even time-sensitive items, such as front-row tickets to a play or sporting event, not only help you but also help the organization that makes them available.

Encourage your donors to provide services and events that reflect well on their organization, because the publicity they get can be of tremendous PR value. When the city of Chicago held its eBay fundraiser, the event garnered nationwide attention. That wasn't just because the sale was being held online. Many of the items, such as a Playboy Bunny costume, attracted the attention of the news media, who photographed it frequently. Bringing up these sorts of examples can encourage your donors to provide high-profile items. Remind them that they can get great exposure and positive public relations from an eBay event, which can have longer lasting benefits than a simple tax write-off.

Don't Overlook the "Leftovers"

Nonprofits can't always be choosy. When a donor comes to your door with a box full of household goods, you can't simply turn the person away. You also can't afford to alienate the generous individual by standing in front of him or her and proceeding to sort out the "good" from the "bad" items. You're best off taking what everyone gives you. That doesn't mean you have to *sell* what everyone gives you, of course. Sort out the items that seem desirable and that are likely to attract attention on eBay. The items that don't seem worth selling on eBay can then be handled in one of several ways. You can:

- *Throw them in the trash.* When you have a lot of other work to do in preparation for a fundraising event, this can be the most efficient option.

- *Donate them.* By giving the merchandise to a second-hand store, you might be able to earn a small tax deduction for your organization.

- *Save them for a garage sale or rummage sale.* You can hold a sale after your online fundraiser. This is a good way to get rid of any items you didn't sell online.

- *Sell all the excess merchandise as a wholesale lot.* You can pack all of your leftovers up in one big box, or group them all together as a single unit, and offer them on eBay at a bargain price. You might clean out your storage area and make a few dollars at the same time.

eBay's Wholesale Lots category (**http://pages.ebay.com/catindex/ catwholesale.html**) is set aside for sellers who want to sell large quantities of merchandise as a single unit. Bundle all your items together in one group and see what you get for them; you probably won't get a large amount, but you might make enough to compensate for a few insertion fees. The sale shown in Figure 4-5 offered a bulk lot of 35 Sony PlayStations; 10 percent of the proceeds were designated for a relief organization.

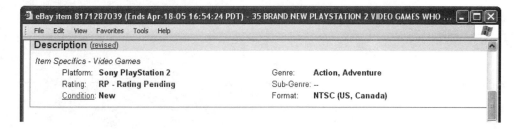

FIGURE 4-5 You can sell a bulk lot consisting of items you don't want to offer individually on eBay.

must have

- Don't try to plan out what will sell on eBay. Be open to whatever is donated. Often, the most popular items come as surprises.

- Look for vintage and collectible items that have recognizable brand names and are in reasonably good condition—you're likely to find buyers.

- Search on eBay itself to determine the kinds of items that are in demand and how much they might be worth. You can then instruct your donors and volunteers to look for such merchandise.

(continued)

- When selecting which items to list online, try to focus on things that are likely to make you at least $25 in profit.

- Look around your own home or business for items that can be reused and offered at auction.

- Try to make your auction merchandise appeal to your core constituency—the people who share your interests and values and who are likely to contribute to your cause by bidding or buying.

- Before you put something up for sale, make sure you're able to ship it economically and that you have an idea of how much shipping will cost.

- Be sure to consider auctioning off one-of-kind experiences, such as a behind the scenes tour, as well as physical items.

Chapter 5
Deciding How to Raise Funds with eBay

It [eBay Giving Works] is a nicely secured, safe environment. We feel comfortable referring people there because the accounting is in place and the process is worry-free.

—Tatiana Shulzycki,
U.S. Fund for UNICEF

What We'll Cover in This Chapter:

- Registering with eBay—first as a member, then as a seller

- Registering for a PayPal seller's account

- Understanding the benefits of using eBay Giving Works

- Deciding whether or not to sell through eBay Giving Works

- Knowing how to sell as a nonprofit through eBay Giving Works

- Doing "community selling" on behalf of a nonprofit

Once you know what type of event you'd like to create and whether you'll be doing it yourself or working with others, you need to understand the options available for selling on eBay and how to get started. First, you'll need to register on eBay and create a seller's account. You should also sign up with PayPal or another online payment solution to ensure you'll be able to receive payment in a variety of ways, including credit cards.

With those formalities taken care of, the next thing you need to do is decide whether or not to use eBay Giving Works, eBay's dedicated program for charity listings. For the great reasons we'll discuss a bit later, eBay Giving Works is generally the way to go. There are, however, a couple of situations where you might choose to list your items as a "regular" seller on eBay instead. If you go that route, you'll need to adhere to some additional rules. In this chapter, we'll show you how to get off the starting block so that, when you're ready to start selling, you'll be off and running.

Registering on eBay and PayPal

You can't win the lottery if you don't buy a ticket. Likewise, you can't raise money on eBay unless you become a registered member. Registering on eBay is easy as long as you're an individual planning to buy or sell solely for yourself. If you're planning to use eBay to raise funds for a nonprofit institution you work for, you have to decide what name you're going to use when you register. You'll also need to determine what kind of financial account (a credit card or a checking account) you're going to use when you register with eBay and its electronic payment service, PayPal. We address those decisions in the sections that follow.

Becoming a Member of eBay

You don't have to be a registered member of eBay if you want to shop for items that are currently up for sale, or read about how to use the site. But if you want to actually place a bid, post a message on the community discussion boards, or post an item for sale, you need to be a member. Registering with eBay means that you identify yourself to the site, provide your contact information, and choose a User ID and password.

Registering with eBay

As long as you're 18 years or older, you can register with eBay. But keep in mind that eBay is going to ask you for a name, address, phone number, and e-mail address at the outset. If you work for a nonprofit institution, your first task might well be to ask around on staff to see if someone already has a User ID and password on eBay. If you already have an experienced eBay user on hand, you may want to use that person's existing account for your organization's fundraising sales. The advantage is one of trust: if the member has been on eBay for a while and accumulated a high feedback rating, prospective buyers will be more likely to trust that person, and are more likely to bid.

If, on the other hand, you open a brand new account and have a feedback rating of zero, buyers might well be skeptical about buying from you because you're an unknown quantity—unless your nonprofit organization is so well-known and has such a good reputation that your good name will overcome your feedback number.

note *Feedback is a rating system in which a user receives a number value based on the trust and level of satisfaction other eBay members have had in past transactions with that user. Each eBay member is encouraged to leave a feedback comment in eBay's Feedback Forum (**http://pages.ebay.com/services/forum/feedback.html**). A positive comment (+1) is for a transaction that went well, where a member behaved in a trustworthy way. The member can leave a negative comment (−1) if a buyer didn't pay up or a seller didn't ship what was purchased. The member can leave a neutral comment when the member didn't provide the desired level of service—a buyer paid slowly, for instance, or a seller packed an item poorly or communicated slowly. Neutral comments don't add or subtract from a member's current feedback rating.*

If no one in your organization has an eBay membership, you might want to designate yourself or another person as the "contact person" for eBay. eBay will use this individual's office phone number and e-mail address in its communications. Let's assume you've determined whose name the membership will be in. You'll follow these steps next:

1. Click the Register button on the eBay home page, **www.ebay.com**).

2. On the Registration: Enter Information page, type your name, address, phone number, and e-mail address. Also choose a User ID and password.

(continued)

> **tip** *Pick your User ID carefully: it will "follow" you on the site as long as you use it (unless you change it at some point) and it can reflect on your organization. Choose a password that has at least seven characters and a mixture of letters and numerals for extra security.*

3. Click Continue. If the User ID you choose is available (in other words, none of the millions of eBay users around the world are using it yet), your browser will move to the next Enter Information page. If the User ID is unavailable, eBay provides a page suggesting similar User IDs and includes a box to type in a new one.

4. When you've chosen a new User ID and the Enter Information page appears, you're asked to enter a credit card number. eBay says this is for identification purposes only. You don't have to provide a credit card number at this point—though you will have to when you register to sell on eBay (a separate process) and when you use PayPal (another process). If your nonprofit doesn't have a credit card, you can use a checking account number—but you'll need one or the other eventually. At this point, if you don't want to enter a credit card number, you will need to enter an alternate e-mail address from a provider that's different than the one you used in Step 2. Click Continue.

5. When the Registration: Agree to Terms page appears, read the user agreement and check the boxes at the bottom of the page. Then click I Agree to These Terms.

6. A page appears asking you to check your e-mail inbox. Look for a message from eBay containing a special number that lets you confirm your registration. When you receive that message, click the Confirmation Registration Form link in the message. This link takes you to the Registration – Step 1 Complete page. Enter the number you received and click the Complete Your Registration button.

That's it; you're now a member of eBay. A web page appears confirming your new membership. You can now place some bids if you want to; but what you really want to do is put items and experiences up for sale, and that requires a separate registration.

Register as a Seller

Once you've registered to place bids on eBay, you can move to the next step: registering to sell. You can use the same User ID and password that you set up in the preceding section. You only need to provide a checking account or credit card number. eBay uses one of these to deduct your selling fees. Once you have one of the account numbers ready, click Sell in the eBay navigation bar. When the sign-in page appears, enter your User ID and password and click Sign In. Click Create a Seller's Account. One of two things happens:

- If you have a credit card number on file already, your browser goes to the Create a Seller's Account page, where you're prompted to sign in again. Enter your User ID and password and click Secure Sign In.

- If you don't have a credit card on file as yet, the Create or Update Your Credit/Debit Card page appears. Fill out the form and click Submit. When the Create a Seller's Account page appears, enter your User ID and password and click Secure Sign in.

When the Seller's Account: Verify Information page appears, review the information you've already placed on file with eBay. Then click Continue if you have a credit card you want to use, or click ID Verify to have eBay verify your information using its ID Verify program (this costs $5.00 and is optional). If you want to use a credit card, enter the information and click Continue. You're then asked to enter a checking account number for extra security protection. Enter the information and click Continue.

Suppose your nonprofit has a checking account on file, but not a credit card. In that case, you should enter a valid credit card number, even if it's only your personal credit card. Why? eBay uses both a credit card and checking account number to identify sellers. And you don't have to have eBay charge to your credit card even though you've submitted it. When the Sellers's Acount: Select How to Pay Seller Fees page appears, check one of the two options to determine which account you want to use—your credit card or checking account number. Then click Continue.

 tip *You can always change your account information by clicking My eBay in the navigation bar, clicking Preferences, and then clicking Change My Registration Information.*

Register with PayPal

Once you've registered with eBay, it's easy to sign up with PayPal, eBay's payment service. Why should you sign up with PayPal? It's a reasonable question, especially since, after you successfully sell an item, eBay will charge you its selling fees, and PayPal will charge you a fee if you receive money from a buyer who pays by that method.

The fact is that many eBay buyers like to use PayPal, and they expect sellers to accept payments with it. For you, as a seller, PayPal is a convenient and rewarding option. Many buyers purchase items and decide to pay for them instantly—the faster they pay, the faster they'll get their merchandise. Don't be surprised if you sell something and, five or ten minutes later, you receive an e-mail message from PayPal notifying you that the buyer has already sent you a payment for it through PayPal.

To register on PayPal, you can either go to the PayPal home page (**www.paypal.com**) or go to your My eBay page and click PayPal under the Related Links heading on the left-hand side of the page. When the PayPal: New Buyer Overview page appears, click Sign Up for a PayPal Account. Enter an e-mail address (make sure it's the same e-mail address you use for eBay) and assign yourself a password. Follow the steps shown on subsequent pages to sign up.

The process for signing up on PayPal is similar to that for registering on eBay. Once you've signed up with a basic account that lets you pay for items you've purchased, you'll need to sign up for a seller's account. You want to choose either a Premier Account or Business Account—these two accounts enable your buyers to pay for their purchases with a credit card, and have the funds transferred directly to your PayPal account. Such payments can take place only minutes after the sale ends; you'll receive an e-mail notification from PayPal like the one shown in Figure 5-1.

The third option, a Personal Account, doesn't enable you to receive credit card payments. That's why many buyers use PayPal: they want to pay for merchandise with a credit card and send the payment to the seller quickly, so the seller ships the merchandise out as quickly as possible.

note *PayPal offers the option to create Multi-User Access to your account as one of the preferences. You can establish separate log-ins with different levels of access, such as the ability to view all data but not withdraw funds. This is handy if, for example, you have people specifically handling shipping but who also need access to account information to see if payment has been received before the shipment is made.*

What Fees Can You Expect to Pay?

The amount of profit you make for your fundraiser depends in part on how much someone is willing to bid. But it also depends on how much eBay and PayPal subtract from purchase prices in the form of fees.

note *It's important to remember that, if you donate 100 percent of a sale's proceeds to a nonprofit institution, eBay will donate 100 percent of its listing and final value fees to the nonprofit, as described later in this chapter.*

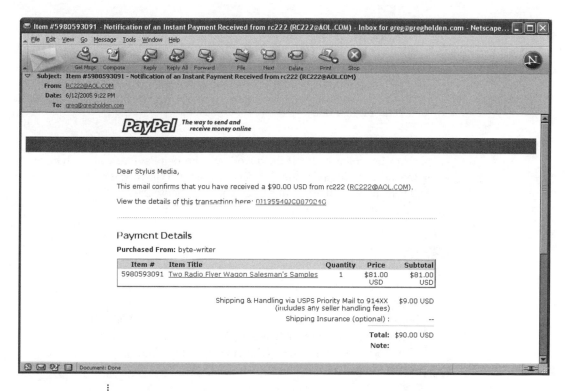

FIGURE 5-1 With a Business Account or Premier Account, you can receive payments shortly after a sale ends.

Here's an example: Suppose you conduct the sale of a set of golf clubs. You set a starting price of $9.99 for the sale. You take several photos of the image, including a thumbnail Gallery photo that will appear next to the auction title in a set of search results. You upload four photos with your description and host them with eBay's own Picture Services. You prepare the sale on a Wednesday, but you schedule it to start on the following day, a Thursday. You hold the longest sale possible, a 10-day sale, which will end on a Sunday when many bidders are at home and able to bid. The final sale price is $82.75. In this case, eBay's fees would look like this:

- Insertion fee: $0.35 (depends on the starting price)

- Gallery photo fee: $0.35

- Picture Services fee: $0.45 (first photo is free; subsequent photos are $0.15 each)

- Scheduling fee (fee for starting a sale at a predetermined time): $0.10

- Ten-day-sale fee: $0.10

- Final Value Fee (eBay's fee if an item sells successfully): $2.90

Total Fees: $4.25

You actually receive $78.50 in profit. That's if your buyer sends you a check or money order. If the buyer pays through PayPal, you're charged a fee for receiving payment through its system. Typically, the fee is 2.9 percent plus $0.30; in this case, you pay about $2.69 to PayPal. Your final profit is $75.89.

Many eBay sellers make up for such fees by charging a handling fee, a fee added on to the shipping charge that's intended to cover the time and effort of packing and shipping the merchandise. Many eBay sellers charge several dollars in handling fees, but a more reasonable handling fee of $1 is recommended. (Buyers may complain if they feel they're being gouged.)

You can save some money by finding your own web site to host your photos, for instance, or by starting a sale as soon as you upload the description to eBay. If you hold a five- or seven-day sale, for instance, you save the 10-cent fee for a 10-day sale. Some of the more common fees charged by eBay are shown in Table 5-1.

You'll find a complete rundown of eBay's fees at **http://pages.ebay.com/help/sell/ fees.html**.

Reasons to Consider eBay Giving Works

Whether you're an individual, corporation, or nonprofit, you can use eBay Giving Works and its charity partner MissionFish. eBay promotes the Giving Works charity auctions to make it easier for philanthropic-minded people to purchase items where the proceeds will benefit a nonprofit. You can tell which sales have been listed under the MissionFish auspices by

Fee	What It Means	How It Is Calculated	Example
Insertion (Required)	A fee for listing an item for sale.	For standard auctions, the fee is based on the starting price. For reserve auctions, it's based on the reserve price. For Dutch auctions, it's based on the opening value of the item for sale.	If the starting price or reserve price is $9.99 or less, the insertion fee is 35 cents.
Reserve Price (Optional)	A fee for listing an item with a reserve price.	It depends on the reserve price.	If the reserve price is $100, the fee is $2.
Picture Services (Optional)	A fee for having eBay's Picture Services host your photo on the Web so it appears with your auction.	The first image is free; each additional image is $0.15.	
Listing Upgrade (Optional)	A fee charged for making an item bold, or highlighting it so it gets more attention.	A flat fee; it depends on type of highlighting chosen.	For standing and reserve auctions, formatting the title in bold costs $1; highlighting with a color costs $5.
Final Value (Required if the item sells)	A fee charged for selling an item on eBay. (You don't pay this fee if the item doesn't sell.)	This is complex; the exact formula depends on the type of sale and sale price.	An item that sells for $100 has a Final Value Fee of $3.37.

TABLE 5-1   Typical eBay Seller's Fees

a "blue and yellow ribbon" icon that appears alongside the charity item listings. The charity items are also aggregated and promoted on the eBay Giving Works page, accessible from the eBay home page, and buyers can search and browse items for sale for charity here.

Behind these promotional features, though, lies the major benefit of using eBay Giving Works—credibility. eBay wants to help ensure the legitimacy of the charity auctions for the benefit of the both the nonprofit recipients and the buyers. This is where MissionFish comes in. They certify that sellers are a legitimate 501(c)(3) nonprofit institution (in other words, it is classified by the Internal Revenue Service as either a "public charity" or "private foundation" and is thus able to receive tax-deductible contributions), and ensure that the portion of the proceeds specified by an individual seller will, in fact, go to a legitimate cause.

MissionFish is two things:

- A nonprofit arm of the Points of Light Foundation, which is dedicated to engaging people more effectively in volunteer service to help solve serious social problems.

- A partner with eBay. Together, eBay and MissionFish vets nonprofits and provide a system for making donations through transactions conducted on eBay.

You don't have to use eBay Giving Works and MissionFish to fundraise on eBay (we'll discuss other options at the end of this chapter), but we recommend you first take a look at the various benefits of using the program for your eBay fundraising.

Legitimacy

Consider the following questions: How do you know that someone online is really going to donate a percentage of a sale to a charity? How do you know that an organization that calls itself a nonprofit is really going to help other people when it receives your money, rather than keep the money for itself? When you attend a charity ball and dance to a band that has been brought in for the occasion, you can be certain that the group that went through all the trouble to organize the event is a real, trustworthy entity. On the Internet, you don't meet a seller face to face. eBay doesn't want to run into fraudulent sellers passing themselves off as charitable organizations any more than you do. Not only that, but state and federal laws regulate just how charitable fundraising works. That's why eBay partnered with MissionFish.

You might think of MissionFish as functioning like a clerk in a store who checks your identity card and writes down your contact information when you hand over a check. They make sure you are who you say you are to help ensure that the transaction will proceed correctly.

Increased Marketing and Exposure for Charity Auctions

eBay strongly encourages sellers to use eBay Giving Works for their charitable donations, not only because it helps create trust, but also because it makes it possible for eBay to help buyers find all the great charitable offerings. The Giving Works hub page enables buyers to browse or search charitable items for both specific items and specific causes. The promotional space on the page allows eBay to showcase some of the unique charitable events to drive even more buyers to special events.

When you sell via eBay Giving Works, your item listings also are marked with a blue and yellow charity ribbon icon, which generates extra attention for sales. Much like highlighting your auctions with a marker or drawing a star next to your listings, the charity icon helps your items stand out from the other listings on eBay.

More and Higher Bids for Charity Auctions

More visibility means more people look at your items and more people bid, which results in higher final sales prices. But there is more to it than that. People like to support a good cause and they like to support sellers who are donating their time and energy to help nonprofits. As a consequence, people will tend to choose a charity item over a comparable noncharity item, and many buyers also bid higher because a donation is involved.

> "Items sold through Giving Works receive 75 percent more bids, are 35 percent more likely to sell, and on average sell for 40 percent more than regular items, so nonprofits and individual sellers will generally get more money for their merchandise," says Clam Lorenz of MissionFish.

For nonprofits, it means realizing more value for their donations. For individual sellers, the increased proceeds may mean you can donate a percentage to charity and still end up netting more dollars for your business. For example, you could give away 10 percent of proceeds and still net 30 percent more revenue. Some individual sellers, as you saw with artist Laura Iverson in Chapter 2, have made giving a successful part of their marketing and business strategy.

eBay Donates Fees for 100-Percent-Charity Auctions

There's another advantage: If you donate 100 percent of a sale's proceeds to a charity, eBay donates 100 percent of its Insertion and Final Value Fees on successful sales to the nonprofit organization designated to receive proceeds (whereas if a seller doesn't use Giving Works, eBay keeps the fees just as they would any other sale). For more on eBay's Donation Policy, see **http://pages.ebay.com/help/sell/givingworks-fee-policy.html**.

How to Use eBay Giving Works

Registering on eBay is free for everyone but how you register and the costs to use eBay Giving Works depend on whether you're selling on behalf of a nonprofit as an individual seller or whether you're selling directly as a nonprofit. In this section we're going to take a closer look at these two ways of using eBay Giving Works. Both reap the benefits we mentioned earlier, but the costs to nonprofits for *direct selling* are less than those for individual sellers. That's because eBay's partner MissionFish acts as a clearing house for *community selling*, processing payments and generating donor receipts, whereas when nonprofits sell themselves, they receive payments directly rather than through MissionFish.

eBay Giving Works for Nonprofits

Regardless of whether you're planning to sell immediately or not, if you're a nonprofit institution, you should become certified with MissionFish. Not only will registering with MissionFish allow you to sell, but it will also allow others to sell on your behalf. Once registered, your nonprofit will show up in the list of nonprofits community sellers can choose from when making donations.

Registering Your Nonprofit

Go to MissionFish (**www.missionfish.org/cgt/nonprofit/np.reg.intro.do**) and click the Start button. Be prepared to provide the following:

- A working e-mail address
- An electronic copy of your logo (JPG or GIF format, 50KB maximum)
- A mission statement of 512 characters maximum (about 40 words)
- Your 501(c)(3) letter or other proof of tax-deductibility
- A voided organization check

Once you've registered, MissionFish screens your nonprofit and adds it to the database. At this point, you, the nonprofit, as a direct seller will need to connect your eBay seller and MissionFish nonprofit accounts, and then register for a free MissionFish seller account. Once you've completed these steps, you can start listing items through the eBay Sell Your Item form as we describe in Chapter 7.

Coordinating Multiple Chapters of a Nonprofit

If your nonprofit has multiple chapters, you have two options: You can create a single account through the national headquarters or you can sign up all the chapters separately. The advantage of the first choice is that there is clearly one entity representing the organization and revenues that come in centrally from community selling (people selling on your behalf). Funds raised can be allocated to program needs from the headquarters or disseminated out to the chapters based on the seller's zip code, so that donations go to the local chapter.

Alternatively, the advantage of signing up all the chapters separately is that when people search on MissionFish by state, all your local nonprofit chapters will show up in the results, allowing people to designate the chapter they wish to support. To have chapters listed separately, either each chapter can sign up individually or your national office can contact MissionFish and provide a data file to register all your chapters at once. Note that the separate registration option is probably better if your chapters intend to sell directly themselves. This way they can build their own reputations rather than share feedback with other chapters.

Receiving Donations from Community Sellers

During the registration process, you'll have the option to configure how you would like community selling to be handled. You may choose whether to be notified when someone lists, or changes a listing, for an item for sale with you as the beneficiary. Why would a nonprofit wish to be notified? Of the two main reasons, one is to know what items are being sold just so you can promote them. The other is to allow you to review the items to make sure they won't negatively affect your brand. For example, if you are an animal rights organization, you may not want people selling a fur coat on your behalf—even if the proceeds help your bottom line.

For this reason, MissionFish offers nonprofits the chance to be notified of new listings and changes to listings. This way, nonprofits have a chance review listings and request an auction be cancelled if they find it inappropriate. For nonprofits that receive many donations, this could become onerous, however, so they may opt to not receive notifications and rather just let people sell whatever they want and simply receive a check for any proceeds. Another option nonprofits have is to create a list of trusted sellers for which they no longer need to receive notifications of listings. This way, the nonprofit is only notified when a new seller has listed an item on its behalf.

After about a month and half (when the refund period has ended), MissionFish will distribute funds raised to the nonprofit and issue receipts to the sellers for their gifts.

Encourage Others to Sell on Your Behalf

You, as the nonprofit, don't always need to sell yourself. Members of the public can sell items to raise funds for a nonprofit organization. Many eBay sellers choose to donate a percentage of the sales price for their items to a charitable cause. It's to your advantage to encourage community selling. You can do so by including links to the community selling page on your web site, linking to "selling on eBay" tutorials, or even holding information nights. You can show your constituents how to do community selling and encourage donations in this manner from your own web site. Sellers simply choose an option on the Sell Your Item form, and are led in a user-friendly way through the ensuing steps, such as the need to register with MissionFish (described later in this chapter).

Many eBay PowerSellers (sellers who consistently earn a minimum of $1,000 in gross sales each month and maintain a high-level of positive feedback) routinely donate a percentage of their sales to charitable causes. Why do they do it? Along with altruism, there's some healthy self-interest involved. As we discussed earlier, when charitable donations are mentioned in auction descriptions, sellers tend to get more bids and higher prices for what they sell. Of course, you don't have to be a PowerSeller to donate to a charity or to make a sale at the same time. As shown in the image on the opposite page, an artist named Teresa Turner (User ID **teresasart**) has decided to donate 40 percent of the sales of one of her paintings. The savvy thing is that she matched the content of the painting with the designated charity. The painting attracted eight bids and the artist's reserve price was met.

eBay Giving Works Costs for Nonprofit Direct Selling

Suppose your nonprofit institution sells something through Giving Works for $1,000. All proceeds will go to your nonprofit, so there is no MissionFish fee. eBay initially charges a Listing Fee and a Final Value Fee, but donates those fees back to you, so it's wash unless you have purchased upgrade features. If you receive payment by check or money order, there is no payment processing fee and you net the full $1,000, but if you use PayPal, you will have to pay their fees. Here's a breakdown of the transaction:

- Final value of transaction: $1,000
- eBay Listing Fee: $0.35
- MissionFish fee: $0.00
- Payment processing fee—PayPal ($0.30 + 2.9 percent of $1,000): $29.30
- eBay Final Value Fee: $28.12
- eBay's donation: $28.47 (paid to nonprofit on a quarterly basis)
- Your payment: $28.47 (unless you've purchased upgrade features)

Nonprofit Receives: $970.70 ($1,000 − $0.35 − $29.30 − $28.12 + $28.47)

 tip   *You can find the current eBay Giving Works/MissionFish fees at **www.missionfish .org/Help/helpAboutMoney.jsp#fees**.*

Whether or not you decide to use MissionFish, it's important that you convey to your volunteers just how to comply with eBay's rules for fundraising sales. If you don't, eBay will cancel your sales and you'll have to relist them. It's better for all concerned if you do it right the first time. See Chapter 5 for detailed instructions on how to register with and use MissionFish and Giving Works.

eBay Giving Works for Individual Sellers: Community Selling

If you're an individual seller (not a nonprofit institution) who wants to donate a percentage of your sales to a charity, you'll register with MissionFish when you list your first charity item for sale on eBay. In the eBay Sell Your Item form (which we discuss in detail in Chapter 7), you'll have the option to donate 10–100 percent of a sale's proceeds to a certified nonprofit through Giving Works. Simply specify the charity and percentage you wish to donate (see Figure 5-2).

FIGURE 5-2 eBay's Sell Your Item form allows you to specify a nonprofit to donate a portion of your sale proceeds to.

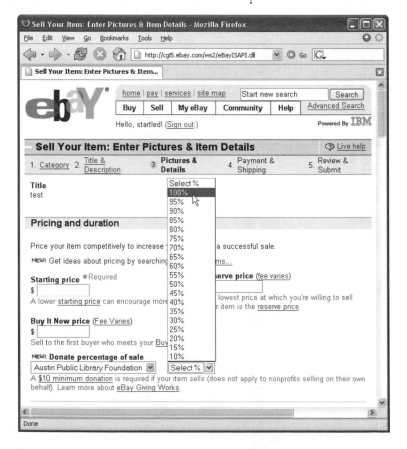

Selecting a Charity

You may select a nonprofit from a list of certified charities by typing
in a specific organization or by browsing lists of certified nonprofits. If
you don't have a specific charity in mind but you want to find one with
a specific purpose, you can look for registered nonprofits that support
that cause. For instance, someone looking to sell items for organizations
benefiting cancer research will be able to obtain a menu of relevant groups
by using either a keyword search of the nonprofit missions for "cancer" or
by browsing a list of nonprofits sorted by specific type of charity using pull-
down menus (see Figure 5-3).

FIGURE 5-3 To choose a nonprofit to support, type in its name, search for it by
keywords, or browse lists of certified nonprofits.

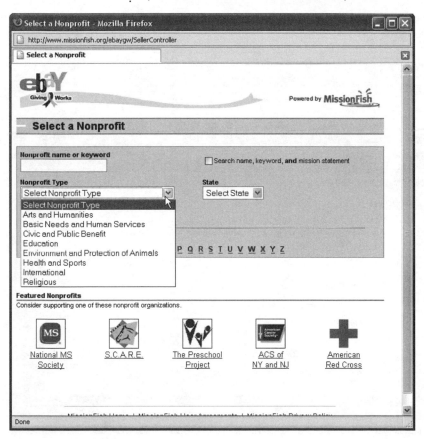

Adding a Specific Charity

What if you have a specific nonprofit in mind but it isn't in the list of more than 5,000 registered charities on MissionFish? MissionFish makes it easy for you to recommend a charity if you have a contact and an e-mail for the organization. By clicking on the Recommend a Nonprofit link, you can suggest a nonprofit and MissionFish will contact the nonprofit on your behalf to invite it to register on MissionFish (see Figure 5-4). Or if you know people at the nonprofit, you could just call the nonprofit and tell it you wish to donate through your eBay sales and request that it register on MissionFish (**www.missionfish.org/cgt/nonprofit/np.reg.intro.do**). Once you've used MissionFish, the next time you go to list an item for sale, the charities you've selected in the past will be available right from the Sell Your Item form. How handy is that?!

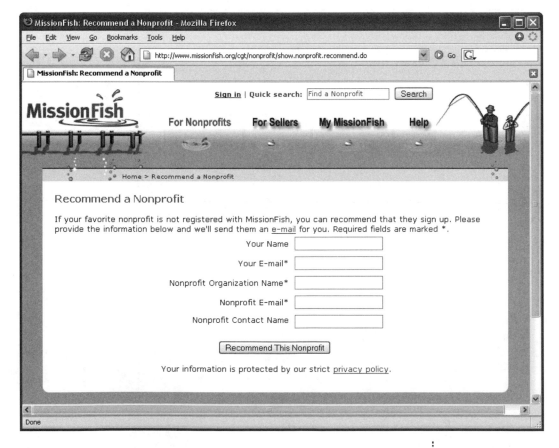

FIGURE 5-4 Recommending a nonprofit is one way to have a specific nonprofit added to the list of certified nonprofits on eBay.

If you want to donate to an organization that isn't on MissionFish's approved list, you also have the option of selling outside of eBay Giving Works as we describe later in this chapter.

> **note** *If you're looking to benefit a cause or group of people outside of the United States, you can choose International from the mission area drop-down list. However, the MissionFish Help page states that only U.S. nonprofits can currently benefit from eBay's Giving Works listings. eBay plans to eventually expand Giving Works into its international sites starting with the U.K., but until then, you need to find a U.S.-based nonprofit that will help people living outside of the United States.*

Registering with MissionFish

When you select a charity to receive a portion of the sale proceeds, eBay then checks your User ID to see if you're already a registered MissionFish seller. If you aren't, you are prompted to register. You'll need to read a MissionFish Authorization page and click Agree and Continue. Next, you verify your contact information and put a credit card on file with MissionFish if needed, and click Continue. At the conclusion you'll return to the Sell Your Item page with the nonprofit and percentage now filled in. Now simply complete the listing form.

Once you've reviewed and submitted your listing, your item is uploaded to eBay's servers. It might not go online immediately; new listings by nonprofits are uploaded immediately, but if you yourself aren't a nonprofit, you might have to wait until a quarter past the hour to see your sale actually appear online.

> **note** *To register with MissionFish, you must already be registered with eBay, and you must have a credit card number on file with eBay. Only sellers from the United States can use MissionFish at the time of this writing.*

Managing Your eBay Giving Works Listings

After you've registered, you can refer to a page you're given on MissionFish that enables you to track your current sales activity on the site. The page is the equivalent of the My eBay page that each member of eBay receives. The page, which is called My MissionFish Account, lets you track which sales are online, which have ended, and how much money you've raised through MissionFish. To access this page go to MissionFish (**www .missionfish.org**), click My MissionFish at the top of the page, and sign in if needed. (If you're already signed in to eBay, you won't need to sign in; you'll immediately see the My MissionFish page.)

After you submit your listing, it will be moved to the Live on eBay area, which means it's online and up for sale. At the same time, the nonprofit you've chosen is notified that you are selling on their behalf; they can let the sale go through or cancel it if the item being sold clashes with their mission, for instance.

If your listing is rejected by the nonprofit you initially chose, you can re-list it from Giving Works by using the Resubmit feature; this allows you to relist your description without having to recreate it. You sign in to MissionFish to access your My MissionFish Account page, check the item you want to resubmit, and click the Resubmit button.

If you need to revise your listing, you can access it from the My MissionFish Account page. Check the item you want to revise, and click the Revise button. You'll access a form that will enable you to change your listing. When you've completed your changes, click Submit. Be aware, though, that you can only edit the description if there are more than 12 hours left in the sale. Within the 12-hour period, you can only add new information to the description.

eBay Giving Works Costs for Community Selling

When you sell using eBay Giving Works, you'll have some fees in addition to the eBay fees we discussed earlier. Keep in mind that for these fees, MissionFish is handling payment and donation processing, including issuing you a receipt for your donation. There's a $3 per-transaction fee from MissionFish when you create the listing. You still pay eBay's Insertion Fee and if the item sells, eBay's Final Value Fee. You also pay credit-card processing fees of 2.9 percent of the donated amount (if you use a credit card) or a $15 fee (if you use an electronic funds transfer (EFT) or a check for payment). The fees are shown in Table 5-2.

Fee	When You Pay It	Where It Comes From	Who Receives It
$3 MissionFish fee	When an item is sold by an eBay user on behalf of a nonprofit	The donated amount	MissionFish
2.9 percent credit-card processing fee	When donations are made by credit card	The donated amount	The seller's credit card company
$15 EFT/check-processing fee	If donations are made by EFT or check	The donated amount	MissionFish

TABLE 5-2   eBay Giving Works/MissionFish Fees

Even if you're not a nonprofit institution yourself, if you decide to donate 100 percent of an item's final sale price to a nonprofit institution (whether or not the institution is your own), eBay will donate the listing fees you pay to the charity. Your transaction looks like this:

- Final value of transaction: $1,000
- MissionFish fee: $3.00
- Credit card fee (2.9 percent of $1,000 donation): $29.00
- eBay Listing Fee: $0.35
- eBay Final Value Fee: $28.12
- eBay's donation: $28.47
- Your payment: $28.47

Nonprofit Receives: $996.47 ($1,000 – $3.00 – $29.00 + $28.47)

warning *The credit card fee mentioned here is the cost of processing the payment of the donation from you to MissionFish. You still have to factor in the cost of processing the payment from the buyer. If you receive a check, you pay nothing, but if you use PayPal, you pay $0.30 + 2.9 percent.*

So, how can you make sure you do not go out of pocket? You can increase shipping and handling costs, or you can donate a lower percentage to the nonprofit, say 90, and use the 10 percent to cover the Listing and Final Value fees. This means, however, that eBay would not donate the Listing Fee to the nonprofit.

Here's what the same transaction looks like if you donate 10 percent:

- Final value of transaction: $1,000
- MissionFish fee: $3.00
- Credit card fee (2.9 percent of $100 donation): $2.93
- eBay Listing Fee: $0.35
- eBay Final Value Fee: $28.12
- eBay's donation: $0.00
- Your payment to eBay: $28.47

Nonprofit Receives: $94.07 ($100 – $3.00 – $2.93)
Your Proceeds: $871.53 ($1,000 – $100 – $28.47, less PayPal fees, if used)

warning *If the donation turns out to be less than $10, MissionFish will still charge you $10, because that is its minimum donation per auction at the time of this writing. For example, if an item sells for $50 and you are donating 10 percent, that would be a $5 donation but MissionFish would charge $10, of which all but MissionFish's $3 fee and 2.9 percent credit card fees would go to the nonprofit. (The seller would also still pay the regular eBay fees.) The donation is also per transaction, so if a seller creates a listing with a quantity of more than one item available, then each item must reach at least $10 in value. See more examples at* ***http://pages.ebay.com/help/sell/contextual/minimum-donation-information.html.***

If You Don't Use eBay Giving Works ...

With all those great benefits of using eBay Giving Works, why might you consider not using the service? Well, for individual sellers, there may be a reluctance to pay the MissionFish fees, or if your items are low priced, it won't make sense to use eBay Giving Works when the minimum donation is $10. For nonprofits, really the only reason you might not choose to use eBay Giving Works is if you have hundreds or thousands of items to list. At the time of this writing, eBay's "bulk listing" tools, such as Turbo Lister and a number of other auction management tools that allow you to list large numbers of items quickly, don't support eBay Giving Works functionality. They expect to have this working by the end of 2005. In the meantime, this means if you have to list a lot of items, you either have to do it one by one using the Sell Your Item form to use eBay Giving Works or use a bulk listing tool and not use eBay Giving Works. Obviously the former's not really practical, so there is an alternative.

If you choose not to go through eBay Giving Works, there is this alternative and you must carefully observe the following requirements:

- You must be, or be donating to, a recognized 501(c)(3) or 501(c)(4) charitable organization. The 501(c)(3) designation allows you to deduct gifts and donations; the 501(c)(4) designation, used for social welfare organizations, does not allow this.

- You must have consent from the organization to solicit donations for it, and you must prove that you've obtained consent by showing a picture of the letter granting you that consent in all your sales listings.

Figure 5-5 shows an example of a letter from a 501(c)(3) organization called SmileTrain as displayed by an eBay seller.

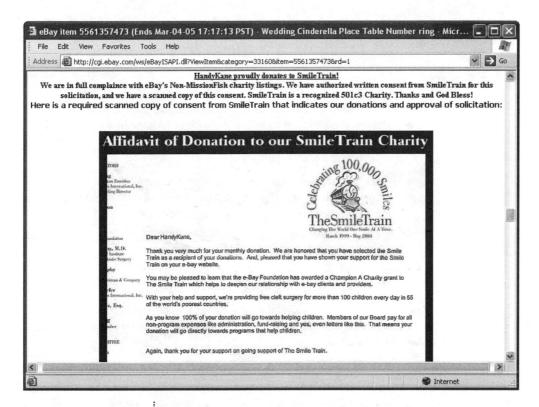

FIGURE 5-5 If you don't want to go through eBay Giving Works, you need to display a letter of consent from a nonprofit organization.

warning *When you choose not to use eBay Giving Works to donate a percentage of a sale to a charity, you describe how much you want to donate in the body of the listing as well display the letter of consent from the charity. Keep in mind you won't check the charitable donation box in the Sell Your Item form.*

The official process prescribed by eBay for such sales goes like this:

1. You need to approach the nonprofit agency of your choice and tell the agency you want to sell on its behalf.

2. You need to get a letter from the nonprofit stating that it's approved you to raise funds on its behalf.

3. You need to scan the letter or photograph you received from the nonprofit, and display it in each of your auction listings.

That's the official series of steps according to eBay's policy (at **http://pages.ebay.com/help/policies/fundraising.html**).

must have

- Before you can start to sell or even place bids on eBay, you need to register. Choose a User ID that reflects your nonprofit's identity, and choose a secure password.

- Once you register as an eBay member, you need to take the additional steps to register to sell on eBay and then register with PayPal so you can accept credit card payments.

- eBay Giving Works, eBay's program for charity listings, has plenty of advantages for nonprofits, including legitimacy, better marketing, more bids, and the potential for having eBay donate back its fees.

- In order to sell through eBay Giving Works, you have to register as a nonprofit and add your organization to the MissionFish database.

- Individuals on eBay can sell on behalf of a nonprofit in what's known as *community selling*.

- If you don't use eBay Giving Works, you need to display a letter of consent from a nonprofit in order to sell on its behalf.

Chapter 6
Building Your Credibility—and Your Donor Base

Nonprofits need to think of themselves as a "brand" just like Coca-Cola does. Think about how you can use the eBay platform to market yourself.

—Jenny Kompolt, Kompolt Online
Auction Agency

What We'll Cover in This Chapter:

- Setting a goal of building trust and credibility among your potential donors

- Registering your nonprofit with an online database

- Obtaining a "seal of approval" from one of several online regulators

- Taking steps to protect your donors' privacy

- Registering with eBay's ID Verify program

- Creating a logo that helps establish your identity

- Crafting an About Me page that lets donors find out more about you

- Opening an eBay Store so you can sell year-round

- Keeping in touch with your donors by adding them to a mailing list

Millions of sales go online on eBay every day, and eBay has millions of members around the world. Technically, the software and hardware that make up the online auction mechanism is complex in its operation. But the reason the whole system works is simple: it boils down to trust. Bidders and sellers alike feel they can trust one another through not only their feedback ratings, but also through the way they present themselves online and the care they devote to one another in their communications.

The same thing applies to fundraisers. Trust is one of the most important factors in developing a relationship with a donor. When the fundraising takes place on eBay, fundraisers need to build a sense of credibility. In order to attract bids, you need to stand out from the crowd and project the image of a reputable and knowledgeable institution or individual. You do that by creating a web page, either on eBay or elsewhere on the Web. You can also boost your credibly by participating on eBay's discussion boards and chat rooms.

Developing a trustworthy image on eBay has other benefits than simply attracting bids. An eBay auction gives you a great way to showcase your nonprofit and what you do. It can help you retain your donor base, which builds a foundation for future fundraising efforts. In many ways, simply being a good member of the eBay community—something all buyers and sellers are encouraged to do—is the best way to make your fundraiser a success. In this chapter, we discuss your options for developing a good reputation while marketing your cause at the same time. This way, before you even list your first item for sale, you will have set the stage for success.

Build Your Credibility

Any Internet fundraiser needs to develop trust and credibility with potential donors. It's one thing to trust a seller to follow through with a transaction. Many beginning buyers have a hard time getting over that hurdle. It's another matter altogether to trust whether some or all of a purchase price is going to the cause that's been advertised. When fundraising is involved, prospective bidders are prospective donors as well.

Register Your Nonprofit

Any nonprofit organization, as well as individuals who sell on behalf of a nonprofit, can build trust by ensuring your donors' security online. Security is a big concern on the Internet, and that applies for nonprofit as well as for-profit sellers. By getting the "seal of approval" from an organization that's recognized as reputable, you tell buyers that you're interested in their confidence and you take their privacy and security needs seriously.

GuideStar

When you're in a group situation and those in attendance don't know you well, you need credentials that inform others who you are and what you do. When you're at a convention or other gathering, you need a badge or name tag. When you're a nonprofit trying to raise funds on eBay or another part of the Internet, you need to register with a nonprofit database.

GuideStar (**www.guidestar .org**) is a database of all tax-exempt organizations registered with the IRS. If your nonprofit has received tax-exempt status from the IRS, such as 501(c)(3), you're already on GuideStar and prospective donors can look you up to verify that you're legitimate.

> **warning** *If you are a faith-based 501(c)(3) that has not registered with the IRS, you will not automatically be in GuideStar, and will need to provide GuideStar with proof of your 501(c)(3) status to be added to the database.*

By registering with GuideStar and filling out the GuideStar Information Form (GIF), you can submit more detailed information about your organization, even a press release. The form allows you to describe your organization's mission, recent accomplishments, and upcoming goals or objectives. Whatever you submit is reviewed and verified before it's posted online.

note *Registering with GuideStar is not a substitute for creating a web page or an About Me page. Rather, you should try to make the different venues work together. The GIF has a space where you can enter your web site URL, for instance. Your web site can point visitors to your GuideStar registration data, and to your current eBay sales as presented on your About Me page. The resulting synergy between online information sources not only increases the chances that someone will make a donation, but it also improves your visibility on the most popular search service, Google. The more links that lead to a web site, the higher the site appears in a set of search results.*

SquareTrade

For-profit businesses know how good it is for them or their products to receive a "seal of approval" from an unbiased organization such as Underwriters Laboratories (UL) or Consumer Reports. SquareTrade (**www.squaretrade.com**) is one of several web sites that provide seals to organizations that do business online. If you commit to maintain the privacy of your customers and adhere to principles of consumer safety, you get a "seal of approval" in the form of a graphic icon you can display on your web pages or in your eBay auction descriptions. The seal ensures that the web site is safe and that the site's owner is taking measures designed to adhere to principles of consumer safety. Prospective buyers can tell from the icon that you're concerned with their privacy. They also learn that you're a verified and reputable seller, because SquareTrade verifies your business information as part of the process of granting you a seal. Figure 6-1 shows an example of SquareTrade's seal as displayed by an eBay seller.

SquareTrade Member Services
memberservices@squaretrade.com
575 Market Street, 10th Floor
San Francisco CA 94105
ph. 800 686 6007
www.squaretrade.com

SQUARE TRADE
"Building trust in transactions"

note *Other organizations that issue "seals of approval" include VeriSign (**www .verisign.com/products-services/security-services/secured-seal/index.html**), BBBOnLine (**www.bbbonline.org**), and TRUSTe (**www.truste.org**).*

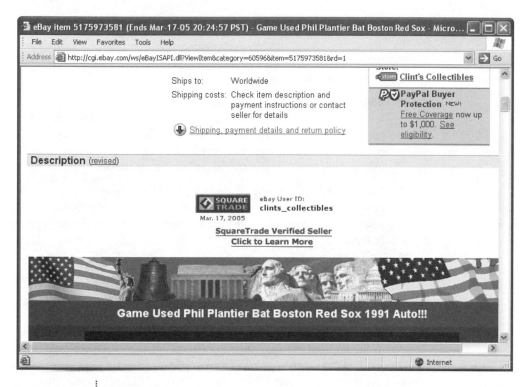

FIGURE 6-1 A seal of approval can enhance your reputation with prospective bidders.

what you'll need

You don't have to rely on an outside organization to vouch for the fact that you're trustworthy. You can and should follow some best practices for ensuring the safety and privacy of your customers' information. Do the following:

❑ **Use encryption** If you have your members or customers submit information to you online, make sure the data is encrypted. Use a secure server—a web server that uses Secure Sockets Layer (SSL) encryption—to protect information submitted from individuals.

❑ **Create a privacy statement** Post a statement on your web site that describes exactly what steps you have taken to keep anyone's online donation safe. You might say something like this:

"We take the privacy of our donors seriously and we make every effort to protect their privacy. For this reason, we use Secure

(continued)

Sockets Layer (SSL) technology to encrypt your information before it is transmitted to the financial institution for processing. We store your information securely and at no time is it made available to outside parties."

❑ **Shield your customer information**   To prevent hackers from breaking into your web site and stealing customer credit cards and other data, store the information on a computer that is not connected to the Internet, and regularly erase any customer information that's stored on computers that are online.

❑ **Have customers opt-in**   Rather than simply mailing out newsletters and other communications on an unsolicited basis, ask your members/customers if they want to receive such mailings beforehand.

ID Verify

eBay has its own way to answer the all-important question: how do you know whether that person on eBay is really the person they say they are? It's called the ID Verify program. ID Verify is an identify verification service available to all eBay users. You pay a $5 fee, submit your personal or business information, and it's checked against databases for consistency by Equifax Secure, one of the nation's largest credit verification companies. Equifax doesn't do a credit check, however; instead, only your identify is verified against information in the databases. After you've been verified, eBay adds a special ID Verify icon to accompany your User ID.

note   *ID Verify is a good way to improve your credibility, but it's also a requirement under certain circumstances. You need to be ID Verified in order to sell anything on a Buy It Now basis, or to place bids higher than $15,000.*

Become a Verified PayPal Member

PayPal, eBay's official payment service, is an increasingly popular solution for sellers and buyers who want to pay quickly and safely. Like many sellers, your nonprofit institution should strongly consider signing up for a PayPal account. The most direct benefit of doing so is the ability to have your donors make purchases from you with a credit card.

Another benefit (though it's a little indirect) is credibility. When you sign up for a PayPal account, you have the option of verifying your bank account information. To do so, you have PayPal make two small deposits into your bank account. You then check your account records and tell PayPal exactly how much was deposited. By doing so, you verify to PayPal that your bank account is really yours. Instead of the word *Unverified* next to your PayPal username, you get the term *Verified*. It lets prospective buyers know that you care enough about your reputation to go through the few steps involved in the verification process.

Develop an Online Identity

When you meet someone at a dinner, raffle, or live auction, you form an opinion about the person because you meet her face to face. On the Internet, you have only someone's word when he says who he is. One of the advantages of selling on eBay is the ease with which you can establish a reputation that your prospective customers can verify through the feedback system. But everyone on eBay has feedback. With thousands, and perhaps even millions, of different sellers posting sales on the auction site at any one time, you need to use other tools to convince bidders that your cause and your organization are real and that you can be trusted. Next, we'll describe some must-haves for establishing your online identity.

Create a Logo

If you work for a nonprofit organization, chances are you already have a logo—a visual image that conveys your group's identity in a glance and that's displayed on your letterhead, envelopes, and advertisements. A logo is a central part of the design element that, together with content and follow-up, works together to create a positive image of your organization online. When you add your logo to your eBay sales descriptions it gives them an added air of credibility. It tells shoppers that you have an identity beyond your name: You might run a business on eBay, or you might sell on a regular basis on behalf of charities.

Logos don't take long to design, but they have a long "shelf life." For a little effort at the outset, you might conceivably get years of use from your logo. It's cost effective to hire a professional graphic designer to create a logo for you or your group. It might cost between $200 to $500, depending on the number or size, and graphic variations, you require. But professional designers usually come up with logos that are smoother and more professional in appearance than you could do on your own.

tip   *If you're looking for a designer, look no farther than Elance Online (**www.elanceonline.com**), a web site that's affiliated with eBay where contractors bid on jobs that employers make available.*

However, if you're on a budget, you can create your own logo. You might use a software program you download and install on your computer (such as Paint Shop Pro, SuperPaint, or Photoshop). Or, if you really want to minimize expense and computer overhead, connect to a web site that provides an interactive form you can fill out in order to create a logo yourself.

Create a Text Logo with CoolText

CoolText gives you an easy-to-use interface that enables you to create your own simple textual logo. There's nothing wrong with having a text logo. If you choose the typeface and the colors correctly, you can have a perfectly professional appearance. Follow these steps to set one up:

1. Go to the Cooltext web site (**http://cooltext.com**).

2. Click Render a Logo.

3. When the Choose a Logo Style page, as shown here, appears, click on the graphic style of your choice. In keeping with your status as a nonprofit fundraiser, we suggest you choose a restrained design such as Starburst.

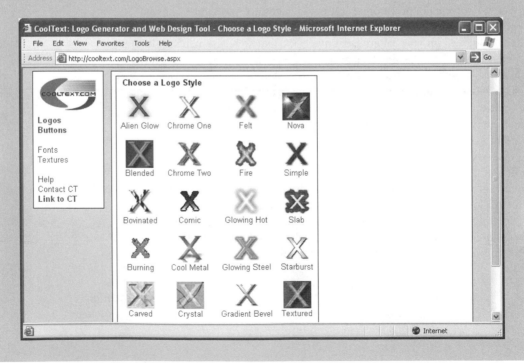

4. The web page refreshes to display the chosen style (for instance, Starburst) along with color and type information. Type the text you want your logo to display in the Logo Text box. You'll probably want to type the name of your organization.

5. If you want to change the type font used, click the sample text next to Font. When a page full of font samples appears, click the one you want to use. You'll automatically return to the previous page.

6. Be sure to change the Text Size reading to something smaller than the default 70 points, such as 30 or 36 points, which will be easier to fit on a web page.

7. If you want to change the color from the default green, click the block of color next to Burst Color (shown here). When a page full of colors appears, click the name of the new color you want.

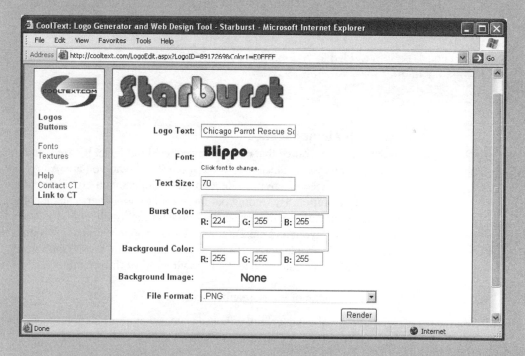

8. When you're done making changes, click Render. Your logo appears on a new page.

(continued)

9. Click the highlighted link Click Here to view your logo in a new window (shown here).

10. To copy the logo, right-click it and choose Save Image As from the shortcut menu that appears (on a Macintosh, click and hold down on the logo image and choose Save As from the context menu). When the Save Image As dialog box appears, choose a location for the file on your hard disk, and click Save.

You'll need to copy your logo to your hard disk soon; Cooltext only stores it on its servers for an hour after you create it.

Create an About Me Page

About Me is a resource that every eBay seller should use. It's free, and it gives your buyers a chance to find out more about who you are. An About Me page is a place where you talk all about you personally or about your nonprofit institution. By finding out more about you, buyers can be better equipped to decide whether or not to follow through with a purchase/ donation. The layout and presentation on your About Me page has a direct impact on how people perceive you or your organization. For a nonprofit, an About Me page can provide the following bits of information:

- The name of your organization.
- A mission statement: a few sentences that describe your goals, and the people you're trying to help.
- The names of some important donors or partner organizations.
- A set of links to your current auctions. You might also include links to any other web pages or web sites you've created.
- Contact information.
- Optionally, you might also want to include photos of yourself or your employees, or a frequently asked questions (FAQ) section about your organization.

The amount of detail you provide depends on how active a seller you are, how many different kinds of items you sell or collect, and whether your page is about you personally or just about your auction activities. The best way to find out what to say on your About Me page is to search the About Me pages of other sellers. Unfortunately, there's no eBay page that gathers all the About Me pages in one set of links. Instead, find a seller who's reputable and presents sales items in a professional manner, and click that seller's About Me link.

Once you've gathered some basic information about what you want to present on your page, you only need to go to the About Me Login page (**http://members.ebay.com/ws2/eBayISAPI.dll?AboutMeLogin**). Click the Create or Edit Your Page button, then follow the steps to create your page.

success

The House Ear Institute (HEI) holds an annual Hollywood Auction for Hearing Health on eBay. The event in 2004 resulted in 146 items being sold, which raised $34,000. The group sees its eBay events as a way for people around the world to support its nonprofit hearing health research endeavors. Entertainment and travel organizations, corporations, celebrities, and other individuals donate items. The group's web site (**www.hei.org**) directed visitors to its eBay About Me page, shown here, which contains links to all of the items for sale.

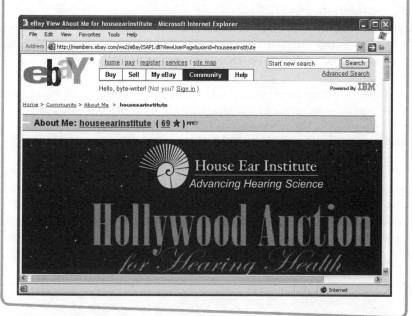

You need to anticipate what prospective donors need to know from you—not only what they want to know, but also what they *expect* from a charitable or other nonprofit organization. Many online buyers expect to be able to call a staff person on the phone whenever they run into problems with an online form, or whenever they have questions. If you think your donors are of this sort, be sure to include a phone number where they can contact customer support.

tip *Some places even include Live Chat or Live Help. If you don't have the staff people available to handle the extra load, you can hire services to handle the customer service load for you.*

Create an eBay Store

Visibility is of great importance for nonprofits. The better known you are in the marketplace, the greater your chances of attracting donations. An eBay Store gives you even more credibility than an About Me page and more visibility than auctions or fixed-price sales. We'll talk about how to open an eBay Store in Chapter 9, but here is a quick overview.

An eBay Store is a web page that eBay allows you to rent for a monthly fee and that can contain fixed-price items you have for sale for 30, 60, or 90 days, or even indefinitely. An eBay Store can be compared to setting up space in a shopping mall: you list items for a fixed price, and you attract shoppers who might visit the mall looking for other things. In this case, since the "mall" is eBay and as many as 17 million visitors browse through it every month, you have a large number of chances of having your store merchandise turn up in eBay searches. Not only that, but a store's contents can appear in the results of a search done on search engines outside of eBay, such as the popular Google (**www.google.com**).

note *In order to open an eBay Store, you need to have a minimum feedback rating of 20 or have your identity verified through eBay's ID Verify program. Be aware that eBay Store listings do not show up in eBay searches unless there are less than ten or fewer auction-style listings returned in the search results.*

When you open a store, you also get a Stores logo that appears next to your User ID. For example, the Stores logo for the Points of Light Foundation (**http://members.ebay.com/ws2/eBayISAPI.dll?ViewUserPage&userid= pointsoflightfoundation**) appears at the far right of the icons that accompany the User ID **pointsoflightfoundation**, shown in Figure 6-2.

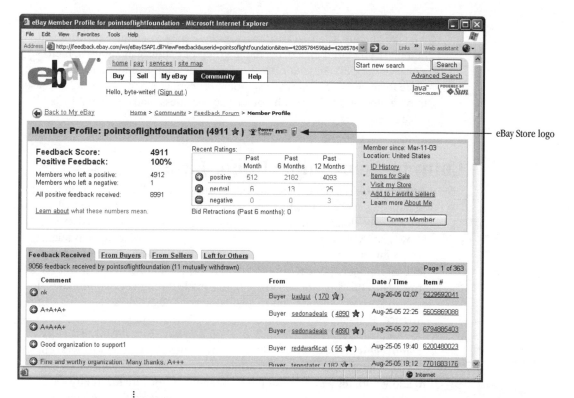

FIGURE 6-2 A Stores logo tells bidders that they can find more merchandise in your eBay Store.

success

The Points of Light Foundation (**www.pointsoflight.org**) runs a fundraising store on eBay. Its corporate and individual supporters routinely donate goods in-kind, which are then sold to support the Foundation's work.

According to Robert Goodwin, President and CEO, "In a giving climate that is challenged, to say the least, offering donors the option to support us in-kind has yielded very promising results. The Points of Light store on eBay has given us an exciting new venue for turning donations that were heretofore unusable items into much needed financial support and awareness. It's a great marketing tool for our donors, and people feel good when they buy from a nonprofit. The unrestricted revenues we have gained through this effort have been invaluable to our mission of expanding volunteering across the country." (as quoted on eBay in their Success Stories page at **http://givingworks.ebay.com/success/**).

An eBay Store gives you the advantage of being able to sell to people who are already satisfied customers because they've purchased from you before. If you build up a dependable group of enthusiastic donors, there's a chance they'll visit your eBay Store. People want to shop at an eBay Store for many different reasons. Some of them come to your store because they're already familiar with you or your business, and they want to see what else you're offering.

Cultivate Your Online Donor Base

Attracting online donors by cultivating trust and credibility is a step toward fundraising success. But for long-term results, you need to retain and cultivate the donors who came to you through eBay. Experienced sellers know that. After a transaction is complete, it often pays to keep in touch with regular customers through e-mail. Customers who are satisfied with their shopping experience are likely to return again once they know they can trust you. The same applies to donations made through eBay purchases: it pays to keep up with the donors you attract online. To do so requires a little advance planning on your part.

An article in *The Chronicle of Philanthropy* (**http://philanthropy .com/free/articles/v16/i17/17002501.htm**) suggests that donors who come to your cause online may not continue to donate that way. Once they get to know you, they may prefer to be solicited by direct mail. At any rate, you need to leverage the potential long-term donors you acquire through selling on eBay. In the sections that follow, we suggest some ways to build rewarding ongoing relationships.

Develop a Mailing List

As you probably know already, a mailing list is a set of contacts that receive communications periodically by e-mail or "snail mail," and a list you can use to approach potential donors. One problem with mailing lists is that they go stale—addresses change, and messages "bounce back" to the sender. Another is overload—after a number of solicitations, donors experience burnout and stop responding.

eBay gives nonprofits a new source of fresh contacts. Once someone has made a purchase from you, that person can be invited to receive your newsletter or be on a mailing list for announcements of future sales. Be sure to compile the e-mail addresses and other contact information for your online donors so you can add them to your existing databases.

tip   *Hopefully, your satisfied customers won't mind receiving e-mails from you announcing future fundraising events. But many online shoppers are touchy about unsolicited e-mail. It's good business practice to invite someone to receive your newsletters or announcements before you actually send them—you can do this in an e-mail message that you send at the end of a transaction, for instance. Alternatively, you can send your communications out, but always invite recipients to send you an e-mail informing you that they don't want to receive your messages in the future. You don't want to risk alienating your valued customers.*

Be a Link-Maker

In all of your communications with online donors, be sure to make as many links as you can to your web site or your About Me page. Include the links in your e-mail messages; a common location for them is the area beneath your signature. You can set up a special text document called a signature file and configure your e-mail application to automatically append it to your outgoing messages.

tip   *You can also include your web site or eBay Store URL in your business card, and instruct your volunteers to drop it in each of the boxes that go out to your buyers. The more links you make, the easier you'll be to find on Google (and the more likely people are to find your sales, if you open an eBay Store).*

The following steps show how to create a signature file in Outlook Express:

1. Open your favorite word processing program to type a signature file.

2. Create a dividing line by holding down the asterisk (*) or hyphen (-) key. This line will set your signature file off from the rest of the message.

3. Type your signature and information about your organization, pressing ENTER after each line. For example:

   ```
   *********************************
   Greg Holden, donations coordinator
   Chicago Metropolitan Parrot Rescue Society
   1234 Anywhere St., Chicago, IL
   555-1212
   ```

greg@parrotrescuechicago.org
Web site: http://www.parrotrescuechicago.org
eBay Store: http://members.ebay.com/ws2/eBayISAPI.dll?
ViewUserPage&userid=chicagoparrotrescue

4. Save the file on your computer as a plain text document.

5. Launch Outlook Express and choose Tools | Options.

6. When the Options dialog box opens, click the Signatures tab, and click New.

7. Click File, and then click Browse.

8. When the Open dialog box appears, locate the plain text signature file you created earlier. Click the file name and then click Open.

9. Click the Add Signatures to All Outgoing Messages check box, then click OK.

It's a good idea to test your signature file out before you send it. Open a new message composition window; your signature file should appear in the body of the message. You can now compose a message by clicking anywhere above the signature file and typing what you have to say. You can also delete the file by scrolling across its contents and pressing DELETE.

Don't regard your eBay nonprofit auction customers simply as future auction customers. Promoting your web site has other benefits. Past donors represent a built-in new audience of people that will be visiting your web site and eBay Store as well.

$$$ moneymaker

Making links to your web site is only part of the online fundraising equation. You can also use your web site to direct the public to your eBay sales, or your eBay Store if you have one. You can also ask the public to donate to your cause. The Points of Light Foundation does this on its Shop Our Online Auctions page (**www.pointsoflight.org/about/support/individual/shop.cfm**) shown next. The links on this page direct the visitor to the Foundation's eBay Store; it also encourages eBay sellers to donate some of their sales income.

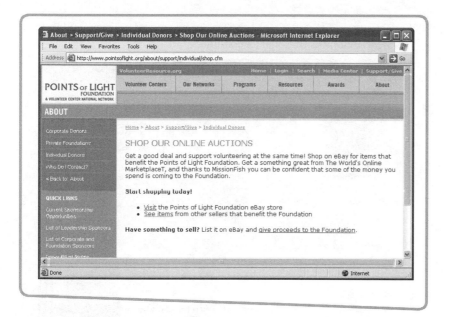

Develop a Sense of Community

Even though eBay is increasingly populated by businesses, it's still at its core a lively community of individuals. By participating in that community, you not only get more attention for your current sales, but you stand a chance of receiving new donations, too. The community spirit is alive on eBay to the extent that people who see nonprofit auctions for causes they're interested in frequently end up making new donations to those causes.

success

Cure for Cancers (**www.cureforcancers.com**, User ID **cureforcancers**) received more donations for its cause—cancer research and development—after eBay members responded to seeing its sales online. The group was founded by sports collectible store owner Mitch Uritz, who was stricken with lymphatic cancer in 1997. Today, Uritz is a cancer survivor who sells on eBay to provide funds for cancer research and development.

Cure for Cancers doesn't overtly call for other eBay sellers to make donations to its cause. It gets attention from the brief human interest story that accompanies their eBay sales, such as the one we've included here.

(continued)

Whenever possible, tell a story about your group and mission, and keep your descriptions as personal as possible.

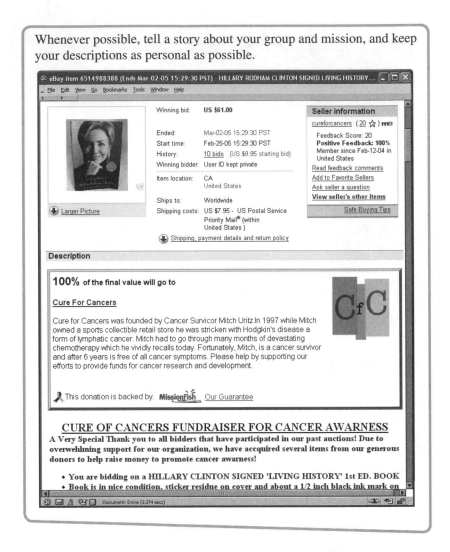

It's also important to be an active member of the eBay community forums—the help boards, general discussion forums, and workshops. These forums aren't just the best places to get inside information about how eBay works; they're also a place to help out others, get tips and suggestions, make friends, and talk up your nonprofit cause.

The entry point for eBay's public forums is the Community Overview page (**http://hub.ebay.com/community**), shown in Figure 6-3.

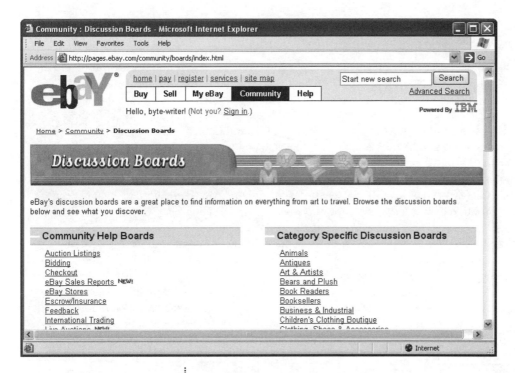

FIGURE 6-3 Participating in the eBay community can help you spread the word about your nonprofit cause.

This page leads you to several subcategories. The Community Help Boards address many subjects of interest to all eBay members, such as Auction Listings, Bidding, and Packaging & Shipping. The General Discussion Boards, such as The Front Porch and The eBay Town Square, are the places to go to meet other users for gossip and talk about anything you please. The Category Specific Discussion Boards are designated for discussion pertaining to eBay sales categories, ranging from Animals to Vintage Clothing & Accessories. The most important forum for nonprofits is the eBay Giving Works Board (**http://forums.ebay.com/db2/forum.jspa? forumID=4001**). Here, you'll regularly find requests for donations, questions about MissionFish, and suggestions on how to hold fundraisers.

Chicago's Successful Civic Pride

Several years ago, Chicago gained national attention for a fundraiser that featured life-size fiberglass cows decorated by artists and designers. In 2004, the city undertook a new and equally ambitious event, when it became the first municipality to conduct a major fundraiser on eBay. From December 2 to 16, 469 items were sold on eBay to benefit the city's Department of Cultural Affairs, the Chicago Cultural Center, and other cultural organizations. Many of the items sold were unusual, one-of-a-kind experiences: a wedding beneath the Tiffany dome in the Chicago Cultural Center (high bid: $21,000) and a chance to dye the Chicago River green on St. Patrick's day ($7,600). A total of $243,000 was raised.

Joan Greene, a consultant to the Department of Cultural Affairs and head of Joan Greene Design Group, Inc., was responsible for implementing the donations and working with the trading assistant hired to create the auction listings, Auctions for Everybody (**www.auctionsforeverybody.com**). Greene says building a sense of community was essential for the auction's success. "It's very important to develop a sense of community among your volunteers and staff. It gives people a chance of being part of a whole and not being isolated. My belief is that when you are doing something in the charity realm, it's not just about the money. The intangibles, in my opinion, are just as important as the hard dollars. For instance, we held a kickoff party for all the people who donated and for the press. It was really neat to have my own hairdresser there—an average person who wanted to donate a $100 package to the cause. There were people with all kinds of talents, from the shoe store to the fire department. You walked away with a sense of community because all of those people make up Chicago—Chicago is nothing without them." It's also important to use a web site to publicize your event and to give visitors a gathering place, a place where they can contact you, find out more about your cause, and get their questions answered. The web site devoted to the fire sale (**www.greatchicagofiresale.org**, shown opposite) received 60,000 visits; more than 160,000 bids were placed on the sale's items on eBay.

The fact that eBay attracts bidders from all over the world resulted in some surprises. A bidder from the East Coast was the winner of the chance to dye the Chicago River green. The chance to turn on the Buckingham Fountain with mystery novelist Sara Paretsky went to a woman from Canada. "It turned out that she had met her husband when they were both walking around the fountain, and they were married by the fountain," Greene recalls.

One tip Greene passes along to fundraisers is the need to find a good chairperson. The Chicago sale's chair, Leslie Hindman, was instrumental in drumming up donations from people and institutions around the city. "It works well because you have the chairperson, who is well connected and who can ask others for a favor. Then you also need someone like me who can follow through on the details and make sure things got completed."

Another suggestion: use your descriptions to educate bidders on who you are and why you or your cause is noteworthy. As Greene says, "I knew that bidders would go on eBay to place bids, but they would read about Chicago at the same time. In the write-ups, I tried to include something about the history or exceptional features of Chicago so that, even if they didn't win what they bid on, they might want to come to Chicago to see it."

must have

- Make an effort to understand your donors' needs and present them with the information they want so you can build a good image online.

- Improve your credibility by getting a seal of approval and creating a logo to build your online image.

- Consider opening an eBay Store or creating an About Me web page also to help induce potential donors to bid on what you have for sale.

- Once you have a set of buyers and have completed transactions with them, cultivate these buyers by sending communications that alert them to upcoming events.

- Develop a spirit of community that encourages your volunteers and colleagues to interact and that attracts further donations as well.

Chapter 7
Listing Your Items for Sale on eBay

The dollars raised on eBay almost all came from outside the school community, which took the burden off the school families to buy all the items.

—Mark Silver, DaddyMade
Trading Assistant

What We'll Cover in This Chapter

- Creating sales descriptions that attract donors

- Searching for the right category in which to list your items

- Writing the right titles and subtitles for your sales

- Taking pictures that show your merchandise in its best light

- Finding a web server where you can host your images

- Training your staff so they can help create sales listings

With your decisions made and the groundwork established, you can now start actually selling on eBay. This involves taking photos, writing up descriptions, putting the information online so shoppers can see it, and starting the sale.

For many institutions, creating eBay sales descriptions is one of the easiest parts of the event. That's because they hire professionals to put their sales online. Often, hiring a trading assistant is an efficient way to start up multiple sales, especially when a large quantity of items needs to go online at the same time.

But for smaller nonprofits, trading assistants cut into vital sales revenue. These organizations prefer to create sales in-house. Plenty of individuals aren't affiliated with a charitable institution themselves, but they want to donate part of their sales revenue to charities they want to help. If you fall into one of these categories, follow the step-by-step instructions we present in this chapter to get your sales online so you can start improving your chosen nonprofit institution's bottom line.

When you display an auction item on a table in the hall where a benefit fundraiser is taking place, you make sure the object is presented in an attractive way. You cover the table with a cloth; you prop the item up if necessary; and you place a tag or piece of paper by the item to describe its attributes. On eBay, the quality of your sales description determines how attractive the item is to potential bidders. When you're raising funds for a cause, descriptions are especially important. That's because you're not the only beneficiary. You want the item to sell in order to help others. How do you improve your description so that it stands out and attracts bidders? We cover the most important attributes of good sales descriptions in the sections that follow.

Fill out the Sell Your Item Form

As you've learned in previous chapters, if you want to raise funds online in a planned, systematic way you need to go through many steps before you actually create an eBay sales listing. After you've chosen your item, decided how you want to sell, come up with a timetable for your fundraising event, and registered as a seller with eBay or MissionFish, the fun really begins. You can actually create your sales description and put your item online, where millions of potential bidders can see it and decide whether or not to bid on it.

> **note**   *Filling out the Sell Your Item form is an important way to get your sales listings online. But before you fill out the form, you may want to take some digital images and save them either on your computer or on a web server, as we describe later in this chapter. When you get to the part of the form that asks you to add digital images to your description, you'll need to have those images "ready to go."*

If you've hired a trading assistant to actually create the sales for your organization, you don't have to go through the step-by-step process of creating eBay descriptions. Even so, it's good to know just what steps are involved, so you know what questions to ask your contractor. And if you've decided to put the sales listings online yourself, you've got to roll up your sleeves and get to work. In the sections that follow, we'll show you how to use eBay's basic sales listing tool, the Sell Your Item form, to get an individual sale online.

> **note**   *The Sell Your Item form is a good place to start, but it isn't the only way to create auction descriptions and get them on eBay. Auction services such as Marketworks, Andale, ChannelAdvisor, SpareDollar, and others all have their own forms that you fill out to create sales descriptions for many items and then submit them all to eBay at the same time. Even eBay software like Turbo Lister gives you an alternate way to create listings fast.*

When Should You Start?

One of the first questions you should tackle even before you're ready to get your sales online is one of timing. Give some thought to how many items you want to sell and how many you want to put online at any one time. The number of auction listings you create depends not on the number of separate items you have available but on the personnel you have to get them online. Not only that, you have to take into consideration how many people you have to answer e-mail inquiries from prospective bidders who have seen your descriptions and want more information.

If you've hired a trading assistant to create your descriptions, these considerations aren't so relevant: you'll need to discuss how quickly your contractor can get the listings online, and whether you want to start all sales simultaneously or space them out over a number of weeks.

On the other hand, if you're doing the work yourself, don't take on more than you can handle at any one time. Suppose you have 1,000 separate auction items to get online. Ask yourself: How quickly can I actually create the listings? You can follow the steps we describe in the upcoming "Create Your First eBay Auction Description" sidebar and try the process out for yourself as an experiment. Experienced sellers who sell multiple items that are almost identical (for instance, a set of men's suits that are the same except for suit sizes and colors) can create a *template*—a standard layout that can be used for many different eBay sales. Only a few details need to be changed in each sale. They can then get several dozen sales online in a single hour.

Chances are good, though, that with your own fundraiser, if you have 1,000 items, very few of them are going to be exactly the same, especially if they come from many different donors. If you only have, say, one or two volunteers available to create the sales, don't expect them to get all 1,000 sales online and starting at exactly the same time. Be conservative, and space things out. You might try to sell only a few hundred items a week. Or, you might start getting your sales listings online in advance and schedule them to start at specific times of your choosing. You can create a listing up to three weeks in advance and schedule it to start at a specific date and time. It's a great way to enter a lot of sales online gradually and still have them all start at once. But keep in mind that eBay charges a $0.10 fee for each item you schedule. (eBay doesn't charge you a fee if you start selling an item as soon as you create its listing.) If you have 1,000 items to sell, you'll have to subtract $100 from your potential sales revenue to do this scheduling.

note *If you use a trading assistant, ask the assistant whether he or she is going to schedule your sales in advance—you should be aware if you're going to be charged the $0.10 scheduling fee. In order to schedule a listing yourself, you need to place a credit card on file with eBay beforehand. Chances are you've already done this when you registered to sell on eBay. But in case you chose to specify a checking account when you registered as a seller rather than a credit card, you'll have to add your credit card number as well. eBay allows sellers to list a maximum of 3,000 items in advance.*

If you don't want to do scheduling in advance and you don't have a trading assistant to do the work for you, find as many people to create sales listings as you can, and get them online gradually. If you have 1,000 total items to sell, you might hold a month-long fundraising event and put 250 sales online each week. You could then create 50 sales listings per day.

Create Your First eBay Auction Description

Once you're ready to create a description, just follow these steps to get started:

1. Click the Sell button in the navigation bar that appears at the top of virtually any eBay page.

2. When the page simply entitled Sell appears, click the Sell Your Item button.

3. When the Sign In: Sell Your Item page appears, type your User ID andPassword in the boxes provided and click Sign In Securely.

4. Click the radio button next to the type of sale you want to conduct (auction, fixed price, real estate) on the Sell Your Item: Choose a Selling Format page.

5. Click Continue.

When the Sell Your Item Step 1 of 5: Category page appears, you can choose one or two categories to list your items in. Listing your items in the right places increases the chances that they'll actually be located by buyers who might be interested in them, so it pays to take a minute or two to choose wisely.

If you have two people doing the work, each could be responsible for getting 25 items online each time, or perhaps five per hour. The same two people could be responsible for answering any questions that come in about the items that have gone online.

shortcut

It's always a good idea to assign the same people who created auction listings to answer questions about those same listings. They're already familiar with the descriptions and accompanying photos and can field inquiries quickly. Someone who's unfamiliar with the item in question will have to look up the description or find the original object in order to answer a question, which will take more time and energy.

Select Your Auction Category

It's a good idea to give some thought to selecting the right category to list your item in to make sure you list it in the place where likely buyers will actually shop for it. You may also want to consider listing the item

in a second category along with the first. Picking a second category costs extra: your insertion fee is doubled, and upgrade fees to make the sale bold, highlighted, or featured are doubled as well. But many sellers (including eBay) report that items listed in two categories simultaneously get more attention than those listed in only one category.

Suppose, for instance, that someone has been generous enough to offer you a baseball signed by the home-run slugger Babe Ruth. This sort of item could be listed in a sports-related category as well as one specific to baseball. But is that the only good location? You could search for a category: Enter the keywords **Babe Ruth signed baseball** in the box labeled Enter keywords to find a category on the Step 1 page of the Sell Your Item form (see Figure 7-1), and click Search.

FIGURE 7-1 Use the Sell Your Item form to suggest the categories where your item will get the most attention.

After you click Search, a window appears with a set of categories and subcategories presented in order. The percentage ranking indicates, on a scale of 1–100 percent, how many sellers with items similar to yours list those items in a particular category. The results shown in Figure 7-2 indicate that 17 percent of all sellers of Babe Ruth signed baseballs list their item in the category Sports Memorabilia, Cards & Fan Shop : Autographs-Original : Baseball-MLB : Balls. You don't have to list your item there, however. You can choose more than one category to list it in. As the list indicates, one of two subcategories in the Art category might be good second choices.

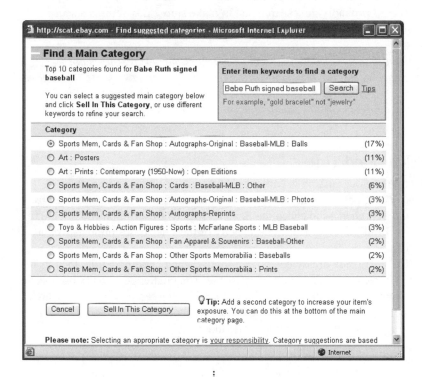

FIGURE 7-2 When you search for a sales category, you'll end up with several choices.

You might well ask why it's important to choose a category at all, given that many (if not most) eBay shoppers actually find items as a result of a keyword search rather than browsing through sales categories. It's true that putting the right keywords in your listings and your title will make it more likely that your sale will be found by a potential buyer. But locating the item in the right category will make it that much more likely that someone who's browsing through a category will find what you have.

If you know what category you want, you can browse for it using the boxes presented on the Step 1 page of the Sell Your Item form. Click the top-level category in the box on the left. A set of subcategories appears in the box next to it. Click the subcategory, and a set of the subcategories beneath it appear in the next box. Keep selecting subcategories until no more appear. Even if you think you know what category you want, you should probably do a search just to make sure. eBay returns a set of suggested categories that are ranked according to popularity.

> **tip** *You can optionally list your item in a second category. Generally this is not recommended because it doubles your listing fees, but it can make sense if you have an item that is cross-collectible. For example, a Snoopy bank might be worth listing in the Peanuts memorabilia category for the Snoopy fans and in the mechanical bank category for bank collectors.*

Pick a Good Title

The title of your auction is without a doubt one of the most important parts of your description. Keyword searches on eBay scan auction titles by default. Searchers who check the Search Titles & Descriptions box in the Search: Find Items form search the body of the sales description as well as the title.

The best piece of advice you can follow when creating a title, then, is to load it with as many keywords as possible. The challenge is to choose the same keywords that prospective buyers are likely to enter when they search for your item. Suppose someone has donated a collection of Loretta Lynn CDs for you to sell. Don't write a title like this:

Loretta Lynn CD Collection

It's too vague. Also avoid unnecessary qualifiers that don't add anything to the description:

@@LOOK@@ Loretta Lynn CD Collection!!!@@LOOK@@

Such add-ons are distracting and look unprofessional because they're so overused. Be as specific as possible to appeal to knowledgeable collectors who crave details and already know about what you have to sell:

Loretta Lynn Like New 6-CD Set Greatest Hits 1959–1999

By including the actual title of the work in the title of the auction, and by including specifics like dates and numbers, you appeal to shoppers who are searching for the exact item by entering its title in the Search: Find Items form. The same advice applies if you're selling general consumer goods rather than collectibles: Be specific and use keywords to increase the chances of having your item found.

Five Tips Toward Tip-Top Titles

It's worth taking time to edit, refine, and rewrite your title so it's most likely to appeal to the shoppers who are actually going to buy your item. When you're titling your item, these five best practices will help:

- *Use all of the 55 characters that are available to you.* Don't fill up the space with exclamation marks and overused words like "minty" and "super," however.

- *Watch your punctuation.* Don't use ALL CAPS since this style is overused and will make your heading look like everyone else's. Simply using upper- and lowercase will make it differ from many others.

- *Be specific.* Use model numbers, dates, and sizes, and add quantities where possible. "Size M Prada Wool Women's Cap in Red" is far better than "Prada Women's Wool Cap," for instance.

- *Add keywords.* "Repair Manual 1959 Ford" is good, but you could also add the name of the repair manual and car in case people are collecting those specific types of items. Many collectors search for such "Mopar" items (items having to do with General Motors vehicle parts, so it's good to know about such terms and add them in: "Chilton Mopar Repair Manual 1959 Ford Galaxie 500 Mint Condition" has more keywords and makes full use of the 55-character limit.

- *Make your item stand out.* So many millions of items are up for sale on eBay at any one time that it's hard to stand out from the crowd. It seems like there's always something similar to your item up for sale by someone else. But what distinguishes your item from the competition? Play up any colors, condition issues, or distinguishing features; words like "Rare," "New," and "MIB" (for Mint in Box) help attract attention.

Your goal is to make your item stand out from the list of search results or category listings by means of your title. After that, it's up to your description and your photos to induce a shopper to actually click the Buy It Now or Place Bid button.

tip *You can also add details about an item by choosing options from the Item Specifics drop-down list. Such lists don't appear in all categories but, when they're offered, they're tailored to the type of item sold in that category. For instance, if you're selling a computer, you can choose the manufacturer, processor speed, monitor size, and other options. The Item Specifics lists appear in Page 2 of the Sell Your Item form—the same page you use to create the title and subtitle.*

Use Subtitles

If 55 characters aren't enough, you can add a subtitle. Subtitles aren't cheap: they cost $0.50 each. But for items that are rare and desirable and for which you expect to receive a sizable winning bid, subtitles can help them stand out from those around it.

You can use subtitles to promote the auction and entice bidders. For example: "Proceeds to benefit Great Oaks Elementary PTA programs." This also helps identify the auction for supporters specifically looking for those items.

Describe Your Items Completely

The same principles that apply to making any eBay sales description attractive and informative apply to nonprofit sales as well. While photos go a long way toward inducing bids, a description holds a shopper's attention and keeps him or her on the sales listing page. It's important to include as many details as you can. Shoppers on eBay love to read as much as possible about the things they're considering buying. Ideally, your descriptions should encourage shoppers to visualize how they might use that bicycle, how snuggly that winter coat might feel, or how they might look driving that convertible car down the street. Also, be upfront about any flaws your item has, such as bumps or cracks. It's better to put out such information up front, so buyers aren't unpleasantly surprised later on.

tip *Details in your item descriptions are very important. If you don't include them, you will get e-mailed questions. For example, if you were selling a pair of shoes worn and signed by Elton John, you would probably include where and when he wore them, but would you think to include the shoe size? eBay buyers will want to know and, although that may leave you wondering if they actually intend to wear them, it will save you time to include these details up front even if you think they're not important or relevant. Similarly, if you have an autographed item, some people will want to know whether it was signed with a Sharpie or paint pen. So, find out, or better yet, include the pen and a photo of the celebrity autographing the item as part of the auction package.*

After you describe the item and before you list the auction policies, include a paragraph about the auction and the nonprofit. For example: "This item is being auctioned by the PTA to benefit additional student learning activities at Red River Elementary. RRE is a Blue Bonnet school located in Anytown, USA, serving 1,000 students. Past PTA-supported projects have raised funds for guest speakers, field trips, a new gymnasium floor, library books, and playground equipment."

If restaurants, service providers, or retailers donate an item, be sure to promote their businesses as well. You might say: "This item is donated by the Big K Family restaurant, a proud supporter of RRE." Include its logo in the listing. This rewards donors and provides them with free advertising—an incentive for soliciting their donations.

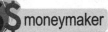

> If you're the nonprofit and you're selling items on eBay on your own behalf, it's obvious why you should include information about your organization in your description. But even if you're an individual selling on behalf of a cause you feel strongly about, it can still have benefits. For one thing, you can have the satisfaction of knowing that the additional information might cause someone to want to find out more about the cause and possibly contribute to it in the future. For another, it makes you look like a knowledgeable and caring seller, which enhances your all-important reputation on eBay.

Consider Formatting Your Listing

If you want to include a graphic image such as a logo in the body of your auction description, you can do it one of two ways:

- You can type the HyperText Markup Language (HTML) commands in the description itself, using the Enter your own HTML tab in the Item description section of the Sell Your Item form. If you already know HTML and have formatted a web-based layout for your auction listings, you can copy the HTML and paste it here.

- If you don't know HTML, don't worry. You can still format your listing using the commands at the top of the Item description's Standard tab (see Figure 7-3). You can select a word and click the Bold, Italic, or Underline button to format it. You can select your auction heading and choose a color from the Color drop-down list to make it stand out from the rest of the listing.

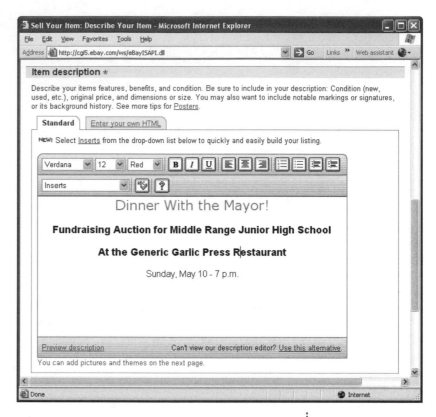

FIGURE 7-3 Format your listing using the Sell Your Item form's built-in controls.

One of the biggest PowerSellers on eBay, Tony Cicalese, uses bright colors, eye-catching typefaces, and a web-page feature called tables to organize the contents of his CDs, DVDs, and other music-related items. It's in keeping with his business philosophy.

"The font matches what's on my business cards," says Tony, who was in the process of reevaluating his sales listing designs as this was being written. "I was in traditional retail management for 12 years, so I have a good concept of what is 'professional,' and I run my business professionally. But I very specifically want to embrace the informality that is music, the camaraderie, and community among my specific niche clientele and extended target audience. While maintaining standards of professionalism, I want to be seen as approachable, accessible, friendly, fun, etc.—in the way that a local record store might have more personality than a 'big box' type of store."

You can't see it in Figure 7-4, but the backgrounds of his auction listings are bright blue and yellow. The whole listing is contained within a table, which enables a designer to organize contents into rows and columns. To create a table, you need a web page editor such as Macromedia Dreamweaver (**www.macromedia.com**) or the free Netscape Composer, which is bundled with the Netscape Communicator browser package (**www .netscape.com**).

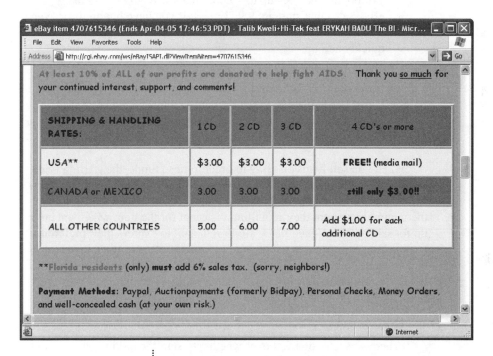

FIGURE 7-4 You can design a layout using tables, copy the HTML, and paste it into the Sell Your Item form.

Set the Starting Price

After you create your description, you click Continue at the bottom of Page 1 of the Sell Your Item form. You move to the next page, which is entitled Enter Pictures & Item Details. The first thing you do is set a *starting price*: the price at which the bidding starts. In any traditional auction (such as the ones held by the longtime British houses Sotheby's and Christie's), the bidding starts at a certain point. On eBay, the starting bid is important for two reasons:

- The starting bid determines how much eBay will charge you for its insertion fee (the fee you pay for listing an item for sale). For instance, if you choose to start an auction with a price of $9.99 or less, eBay will charge an insertion fee of $0.35. If you charge $10.00, the fee goes up to $0.60. That's why you see so many eBay sales that start at $9.99 or less: if you have hundreds or even thousands of objects up for sale, the 25 cents' savings per sale can quickly add up.

- Unless a reserve bid is specified (see the following section, "Set a Reserve Price"), the starting bid is essentially the lowest amount you'll accept in order to sell the item to someone. Because eBay levies an extra charge for a reserve bid, many sellers use the starting price as a reserve price—the minimum amount they'll accept for an item.

When you sell items on eBay in order to raise funds, the starting price takes on extra meaning. Suppose you receive some valuable and rare items from donors around your town. Those donors might have a feeling about the minimum amount they're willing to accept for the item when you put it up for sale on eBay—and many aren't reluctant to express their preferences to you. You, for instance, might want to keep the starting price low in order to pay the minimum insertion fee. (Not only that, but many sellers feel that lower starting prices inspire higher bids from shoppers who feel they're more likely to purchase something for a bargain price.) But your donors might object to having the possibility of selling their cherished object for, say, $0.99 or $9.99.

"There was a lot of angst over whether to start the bidding at $1," says Joan Greene, who organized Chicago's municipal fundraiser, the Great Chicago Fire Sale, in 2004. "There is also pressure to start things at a higher price—donors specified that there was a requirement to start things higher. I will always wonder if we would have gotten more bids by starting with lower starting prices."

Set a Reserve Price

A *reserve price* is a safeguard that a seller can specify in order to prevent having to sell an item for less than it's worth. If you set a reserve of $100 for an item and the bidding only goes up to $99 by the end of the sale, you are not obligated to sell your item because your reserve price was not met. On the other hand, if someone places a high bid of $101 on an item that has a reserve of $100, you *are* obligated to sell.

> note *The bid increment also plays a role in determining exactly how much someone has to bid in order to meet a reserve or win an item. An increment is a minimum amount a bid must increase by in order for the bidder to be a high bidder. An increment prevents bidders from placing tiny bids of, say, one cent at a time just in order to be the highest bidder at the end of a sale. For bids of $100.00 to $249.99, for instance, the bid increment is $2.50; if the seller specifies a starting price of $100.00, the minimum amount that someone must bid in order to win the item is not $100.01 or $101.00, but $102.50. You can find out more about bid increments at **http://pages.ebay.com/help/buy/bid-increments.html**.*

Sellers who want to "protect their investments" place reserve bids on their items to ensure that they don't lose money. If you paid $125.00 for something, you don't want to sell it for $9.99, for instance. But many longtime, savvy eBay sellers stay away from reserve prices because eBay charges extra fees for them, and because there's a widespread perception that auctions with reserve prices don't attract as many bids, because shoppers don't feel they'll get a bargain for what they want. In recent years, the starting price has gained more importance, and many sellers use it as a *de facto* reserve.

> note *The reserve price fee is $1.00 if the reserve price is $49.99 or less; $2.00 for a reserve price of $50.00 or $199.99, and 1 percent of the reserve price if the reserve is $200.00 or higher.*

Set a Buy It Now Price

A Buy It Now price is an alternative to auction bidding. It's a fixed price that you specify for something. If someone agrees to pay your fixed price, they purchase the item immediately and avoid the bidding process altogether. Choose this option if you don't want to have shoppers bid on your item but would rather sell it for a fixed price—or if you want to give shoppers the opportunity to purchase something for a fixed price as well as the chance to bid at auction.

Set the Starting and Ending Time

When it comes to scheduling auctions, you've got two things to decide: How long the sale will last, and when it should start and end. For standard and reserve auctions, eBay gives you six different options for the length of the sale:

- **1-Day** This short time frame is ideal for selling time-sensitive items such as concert or theater tickets.

- **3-Day** This format is likely to attract more bidders on time-sensitive items than a one-day sale.

- **5-Day** This format is useful if you want to start a sale at the beginning of the week and end it on the following weekend.

- **7-Day** Probably the most popular auction length; a sale ends exactly a week after it begins.

- **10-Day** This longest auction format is likely to attract the most shoppers; however, a 10-cent extra fee is charged for ten-day sales.

Regardless of the auction length, it is a good idea to have the auction end when a lot of people on are online, which is evenings and weekends. If choosing a five-day auction, for example, consider starting it on a Tuesday at 8 P.M. so it ends on Sunday. Seven-day auctions can run Saturday to Saturday, or Sunday to Sunday, and ten-day auctions provide the bonus option of being able to run the auction over two weekends. Your auction starts as soon as you submit your listing unless you choose the option to schedule it for a specific time (for an added fee).

note *The definite starting and ending time you specify for a sale can, of course, be undone if you offer a Buy It Now price and someone purchases the item for that price. In that case the sale ends immediately—and hopefully, you receive your money more quickly than you would otherwise.*

Host Your Images Online

Including pictures in your sales listing is essential. Many people will not bid on an item unless there is a photo. Often, the better the picture, the higher the final price will be. Images are so important that we have included a section, "Attract Donors with Photographs," later in this chapter to discuss how to take good pictures. In order for any image to appear online, whether it's on eBay or another web site, it has to be hosted on eBay or a computer called a web server. Once you've captured and edited your digital images, you need to move them from your computer to your host's web server.

Where, then, do you find a host for your auction images? You don't have to look far. eBay provides image hosting through eBay Picture Services. But you don't have to use eBay. It's convenient because the interface you use to upload (the techy term for moving images from your computer to a server) files is built into eBay's Sell Your Item form (see Figure 7-5), but it's more expensive than other hosting options. eBay Picture Services lets you add one photo to an auction for free. After that, each image costs 15 cents. Suppose you put 25 items up for sale each week, and each sale has five photos. That's 125 photos, 100 of which cost a total of $15. Spread that over 50 weeks or so, and you've paid $750 annually to eBay for photo hosting.

FIGURE 7-5 You can post your items on eBay using its Picture Services service.

The least expensive hosting option is your own Internet Service Provider (ISP), the company that gives you access to the Internet. Virtually all ISPs give their clients at least 10MB of storage space on a web server along with Internet access. You can use that storage space to make a personal web site, post family photos—or post auction photos as well. You may already have space available on a server where you can store your images. If you have an account with America Online, you can create up to seven usernames, and each of those usernames is entitled to 2MB of space for web pages and photos. If you don't use one of these options, you have to choose one of these other services for hosting your images:

- **A web-hosting service**   The same web-hosting services that publish your web sites give you space that can be used for posting images and web pages alike. One of the least expensive, Deadzoom (**www.deadzoom.com**), gives you 10MB of hosting space and one gigabyte worth of data transfer per month for $5 per month.

- **An auction management service**   Most services that help you manage your auction sales, such as ManageAuctions.com (**www.manageauctions.com**) and AuctionHelper (**www.auctionhelper.com**) make it easy to upload your image files.

- **A photo-hosting service**   A few web sites specialize in providing space where eBay and other auction users can publish auction images to accompany sales listings. Deadzoom (**www.deadzoom.com**) costs $5 per month for 10MB of server space, which is more than enough for thousands of auction images. No eBay Motors images are allowed, however. A few free services also exist: Auction-Images.com (**http://auction-images.com**) gives you 1MB of space for free. eBay Motors images are not allowed here as well, however.

It pays to shop around and find an affordable option for posting your photos online; the more photos you provide of an item, the more likely prospective buyers are to bid on it. If you don't post your photos using eBay's Picture Services, you make a link to this location on the web server you've chosen from the Sell Your Item form. You can host your photos on any computer that's connected to the Web; you only need to know the image's Uniform Resource Locator (URL). For instance, if your ISP's server URL is www.myisp.com, and you're assigned a folder on that server named ~myfolder and post an image called auctionimage1.jpg, that image's URL is www.myisp.com/~myfolder/auctionimage1.jpg.

Establish Shipping, Payment, and Policies

One of the best ways to make it easy for people to buy from you is to take all forms of payment, including PayPal, to ensure that payment can be done quickly. For people to know the amount to pay, they need to know the shipping cost. As we discussed in the section "Before You Sell, Plan How to Ship" in Chapter 4, there are a couple of ways to determine shipping cost. Whether you use a shipping calculator or select a flat shipping price, make sure that you explain these costs clearly and succinctly in both the description and in the shipping terms. Don't forget to write a return policy. It can be as simple as "All items sold as is," or "Returns accepted for any reason within two weeks, as long as the item is returned in the condition it was sent." How to manage your auctions, including more detail on how to receive payments and ship items, is discussed in Chapter 8.

Consider Listing Upgrade Options and Submit

Near the end of the Sell Your Item form, there are options for additional fees, to upgrade your listing including adding a gallery image, bolding, highlighting, or featuring your listing. eBay has a number of statistics suggesting that these upgrades increase page views, bids, and final selling prices. For lower-priced items, it is typically most cost-effective to only add the gallery image, not the other upgrades. However, if all your items are low priced, it might be worth highlighting or bolding a few of the more interesting items because buyers drawn into those items will often check out your other listings as well. For expensive items, search on eBay to see what other sellers are doing in your category, then choose the options that will make your listing stand out. For example, if many sellers are using bold, try using the highlight feature instead.

Once you complete the form, the only step remaining is to review your auction listing. If you see any typos or errors, return to the prior page and make any corrections. When you are satisfied, submit your listing. If you have not scheduled your auction to begin at a specific time, your auction will be live immediately, although it may not show up in search results for an hour or so.

And now you have successfully listed an item—congratulations! In the next chapter we'll show you how you can answer bidder questions and complete the sale. Before we jump into that, though, we'll give you some more tips in this chapter on how to take great pictures and really make your listings pop.

Attract Donors with Photographs

If your cause is a household name (for instance, the American Red Cross) you might be able to solicit donations without any photos of the merchandise you have to offer. But in most cases, donors, like any bidders on eBay, need to see what they're bidding on. That's where photographs come in. Many eBay sellers consider photos to be the most important part of any auction description on the site. If you're selling on behalf of a well-known cause, photos are perhaps less important overall, because the name and the cause attract bids as well. But photos are always important; the more photos you have and the better their quality, the more likely you are to attract the bids you want. Many new auction sellers are intimidated by the need to take digital photos and put them online. You needn't be; you have several different options for obtaining good photos, and eBay and other hosting services make it easy for you to put them online.

Capture Digital Images

When most people think about taking auction images for sales on eBay, they immediately assume they have to purchase a costly digital camera, figure out how to use it, figure out how to get the images from the camera to the computer, and so on. It's true that, these days, most sellers use digital cameras to capture digital images for their eBay auctions. But it's by no means the only option.

First, though, you need to understand what a digital image is. Digital images aren't the type of images you get back from the photo shop on paper or as slides. Rather, they're images that consist of the digital information that computers can interpret. They exist in the form of computer files. The first requirement for including an image with your auction listing, then, is to obtain images that are in the form of computer files. But any old computer file won't do. The file needs to be saved in a format that compresses the digital information in the image. The most important file format is Joint Photographic Experts Group (JPEG). This format compresses the digital information in an image to keep the file size small; it is especially useful for photos you intend to display on the Web.

note *Another digital image format, Portable Network Graphics (PNG), unlike JPEG, can compress files without losing information in the image, but the files will be larger and take longer to download. If pictures don't load quickly on their computers, people will give up and look at other items. So for this reason, it's better to use a JPEG format in high-quality mode. If you use eBay's own Picture Services to host your images, you can save them in any of the following formats: JPEG, Windows Bitmap (BMP), Graphics Interchange Format (GIF), or Tagged Image File Format (TIFF). If you have the know-how to create an animated GIF image (a series of images that play one after another like a slide show), you can even post such an image on Picture Services.*

Capturing an image means that you convert it from its original form—a real three-dimensional object, or tones on a piece of paper—into those bits of digital information called *pixels*. If you don't want to purchase a digital camera for your auction images, you don't have to. You have two other options: buying a scanner, or letting the photo lab do the conversion to digital format for you. The advantage of letting the photo lab do the work is convenience: you don't have to purchase a camera or scanner and learn how to use it. But there's a big disadvantage: price. Those photo CDs can cost as much as $10 each. After you take pictures of your auction merchandise with your conventional camera, bring them to the photo lab. Check the box on you photo order form that provides an extra copy of your photos on CD-ROM. When you get your photos back, you get both prints and the CD-ROM. The prints can go into your photo album. The compact disc can go into your computer, and you can copy the photos you want to use in your auctions.

 shortcut

> If you want to save a few dollars or don't have time to go to the local photo lab, you can mail your conventional film to a service that will deliver a CD full of auction photos to you by mail. The labs will also post your digital images online so you can download them quickly to your computer. Look into Snapfish (**www.snapfish.com**). At this writing, the service gave new users their first 20 digital images for free. A CD containing 50 photos costs $9.49; photos you can download from the Snapfish web site cost $0.49 each.

You can also capture digital images of objects—especially flat objects such as books, posters, and cards—using a scanner. A scanner is a piece of hardware that connects to your computer and that works much like a photocopier. The scanner scans the object placed on a glass bed with a special lens. But instead of outputting the image to paper as a photocopier does, the output goes to your computer, where you can preview it using software provided with the scanner. You can then save the image to disk so you can use it in your auctions. Note that you can take print pictures of your objects and scan those photos if you wish since prints are pretty cheap to get. Scanners (such as the flatbed model shown in Figure 7-6) are less expensive than digital cameras—you can find them at Buy It Now for prices of $40 to $60.

Of course, if you already have a digital camera or are eager to buy one for either auction or personal use, it's by far the most practical and affordable option for capturing images of your sales merchandise. A digital camera saves the image directly to computer disk. In other words, you

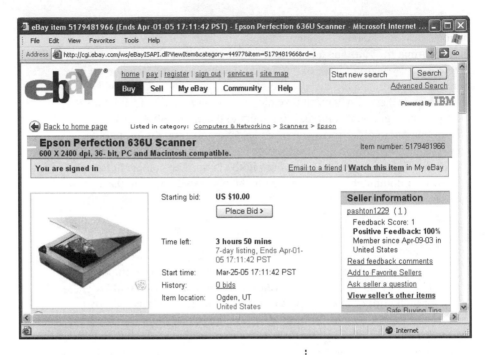

FIGURE 7-6 Scanners are inexpensive and ideal for capturing books, cards, or other flat objects.

don't have to mail your film to a photo lab, and you don't have to wait a day, or even an hour, to get your pictures back. You can immediately see if the picture came out well and take another if you're not satisfied. In just a matter of minutes, you can transfer your photo files from your camera to your computer quickly and easily.

A digital camera is an indispensable piece of equipment for nearly every eBay seller. One of the best places to shop for and purchase a camera is eBay itself. They're getting less expensive and more powerful all the time. The good news, though, is that you don't necessarily need the most expensive and full-featured model around. At this writing, the most expensive and latest models can display as many as seven megapixels of information (that's seven million pixels) within a single image. Such a camera would be good if you intend to use it for your personal photos, and if you plan to print out your digital images and display them in a frame or another format. But an image with that many pixels within it will result in a file that is several megabytes in size—an image that big would be impractical. Why? In order for an image that's contained on a web site to be displayed on your browser, it's downloaded from the server to your computer. The bigger the image, the longer it takes to display.

eBay images (or other web images, for that matter) are only intended to be viewed in a web browser on a computer screen, and monitors are limited in the amount of digital information they can display. Ideally, images on web pages should be a maximum of 50KB (that's 50 kilobytes, or 50 thousand bits) in size so they appear on a shopper's computer screen in a matter of seconds. If images take too long to appear, shoppers might quickly become frustrated and turn to someone else's auction.

The many well-known camera manufacturers such as Canon, Nikon, Minolta, Olympus, and Fuji all produce digital cameras that are affordable and that can capture a moderate amount of information. And at the time this was written, there were more than 22,000 separate listings for digital cameras on eBay. An example is shown in Figure 7-7. The Olympus CAMEDIA shown captures a maximum of 2.0 megapixels. It's far from the most powerful digital camera, but the ones that are less capable are more affordable, and generally simpler to use—this particular model sold for only $86.

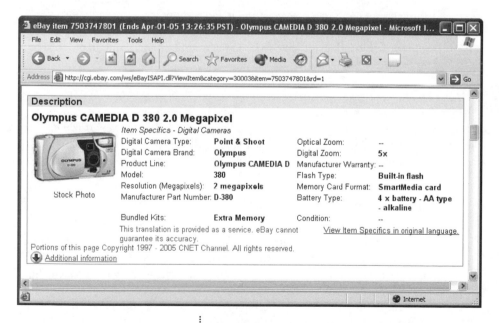

FIGURE 7-7 You don't need lots of megapixels when taking digital photos for eBay.

note *The amount of detail a digital camera can capture is called its* resolution. *Digital cameras give you the capability to adjust the resolution you capture an image at. Even if you have a 5 megapixel camera, you can change the resolution to a lower amount, such as 1 or 2 megapixels, to capture smaller image files that are easier to display on the Web.*

We're not going to go into detail on how to use your digital camera—that's what your camera's instruction manual is for. However, there are a few things to keep in mind. One of the best features of digital cameras, especially for eBay items, is a *macro lens*—a lens that is specially fabricated to capture detailed close-up images of larger objects. It's the best way to obtain sharp, clear images of an item's detailed features. Take as many close-ups as your object warrants with your macro lens, and try to get photos from different angles so prospective bidders can see them from many different perspectives. Also be aware of your camera's options for focusing images so they appear as sharp as possible. Most digital cameras don't let you focus manually. They use a focal area in the middle of the image that controls the focus. If you don't have your image centered quite right, it might not be in focus. Reposition it and reshoot if you're in doubt—or consult your camera's manual to see if you can turn off the auto-focus lock so your subject doesn't have to be in the middle of the frame in order to be in focus.

tip *Many eBay sellers take their objects outdoors and photograph them in natural light. This enables them to avoid problems with flash attachments such as light flares that can appear on a shiny object and make its details difficult to see. If you do photograph outdoors on a sunny day, make sure shadows don't fall on your item. If you can, try to photograph on a bright but cloudy day when the light is more even.*

Show Your Merchandise in Its Best Light

The most expensive camera in the world can be undone by poor lighting and presentation. Along with capturing a sharp image that has good balance between light and dark areas (in other words, good contrast), you need to take care with what's in the background of the image, how the image is lit, and whether it needs to be mounted in a special way.

You want your auction offering to be the "star" of your photo. It shouldn't compete with "costars" such as tools, paintings on the wall, furniture, and other objects that happen to be sitting around it. Position your item against a solid background by draping a sheet or other cloth behind it. Make sure you have both a dark- and a light-colored cloth available: use the dark cloth for light-colored merchandise, and the light-colored one for dark objects.

The built-in flash on a digital camera only goes so far. That's because its light comes from only one direction and is apt to leave shadows around the edges of what you're photographing. Two or three good studio lights with umbrellas to diffuse the light, like the devices shown in Figure 7-8, will enhance your item's existing assets. Simpler and less expensive lighting systems include a small tent-like enclosure that's ideal for tabletop photography.

FIGURE 7-8 Professional studio lights will make your items look better, which reflects positively on your organization.

What happens if you fail to diffuse or balance the light shining on the object you want to sell (especially if it's an object with an especially shiny or reflective surface)? No disasters occur. However, you'll probably have to answer questions from customers as to what exactly they're supposed to be looking at.

You might consider creating a photo "studio" in your home or business where you can place your merchandise. Have a table handy so you can place smaller items atop it. (Larger things can go in front of the table.) If you're selling jewelry, see if you can purchase or borrow a stand that can make small, shiny groups of objects more easily visible. If you're selling clothing, try to obtain a mannequin of the sort used in department store windows—it gives bidders a chance to visualize how such items might look when worn. If you can engage your buyer's imagination, they're far more likely to click Place Bid or Buy It Now.

Edit Your Images

Only on rare occasions does an image come straight from your digital camera, scanner, or photo CD in perfect shape for posting online. In almost all cases, the images are too big, or the contrast and lighting need to be adjusted in some way so the contents can be viewed more clearly. Once you capture an image, you should edit it in a graphics program so it's just the right size and all its contents are clear and sharp.

You might not have to purchase the image editing software you use to adjust your files for eBay. If you've purchased a digital camera or scanner, chances are it comes with a program that enables you to adjust an image's brightness, contrast, and other qualities. Some digital cameras come with an excellent image editor called Adobe Photoshop Elements. This program is ideally suited for working with digital photos, while professional graphic designers use its bigger and more expensive cousin, Adobe Photoshop, to create computer graphics of all sorts.

note *You can find out more about Photoshop and Photoshop Elements on the Adobe Systems Incorporated web site (**www.adobe.com**). Photoshop Elements for Windows costs $89 if you download the software from the Adobe web site; you can download the Macintosh version for $79. Windows users might also want to try Paint Shop Pro by Corel (**www.corel.com**), which costs $129.*

One thing you might want to do to your auction image is *downsample* it for the Web. Downsampling is the process of lowering an image's resolution. You literally reduce the number of pixels in the image so the image file takes up less computer space. You might take an image at a resolution of 300 dpi (dots per inch, which is the same as pixels per inch) but downsample it to 72 dpi, which is a desirable resolution for the Web.

The most common editing functions handled by graphics software are:

- **Adjusting the contrast** This is the difference between the light and dark areas in an image.

- **Adjusting the brightness of the image** Some scanners produce images that are initially too dark and need to be lightened up.

- **Cropping the image** You reduce the image's physical size (its height and width) by cutting out contents that aren't needed and focusing on the most important parts of the image.

In virtually every graphics program, the process of cropping works the same. You click the Crop tool, position your mouse pointer just above and to one side of the image, click and hold down your mouse button, and drag your mouse down and to the opposite side of the image. Release your mouse when the subject of your photo is outlined with the marquee box. An example is shown in Figure 7-9.

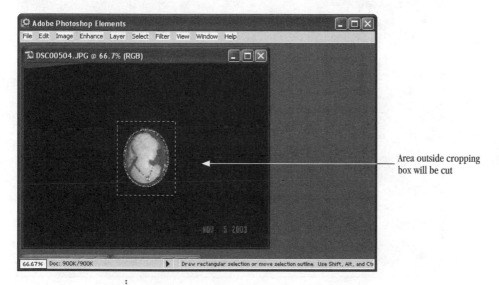

FIGURE 7-9   Crop your images so they take up less space on disk and on screen.

Cropping has the added benefit of reducing the image's file size. But reducing the height or width is important, too. You don't want viewers to have to scroll left or right to see all the contents of an extra-wide image. Such an image doesn't look professional, and it's inconvenient to shoppers who don't have a big enough monitor to display the image fully. Many shoppers don't have 19- or 21-inch monitors at their disposal when they shop eBay. You have to assume that they have the smaller and more common 15- or 17-inch models. (They may be using their laptop computers, after all.) What's the ideal size for a 17-inch monitor? An example is shown in Figure 7-10. We've drawn the height and width on the image to indicate a possible maximum size you should shoot for.

Once you've captured and edited your auction images, you need to save them in a location on your computer where you can find them easily. Save them in either JPEG or PNG format. You can then locate the images and put them online when you create your auction description. The actual mechanics of moving the files from your computer to eBay or another hosting service are described in "Host Your Images Online" earlier in this chapter.

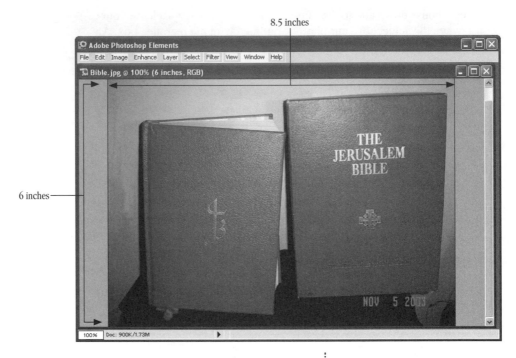

FIGURE 7-10 Limit your images to a height and width that will fit in most viewers' monitors.

Ten Tips That'll Make Your Listings Go from Drab to Fab

What separates a ho-hum auction description from one that attracts attention and encourages bids? It's no mystery. You only have to think about the items you've bid on yourself, and the sales you've visited, to get the answer. Why did you bid on one item and not another, similar one? Here are ten obvious reasons—things that you should try to include in your own descriptions:

❑ **Lots of photos**   There's no formula or rule that prescribes how many you need—just make sure you have enough images to show the object from all possible angles, and to show important details like maker's marks or dates.

❑ **Clear, sharp photos**   Check your photos online to make sure they're bright enough and clear enough.

❑ **Close-up images**   Close-ups that show trademarks, as well as those that clearly illustrate flaws like hairline cracks, increase buyer confidence.

❑ **Details, details** On the Internet, you can achieve a level of detail that you can't approach in sales catalogs, television commercials, or printed ads.

❑ **A good title** The first key step for any sale is making sure it's found. A title full of pertinent keywords will make it easier to find.

❑ **A good location** Placing the item in one or two categories will make it easier for "browsers" (shoppers who browse through categories as well as search) to find them.

❑ **Clear sales terms** The more upfront you are in your description regarding your returns policy (if you have one), your preferred shipping methods, and the types of payment you accept, the more comfortable shoppers will feel about making purchases from you.

❑ **Multiple payment options** Shoppers online want a choice: They want to pick the payment method they're most comfortable with, whether it is PayPal, a check, or a money order.

❑ **Unambiguous shipping charges and procedures** Shoppers are turned off by handling charges that seem unjustified and shipping charges that seem excessive.

❑ **Something that engages the shopper's imagination** An example is a good story. It's also anything that gets the shopper to envision how she or he would use an item.

The "extra" detail that enhances all of these basic steps is to have an item that's in demand—to offer something that people are going to want either because they can't find it elsewhere, because it's one of a kind, or because it's something they need. It's great to think that eBay members will buy what you have to offer simply because they want to benefit your nonprofit cause. But eBay is a marketplace first and foremost; desirable products together with worthy causes result in a winning combination.

Avoid Obvious Problems

Sometimes, success is as much a matter of avoiding mistakes that are preventable as a matter of luck or skill. Selling on eBay is similar. It's easy to avoid having your listing pulled by eBay by not selling items that the auction site considers questionable or prohibited, for instance. (Check the complete list of prohibited and restricted items at **http://pages.ebay.com/ help/policies/items-ov.html**). You can also avoid trouble by:

- Not copying images from other eBay auctions or web pages.

- Not suggesting something "might be" a brand name item such as Gucci if you are not sure. Either it is or it isn't. State only the facts that you know.

- Not using words such as "like" or "not" in titles. Buyers become frustrated when searching for specific items and other items that are similar to but not the items they are seeking show up in their search results.

- Not "keyword spamming" or listing words unrelated to your auction item in the description in order to show up in more search results.

- Not reproducing a company's trademarked logo in your description.

- Not selling counterfeit or illegally copied merchandise.

Don't bid from the same computer that was used to originally list an item. The Atkinson, Nebraska, auction we described in Chapter 4 encountered this problem. A high-school computer lab was made available to volunteers who created sales listings. Those same volunteers wanted to place bids on the auction merchandise, and inadvertently used the same computers to bid that were used to create the listings. To eBay, this looked like a process called *shill bidding*—a practice where a seller improperly inflates bids on an item to get more for it.

tip *One of the problems that can hold you back and potentially turn an enjoyable process into a nightmare is failing to plan for success. You don't know how many donations you're going to get for your auction; you don't realize how many e-mail inquiries you're going to receive, or how many items you're actually going to sell. Make sure you have enough volunteers on hand to handle the load just in case you're flooded with donations at the last minute or you have to ship out dozens of items quickly. It's better to have too many "helping hands" available than an insufficient amount.*

Train Your Staff

Once you've gone through the Sell Your Item form and come up with a system for taking and hosting your photos, don't keep your new knowledge to yourself. Share your expertise with the colleagues who are going to help you conduct the sale. After all, if you're the only one who knows how to create a sales listing on eBay, you're going to be the only one who is capable of writing descriptions and getting them online—a time-consuming and tedious process, especially the first time around.

You can lead your staff through your own personal tutorial. However, if you don't have time to sit down and run through the listing process with them (and you might not have the time, especially if you're also tasked with soliciting donations and coordinating volunteers), keep in mind that there are numerous books on selling on eBay, not to mention countless helpful tutorials on eBay and online training programs. eBay University (**http://pages.ebay.com/university**) publishes a schedule of training so if there's a class in your town in a timely manner, it's a good idea to attend and/or send some staff members from the nonprofit. There are other training programs from companies like M Networks (**www.mnetworks.com**), as well as online courses from CNET.com (**www.cnet.com**) and other sites. You may also be able to tap into local Trading Assistants and certified eBay education specialists who might be willing to come to your location and train staff for a fee.

Your volunteers are the public face of your organization when they work on your fundraiser. That applies whether the event occurs online or in a brick-and-mortar space (or both). When you train your volunteers to help conduct your eBay fundraiser, you might have to do some computer training. But just as important, you need to train your volunteers to spread your message and boost your public image. Some specifics are covered in the sections that follow.

tip *Consider holding a "training party" and hand out training materials and educate volunteers about your group and its mission while entertaining them at the same time. A group session saves you time, and it builds a spirit of cooperation and cohesion among your volunteers, too.*

Be Clear about Your Goals

When you train volunteers, keep in mind that you're likely to be working with people of different ages, with different educational and financial backgrounds, not to mention motives for helping you. Don't be reluctant to explain every step your volunteers have to follow and provide them with instructions on what to say. If there's a specific task you want them to perform, or a set of merchandise you want them to promote, you must educate them. Don't assume everyone is on the same wavelength.

First, make sure your volunteers are familiar with the reason they're helping to raise funds in the first place. They may have to explain your mission to people they meet on the street while putting up posters, or people they meet who might have merchandise to donate. Instruct them to say a standard phrase along the lines of:

> We are raising funds for our youth group to travel to the Misty Shoals state park. There we will help repair the park cabins, clean up damage from a recent storm, and help build a new ranger facility.

eBay sales listings should always carry a clear statement of purpose in the description: "Proceeds will go toward medical expenses of Jimmy Bolen, a six-year-old suffering from leukemia. Blood marrow transfusions and other expenses have put a severe strain on his family."

shortcut

> Provide a script that spells out what your volunteers should say to prospective bidders or donors: "We are working to help the Saline County Nature Center to raise funds for a new sanctuary and walking trail. Our nonprofit organization is dedicated to rehabilitating orphaned and injured animals and educating children and adults about the natural environment in this area."

Keep It Positive

You might feel overwhelmed and stressed out when you're trying to pull your event together, but your volunteers don't need to absorb your anxiety. No matter what's going on, try your best to keep everything very upbeat and positive.

Remember that you're boosting morale for your volunteers. The friendlier and happier your volunteers are, the more positive the sales descriptions they write, and the more courteous and positive their e-mail and phone contacts with potential buyers will be.

Be sure to make your volunteers feel wanted and let them know that their efforts are appreciated. Always remember to thank volunteers for their services. You might consider letting them bid early or have an early chance at placing a Buy It Now bid on items that are being offered at a fixed price. Be sure to supply them with food and refreshments, and give them frequent shift breaks so they can rest and look at the items.

> **tip** *If your volunteers meet with a situation they're unable to resolve and they're talking to donors, instruct them to be courteous and tell the inquiring party to wait until they talk to a qualified individual. Oftentimes, they're confronted with questions they just can't answer. Rather than saying "I don't know" or "I can't answer that," provide them with a list of organizers and their contact information so they can refer the donors to the appropriate people. If the volunteers feel lost, they don't have to feel badly or leave the potential donor frustrated. By having a contact list available, you enable interested parties to go up to the next level of authority and ensure that their concerns will be addressed.*

Be Friendly with Potential Donors

Volunteers are salespeople as well as publicists for your cause and your organization. Tell them that they shouldn't be reluctant to approach someone they meet in person—for instance, someone who's visiting your storage facility and looking over the items that will be placed up for auction. Striking up a conversation with the visitor may help cement a deal for them to purchase or donate. If someone walks away or hangs up without purchasing or donating, it's a good idea for volunteers to be extra polite with statements such as "Thank you for listening" and "Have a good day."

Volunteers—especially children—should be instructed to dress and act appropriately. If you're raising funds for a church or elementary school, they shouldn't show up at your event wearing skin-tight jeans or bare-midriff shirts with sexually explicit slogans on them. This applies whether the event is online or off. If at all possible, your helpers should wear something that has the name of your organization on it to let visitors know they're working members of the group.

> **tip** *If you have a brochure or flyer that describes your fundraising event or the organization you're working to benefit, include it in the package when shipment goes out to a high bidder or buyer. A brochure describing the cause you're trying to address not only builds goodwill and helps publicize your nonprofit institution, but it also might just result in additional donations. See Chapter 8 for more about completing transactions and building good relations with your customers.*

Be Prepared for the Big Rush

As the time approaches for your eBay fundraiser, be ready for a flood of last-minute donations. Many people decide at the very last minute that they're going to make merchandise available for nonprofit events. This can put a great burden on the people who are creating your sales listings, whether they're volunteers or the trading assistants you've hired.

"At the Great Chicago Fire Sale, the write-ups for the auction were very time consuming," says Joan Greene. "As life would have it, auction items seemed to fly in toward the end, thus the need for long hours of writing and great patience from our eBay trading assistant, Auctions for Everybody (**www.auctionsforeverybody.com**) to take our write-ups and get them into eBay format."

must have

- If you want your eBay sale to benefit a specific charity and you are not using eBay Giving Works, you need to obtain the approval of the charity and display a copy of the letter in your auction listing. However, if you donate your overall profits to charities of your choice on an intermittent basis, you don't need to display such a letter.

- By listing with eBay's charitable arm MissionFish, you'll get more bids for your item. You can initiate the process from within eBay's Sell Your Item form.

- Use a scanner or digital camera, or get digital images from your photo processor, to increase interest in what you have to sell.

- Take the time to write headings that use keywords and craft descriptions that are descriptive and detailed to build confidence and answer any questions that occur to prospective bidders.

Chapter 8
Managing Your Auctions and Building Good Donor Relations

I regard this [eBay auctions] as friendraising as much as fundraising. The relationships and public awareness we have been able to raise have made all the difference in the world.

—Elana Viner, Child
Welfare League of America

What We'll Cover in This Chapter:

- Cultivating your donor base by providing good customer support

- Easing the payment and shipping process for your donors

- Managing "back-room" functions such as inventory tracking

- Recording feedback after the transaction

- Obtaining receipts for your organization or providing them to customers

- Tracking your customers to build relationships after the sale

- Making sure your donors' questions are answered

Donors are key to any nonprofit fundraising activity. The Web and eBay give you the chance to personalize relationships with your donors in a way you just can't do in the offline world. Even though you may never meet the donors who purchase your items on eBay, once you establish contact, you have the opportunity to build lasting, long-term relationships with them.

In the field of e-commerce, Customer Relationship Management (CRM) has always been seen as important. CRM holds that a company has the capability to customize the way it interacts with its customers, based on preferences those customers have communicated. Clients on the Web are often given the ability to choose whether they want to receive a newsletter or list of sales from an online merchant; they are also able to specify whether they want to receive the communications in plain-text format or in an HTML-formatted version. Based on this information, as well as items the person has purchased in the past, the company is able to send out information the customer is likely to be interested in.

Any web site that enables merchants to sell products also has the capability to conduct *one-to-one marketing*: the practice of addressing clients or customers—or, in this case, donors—with personalized communications. Nonprofits that efficiently manage inventory and collect information about their donors can provide these Very Important People with excellent, personal service. In this chapter, we address ways you can manage your auctions and develop good donor relations at the same time— follow those proven customer service practices that have always worked in the offline world, but implement the practices in unique ways to reach out to donors online.

> Customer Relationship Management (CRM) is all activities that keep you in contact with your customers and potential customers. CRM activities include keeping track of names and addresses, maintaining records of how your company responded to a customer, and developing standard response templates that everyone in your organization can use. To find out more about how technology can help you practice CRM, read the useful article on the subject at **http://guide.darwinmag.com/technology/enterprise/crm**.

Manage and Cultivate Your Donors

The vast majority of people who buy things on eBay are customers. But as any successful eBay businessperson knows, they aren't *just* customers—the customer is king, the key to maintaining a good feedback rating, and the key to repeat business that can keep an eBay sales effort afloat. Cultivating ongoing relationships with satisfied customers is the key to ongoing business.

To those who sell on eBay to benefit nonprofit causes, customers are even more special: they are *donors*. They're people who keep you going and make your activities possible. As anyone who has participated in one of eBay's community forums can tell you, the Internet is a great place to develop close relationships with individuals who share a common goal or interest—in other words, develop relationships with an online community.

On eBay and the Web, caring for and feeding donors is as important as it is in the offline world. eBay gives you several ways to maintain good relations with other members. The most important is eBay's well-known feedback system, which rewards trustworthiness and punishes dishonesty. You can also volunteer information that helps your donors—providing them with the URLs of web sites they might like to visit, on eBay or elsewhere, or answering questions on the message boards. At the very least, you'll gain the respect of your donors by responding quickly to e-mail inquiries, and making payment and shipping easy.

Customer Support

If you're affiliated with a nonprofit, you already know about cultivating your donor base. It boils down to being nice to your donors: inviting them, feeding them, praising them, and giving them special access and possibly other perks.

On the Web (and by extension, on eBay), cultivating donors is the same as providing a high-level of customer service. But customer service on the Web is different than in other venues. Nonprofits, like other organizations that sell on eBay or online, need to take into account the special way online consumers behave. In the traditional offline world, customer service is a matter of answering questions and solving problems with orders. Customer service representatives make themselves available to field questions and problems as they arise.

Customer service on the Web isn't a matter of publishing a phone number or e-mail address and waiting for consumers to send you questions. Such basics are important, but it's more a matter of making information *proactively* available to consumers. The customer is in charge on the Web, not the seller. Customers choose to view your items for sale or visit your web site; they choose to make a bid or a donation, or go elsewhere with their money.

 shortcut

Many eBay sellers who receive questions from prospective bidders answer those questions quickly. But they go a step further, too. They also publish the questions and answers as additions to their sales descriptions. This reduces the number of similar questions you receive, which saves your volunteers some work; it also raises the level of customer support you provide, which makes prospective bidders more likely to purchase from you.

When you receive a question from a prospective buyer through eBay's message system, you have the option of simply responding to the buyer privately, or adding the question and your response to the body of your sales description. In Figure 8-1, a seller representing the 6th Man Foundation and Project Contact Africa answered a question about a rocking chair once owned by President John F. Kennedy. The seller added the question and answer to the description under the heading Questions from other members.

Ease the Payment Process

Online shoppers want the experience of buying something online to be fast and convenient. If they weren't in a hurry, they would look laboriously around their local area to find just what they're looking for. Online shoppers

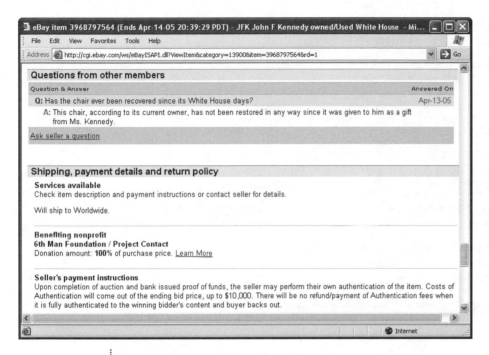

FIGURE 8-1 Adding questions and responses to your sales description after it goes online heads off similar questions from other prospective bidders.

expect sellers to provide a painless process when it comes to paying for an item they've purchased online. Anything less makes them suspicious and prompts them to leave neutral or negative feedback.

The fact that you've chosen to sell on eBay automatically helps streamline the process of purchasing and paying for merchandise. eBay provides the Buy It Now and Place Bid system. After the sale, eBay automatically sends e-mail messages to both the buyer and seller to let them know if the sale has ended with a successful bid or a Buy It Now purchase.

> **tip** *One aspect of payments on eBay is a* handling fee: *a fee that many sellers charge to compensate for the materials, time, and effort they spend in packing, shipping, and making sales. A modest handling fee (say, $1) can help you gain a profit on small-ticket items. But don't gouge the buyer with a high handling fee; buyers can sense that they're being overcharged and might protest with negative feedback.*

Payment Process: Best Practices

You still need to observe a few best practices to make sure everything proceeds smoothly. Make sure you do the following:

- ❏ **Sign up with PayPal**   It's recognized as a standard, reliable method of payment by many sellers.

- ❏ **Verify your PayPal registration**   You do this by noting some small deposits PayPal has made to your account; verification builds trust among buyers.

- ❏ **Accept checks or money orders**   Many buyers feel more secure sending a piece of paper through the mail than paying electronically for something they purchase online. Just make sure you wait until the check clears before you ship the item out.

- ❏ **Accept cash, but only if you provide a disclaimer**   Some buyers insist on sending cash through the mail, even though it's obviously risky.

- ❏ **Consider accepting electronic system payments**   Use a service that's considered a trusted alternative to PayPal, such as Western Union's BidPay (**www.bidpay.com**).

Ensure Smooth Shipments

Providing multiple payment options isn't enough to calm shoppers' uncertainties about shopping online, or their need for instant gratification. Customers want a quick confirmation that the order has been received. They want to know when the item will ship. Web customers don't like to wait for anything—especially deliveries.

Most eBay sellers use one of the "Big Three" shippers: the United States Postal Service (USPS), United Parcel Service (UPS), or Federal Express (FedEx). The shipper you pick depends on your location and your needs. If you're willing to bring your packages to your shipper yourself, you should pick the one that's closest to you; if your main concern is postage cost, choose USPS, as its rates are generally the lowest. If you need to have your packages picked up from your home or office, however, sign up for an account with UPS or FedEx; both enable you to arrange for a pickup at your location.

Many eBay sellers choose USPS Priority Mail as their shipping method of choice because it's relatively fast (delivery is completed in a matter of two days). Even more important, the USPS makes a special line of Priority Mail shipping materials available for free to anyone who uses that method of shipping. The boxes, envelopes, tape, and labels are all clean and new and marked with the Priority Mail logo. For many sellers, the convenience of being able to use the USPS's shipping materials for free is reason enough to choose Priority Mail. You can order the materials online rather than going to the post office for them; find out more at The Postal Store at **http://shop .usps.com/cgi-bin/vsbv/postal_store_non_ssl/home.jsp**, or for the very cool eBay–USPS cobranded boxes, shown here, go to **http://ebaysupplies .usps.com/**.

Boxes Are Just the Beginning

It's becoming increasingly easier to handle more and more of your shipping tasks online from your home computer. The USPS offers a number of services to assist eBay sellers with calculating shipping, printing shipping labels, purchasing insurance, arranging for a carrier pick-up, tracking shipments, and confirming delivery online. One new time-saving product from the USPS is Priority Mail Flat Rate Packaging. Sellers can fill the Flat Rate Boxes for $7.70, regardless of weight, and ship them anywhere in the U.S. (Flat Rate Envelopes are $3.85). For the latest shipping solutions from USPS and other shippers, visit eBay's Shipping Center at **http://pages.ebay.com/services/buyandsell/shipping.html**.

(continued)

Pitney Bowes has integrated their service with eBay and PayPal to make it easy and fast to generate shipping labels complete with USPS postage and addresses already entered. Take a look at their tutorial at **www.pitneyworks.com/ebay/**.

UPS offers helpful step-by-step information for those considering international shipping, including international forms you might need to ship items overseas, through their Global Advisor (**www.ups.com/content/us/en/resources/advisor/intro.html**). They also have useful packaging tips at **www.ups.com/content/us/en/resources/prepare/index.html**.

FedEx shipping can be arranged online and the service provides very detailed tracking (which buyers love!). Another plus, you can usually print the shipping "labels" on plain paper (instead of buying label stock) and attach it to the package with clear packing tape or in one of their clear adhesive pouches. If you know of local companies with FedEx accounts, you could ask them to help with the shipping for your fundraiser so that you can take advantage of their corporate rates. FedEx will also consider in-kind donations of shipping for nonprofits on a case-by-case basis. For information on how to submit a request for charitable shipping visit FedEx at **http://community.fedex.com/** and click on Contribution Guidelines.

Another shipping shortcut is a high-quality postal scale. This enables you to calculate postage no matter which shipper you use. You can find postal scales on eBay itself for less than $20.00; the one shown in Figure 8-2 had a Buy It Now price of $17.50.

FIGURE 8-2 Buy an accurate postal scale so you can estimate shipping costs for your buyers.

A postal scale comes in handy in several ways. When you fill out eBay's Sell Your Item form as we describe in Chapter 7, you can choose to add a built-in shipping calculator to your sales description. This enables prospective buyers to calculate the shipping cost based on their location—as long as you provide the accurate weight of the item being offered. If you don't want to use the calculator, you can state in the form how much the item weighs, and have the buyer calculate the shipping using your shipper's online calculator. The faster you can ship your items, the faster your donors will receive them. And the faster buyers receive what they purchase, the more satisfied they'll be. The fastest way is to calculate your postage yourself and print it out at home. All of the Big Three shippers let you print out your own postage; and many eBay sellers are happy with postage services such as Stamps.com (**www.stamps.com**), which lets you print your own postage at your home or office.

It's also important to instruct the volunteers who are going to pack your items to use as much packing material as possible: you don't want items returned because they've been broken in transit. Buyers who receive damaged items are likely to demand refunds from you. You don't necessarily have to provide a refund, but it is a good idea in the listing to take the precaution of advising or requiring buyers to purchase insurance from the shipper or from an insurance company such as U-PIC (**www.u-pic.com**) if the auction item is something especially valuable or fragile. Nonetheless, many sellers provide refunds to keep customers satisfied and prevent negative feedback. For particularly fragile items, such as those made of porcelain or glass, many sellers have learned to double-box. They put the item within one box filled with packing peanuts or bubble wrap as insulating material. They then put this box into a larger box that's also filled with insulating material. It's more work and expense for you, the seller, but it greatly reduces the chance of damage, and it impresses customers, who are pleased with the care you've taken to send their merchandise.

$$$ moneymaker

Sometimes it pays to sign up with an e-commerce host in order to obtain software that streamlines functions such as tracking inventory and notifying customers about the progress of shipments. Order Manager, a service provided to customers who host e-commerce web sites with Microsoft Small Business Center (**www.microsoft.com/smallbusiness/bc/default.mspx**), enables sellers to track orders and send notifications at critical stages to both you and your customers.

Manage Your "Back Room"

One aspect of customer service is quick and efficient order fulfillment. Customers on eBay are used to getting what they've ordered within days of paying for it (or, if they pay by check, within days of the check clearing). Occasionally, when a customer buys from an eBay seller who's using a drop shipper (a company that provides the merchandise and stores it and ships it, which means the seller never actually sees it), problems can occur. If the item isn't in stock and the drop shipper doesn't have it, the customer quickly becomes dissatisfied and either leaves negative feedback or chooses another seller.

Keeping track of what you have in stock and making sure it reaches its destination efficiently is important for any auction seller. For nonprofits doing fundraising on eBay, it's less complicated than it is for full-time sellers, because the merchandise being sold tends to consist of one-of-a-kind objects (chances are you aren't selling ten identical Christmas ornaments or ten identical dinner-with-the-principal packages, for instance). Still, you need to keep track of the inventory you do have on hand so your volunteers don't get confused and—most important—so your prospective donors get their questions answered or their items shipped quickly.

Manage Your Inventory

Lots of big-time auction sellers use computer systems that automatically manage their inventory: when they sell something, the software records the sale and adjusts the number of identical items that are still in stock. Since you're doing fundraising and you might only hold a fundraiser once or twice a year, you probably don't need a complex system to handle inventory management.

That doesn't mean you shouldn't keep track of what you do sell, however. There's nothing wrong with tracking your inventory in a ledger book by hand the old-fashioned way, or creating a simple spreadsheet in a program like Excel or Access to keep track of items that need to be shipped. The following suggestions address some things to keep in mind for managing your inventory.

Logging

When you have lots of activities to pursue, it's tempting to simply put a pile of items out on a big card table, or on the floor of your meeting room, and keep track of them by sight. Keep in mind that you're going to:

- Photograph each item.
- Match the photograph to the correct description.

- Upload your sales descriptions and photos so the sales actually start on eBay, at which time eBay will assign its own item number.

- Answer questions from prospective bidders about each item you have for sale. Shoppers will refer to your item by its eBay item number, so you'll need to match this item number to your internal item number to know where the item can be located.

To keep track of all this information, consider appointing one of your volunteers to be the Sales Coordinator. The Sales Coordinator should assign each item a number and attach a "sticky note" to the item with the number on it. This individual can then add the item and number to your inventory database list. When eBay assigns its own number to the item and the sale goes online, the number should be added to the database as well. That way, any one of your volunteers will be able to answer a question about the item.

warning *Numbering and labeling items isn't just a matter of keeping a good inventory. Too many things can go wrong if you don't invent some sort of tracking system for your merchandise. You can easily list an item for sale twice; lose track of it when you need to ship it; or it might get "lost in the shuffle" amid piles of other items and never be put up for sale. Number and label your merchandise so everyone can find and track it more easily.*

Coordination with Shipping

When a sale is made, eBay automatically sends you and the high bidder/ buyer an e-mail notification. The message refers to eBay's item number. It's a good idea to use these item numbers in the e-mail messages you send to your customers. For example:

Dear Customer,
Your eBay item number 334567890, the rhinestone studded jacket worn by Robert Redford, shipped today by Priority Mail and should reach you in two to five days. We are enclosing a copy of the eBay sales invoice, which you can keep for your tax records. Thank you for your support of our cause, and please consider us in the future for donations or other forms of support.

Such messages let customers know that you're organized and that they can expect their merchandise soon, which is reassuring to shoppers who aren't used to purchasing at auction.

tip *Your nonprofit organization may want to include a brochure about your organization or a fundraising flyer in the package you send to a buyer with the item purchased. This will help people understand your cause and activities, and could lead to additional donations.*

Complete the Transaction

The Web can be a remarkably personal place despite the fact that individuals use it to share information and conduct sales transactions and never see one another face-to-face. A successful nonprofit (or for-profit) sales effort continually gathers data about its shoppers—both those who simply browse and those who go on to make a purchase—to try and get to know them better. Successful research and site management can attract return donors, which results in improved sales.

eBay, and its My eBay feature, can provide you with information about your customers through reports of web activity. Some eBay sales tools, like Selling Manager Pro, can help you create input forms so your customers can contact you and tell you about themselves, what they think of your web site, and what they need from you. Consider sending e-mail asking shoppers for their opinion of your level of service after they've received their merchandise. It's a way of continuing the dialogue with that customer that might lead to future donations. You don't want information for its own sake, though. You want to analyze and act on it.

Record Feedback

If you're a nonprofit organization, you probably know already that word-of-mouth and reputation play an important role in the number of donations you

Handling Returns

Returns are an important part of doing business, both online and off. Of course, we hope you won't have many returned purchases to deal with, but when you do, you need to process the transaction fairly and quickly to maintain customer satisfaction.

There isn't any rule on eBay about whether a seller should accept returns or not; the policy is up to you. The important thing is to state your policy in your auction listing to eliminate confusion. Some sellers simply allow returns for any reason in order to ensure positive feedback as well as repeat business. Others won't allow returns at all.

You don't have to refund the customer's money in full when they return an item. If the product is in good working order and the only reason for the return is that the customer has changed his or her mind, you might charge a fee for your time, trouble, and shipping costs.

receive. On eBay, word-of-mouth takes the form of an organized system of feedback that collects the comments buyers and sellers register about one another on eBay. After a transaction has been completed, members evaluate the transaction in an online form, and eBay posts the evaluations in its Feedback Forum. Comments from the most recent buyer or seller an individual has done business with are added to comments received for previous transactions.

Feedback can take one of three forms: positive, negative, or neutral. One aspect of managing feedback is to leave it for the person who makes a purchase from you. If the comment is positive, a buyer will be happy to receive it, as it increases his or her feedback rating by one point. You can leave feedback for someone you have completed a transaction with through your My eBay page, or from the Feedback Forum page (**http://pages.ebay .com/services/forum/feedback.html**). In either case, give some thought to your comments, and be specific about the experience you had with someone during the transaction.

Provide Receipts

If you're a registered 501(c)(3) nonprofit with the Internal Revenue Service (IRS), talk to your tax advisor for information on giving receipts. (We are not tax experts and cannot provide advice specific to your organization.) In general, nonprofits need to provide receipts to all of their donors—both the donors who provide merchandise to put up for sale on eBay and the donors who provide your nonprofit with revenue when they make purchases. Your donors can deduct their donation from their taxable income when they declare their income tax. Your receipt enables your donor to support what they claim.

In fact, according to IRS Publication 1771, each donor must obtain a written acknowledgment from a charity for any contribution worth $250 or more before the donor can deduct the donation. The same publication states that charitable organizations are required to provide written acknowledgements to any donors who purchase something from you for more than $75. Find out more at **www.irs.gov/pub/irs-pdf/p1771.pdf**. It's easy to provide buyers with a receipt: just print one out and include it in the package along with the item you ship.

Keep in mind that buyers receive a product or service when they purchase items on eBay, even if the seller is a nonprofit. So buyers will have made a purchase, not necessarily a donation, unless the items sell for more than the fair market value. If you know the fair market value of an item, such as the retail price for a CD, include this information in the listing. If the item sells for $25, and the retail price is $20, then the $5 difference between the retail price and the auction sales price would be a donation. A $100 dinner gift certificate that sells for $150 would be another example.

But what is the market value of an experience such as meeting a celebrity? Unless you can itemize the value of the package being sold, there is no "retail price" and the market price would be whatever it sold for at auction. Generally, most nonprofits assume that the price paid is the fair market value and therefore do not generate a donation acknowledgement for buyers. In those rare cases when buyers pay a significant premium over retail because they want it to benefit a nonprofit, it is often simplest to address them on a case-by-case basis when a donation acknowledgement is requested by a buyer.

tip *When someone donates an item to you, you should avoid placing a value on what's donated. Instead, simply state what was donated. It's the donor's responsibility to place a value on the item, not yours.*

If you sell through eBay's charitable arm MissionFish on behalf of a nonprofit, you'll automatically receive a tax receipt showing that you made a donation as a result of an eBay sale. (You can also get a receipt at any time from the My Donations section of your My MissionFish page.) The proceeds go to the nonprofit you selected, however the receipt comes from MissionFish, also a 501(c)(3) nonprofit organization, so you can deduct the donation from your taxable income.

Similarly, if you are a nonprofit and someone delegates a portion of their proceeds to you, MissionFish will take care of sending the seller a receipt for the donation so you don't have to. On the other hand, you will likely wish to thank this seller for their gift as well and invite them to join your mailing list so you can send them more information about your organization activities and cultivate them as ongoing donors.

note *If you're an individual donating part of a sale's proceeds to a charity, your buyer can't claim a tax deduction from the sale. The buyer can only claim a deduction if a nonprofit is selling an item on eBay on its own behalf, and the item sells for more than fair market value.*

Develop a Set of FAQs

Consumers on the Internet are accustomed to getting nearly all the information they need to make purchases on their own, with just a few mouse clicks. One of the best ways to keep them informed is to develop a set of frequently asked questions (FAQs): questions that donors commonly ask about you or your organization. Instruct your volunteers to make note of any questions they're asked and communicate them back to you. Any questions that are specific to an individual item (for instance, what size is it, or what color is it?) should be answered on the item's eBay description page while the sale is ongoing. However, you can note and answer any FAQs that might apply to a general audience on your organization's About Me page (see Chapter 6 for more on creating an About Me page). Examples include:

- Are you a registered 501(c)(3) nonprofit?
- What's the history of your group?
- What's your mission?
- What kinds of events and programs do you conduct?
- How do donors pay for auctions they win?
- Where can donors find out more about your group?

The nonprofit National Women's History Project has an FAQ on its eBay About Me page, shown in Figure 8-3. This page also includes links to the group's home page on the Web as well as its online sales catalog.

warning *You can include links to your web page and other pages from your About Me page, but not from your eBay sales descriptions.*

moneymaker

Some nonprofits (particularly those with larger budgets) offer their shoppers "live help" and information on their activities. "Live help" means that a person is available during specified hours to answer questions, either by phone or *online chat* (the process of typing messages to another person in real time on the Internet). Some people still harbor a distrust of online shopping and don't want their credit card or personal information floating in cyberspace. Live help also assists donors who want to obtain more information about the group or simply donate money without bidding. Include a statement such as, "For more information, visit our web site or call 1-800-CALLNOW." You can find out more about offering live help at the LivePerson site (**www.liveperson.com**).

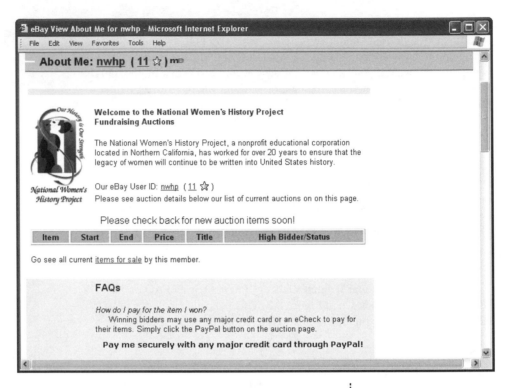

FIGURE 8-3 A set of FAQs helps publicize your group and streamlines the process of completing transactions.

Record Customer Data

Once you make a sale and ship out a product, make sure you or one of your volunteers records the customer's information. Don't simply record the person's name and address; make an effort to also note what the person bought, any questions the person asked, and any comments he or she made about your nonprofit institution or your cause.

Once your fundraiser has ended, you can open up your database of new donors and approach them with information about your organization, such as sending them a newsletter or flyer. Don't immediately try to solicit customers for money; just attempt to strike up an ongoing relationship with them by telling them how you're putting their donations to work. Simply writing down a bidder's contact information is only one way to record data about your eBay donors. We describe some more high-tech options in the sections that follow.

warning *Never lose sight of the need to store customers' credit-card and other personal information in a secure place where hackers and thieves can't reach it. The ideal location is a server that uses encryption to store the information and that is physically separated from your own computers.*

Add a Counter

The first place to look when you want to find out about the number of visits you've had to your web site is to check the list of all the site's visitors. A *hit counter* records the number of visits made to a web page. The counter resides on the web server that hosts your web pages. You make a link to the counter on each page you want counted.

For sites hosted on eBay, you can add a counter to one of your pages for free. Your home page is a likely place to put a counter if you'll have only one page counted. You add a counter from either the standard eBay Sell Your Item form or from Step 5 (Item Pictures and Pricing) of MissionFish's Sell Your Item form. You get the choice of two counters: one in the auction service Andale (**www.andale.com**) style and one in the common "green LED" style. You can also specify that the counter be hidden and only you can see it (see Figure 8-4).

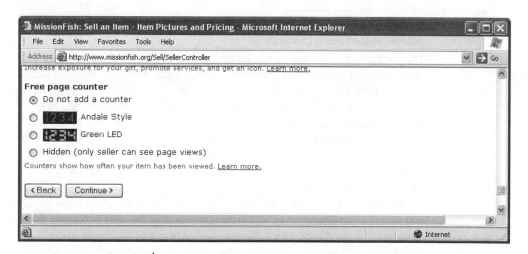

FIGURE 8-4 MissionFish's Sell Your Item form lets you add a counter in one of two graphic styles.

tip *Auction service Andale provides more powerful counters. Its counters (**http://cms .andale.com/auction/counters.html**) come in two versions: Andale Counters, which is free, and Andale Counters Pro, which costs $3.95 per month. The Pro version tracks visits to your auctions on a daily basis or (as shown here) on an hourly basis, so you can determine the best times to list items.*

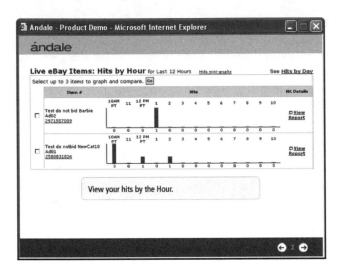

Thank Your Underbidders

The term *underbidder* refers to bidders who placed bids on an item but didn't turn out to be the high bidders or purchasers. You don't have to keep constant watch on a sale and write down someone's User ID whenever he or she places a bid. eBay keeps a list of all bidders for you. After the sale is completed, open the item's description page and click the Bid History link. A list of bidders and their corresponding User IDs appears. Click each bidder's User ID to go to that person's member profile page. You can then click Contact Member to send the individual an e-mail message through eBay's message system.

Experienced retailers know the value of providing excellent service and extending courtesy to all customers, whether or not they actually end up purchasing anything. Many large department stores expressly instruct their employees to greet everyone at the front door when they enter, and to offer to help shoppers before being asked a question. You, too, can take a proactive approach: you can approach everyone who bid on your items and thank them for their interest. Your thank you note can include a link to your web site, a brief explanation of your organization and what you do, and an encouragement to bid on future sales as well. You publicize your institution and your message, and you make contact with potential donors who have already shown an interest in what you do.

When you send unsolicited e-mails to people who only bid on your items and didn't actually make a purchase, does this constitute "spamming" eBay members? Some members would probably answer in the affirmative. But we think that because you're a nonprofit business rather than a for-profit one, you're more likely to spread goodwill when you send a thank you note than producing outrage. But be careful: If you get negative comments from underbidders, be sure not to offend them further. Your top priority should be to preserve your good reputation on eBay.

must have

- Manage your sales inventory so items don't get lost

- Make sure merchandise is shipped out quickly

- Provide receipts to your customers, if you're a 501(c)(3) organization, so they can deduct the value of their purchase from their taxable income

- Keep track of your customers and record information about them so you can encourage them to make purchases from you in the future

- Protect your customers' personal information so it isn't stolen or misused

Chapter 9

Advanced Selling: Using All of eBay's Sales Options

The power of eBay is its ability to draw a mix of individuals to a particular sale. It's an audience that auction houses had no idea how to access five years ago, and it has enhanced their business exponentially.

—Clint Cantwell,
Marc Ecko Enterprises

What We'll Cover in This Chapter:

- Opening an eBay Store so you can sell fundraising items for months at a time

- Putting restaurant coupons, travel tickets, and other specialty items up for sale

- Including one-of-a-kind experiences among your sales options

- Creating a storefront that sells merchandise bearing your group's logo

- Considering eBay's online live auction venue

- Creating a group of like-minded nonprofits

- Exchanging links with other nonprofits that sell on eBay

eBay is best-known as an auction-based marketplace. That's one reason why it's a good fit for nonprofits, which are already used to holding auction fundraisers. But auctions aren't the only game in town where eBay is concerned. You can sell items at fixed prices through an eBay Store and keep them before the eyes of prospective donors for a much longer period of time than you could at auction, for instance.

Consumer goods, collectibles, and one-of-a-kind items aren't the only things you can sell on eBay, either. Because you're holding a fundraiser, you have access to a wide range of services and "experiences" you can put up for sale as well. Dinner with the mayor or principal, a behind-the-scenes tour of a local museum, or a free massage are just a few of the many things you can offer to buyers on eBay, as long as they either live in your local area or are willing to come into town to "redeem" what they've purchased. eBay is already well-known for providing theater tickets and restaurant discounts to buyers. In this chapter, we'll describe these types of items and other ways to use the online marketplace to its fullest advantage.

Opening an eBay Giving Works Store

When you think about fundraising, you normally think about two things: auctions and outright gifts. These are the tried-and-true, traditional ways to receive donations. But when you open your fundraising activities to include eBay, you gain another way to raise funds: you can open your very own store. An eBay Store is a place where sellers—both profit and nonprofit— put merchandise up for sale at a fixed price. It's essentially a web site that eBay allows you to fill with listings for individual items. You'll find out how easy it is to open and operate a store in the sections that follow.

tip *You don't have to have your eBay Store open all the time. You may decide to make merchandise available through your store only during the period when your fundraising efforts are taking place. You may also want to keep the store open all year round. It's up to you; there's no penalty for opening a store and then keeping it "closed" or inactive when you don't need it.*

Understanding How eBay Stores Work

Rather than opening up each sale to bids, you specify exactly how much you want to accept for an item. When you put an eBay Store item up for sale, it stays online far longer than the one to ten days an auction sale lasts. You specify whether you want the item to remain up for sale for 30, 60, or 90 days, or even for an indefinite period. When someone clicks the Buy It Now button that appears along with each eBay Store listing, this person commits to purchasing the item immediately from you.

Having an eBay Store enables a nonprofit organization that lacks a large volunteer staff to have a way to keep sales items up for sale for long periods of time. (In contrast, if an auction that lasts, say, seven or ten days comes to an end without receiving any bids, someone has to relist the item manually.) Selling at fixed price in an eBay Store gives nonprofits a way to deal with donors who require that their items sell for a minimum amount. Some donors specify that particularly valuable items sell for a minimum of, say, $1000. You could sell the item at auction with a reserve price of $1,000 or a starting bid of $1,000. But if the item doesn't sell for one of those prices, you can relist it in your eBay Store for a fixed price of $1,000. That way, it can stay online for a month or more at a time, and you're that much more likely to get bids for it.

warning *Keep in mind that eBay Stores aren't free. A basic store costs $14.95 per month, and a featured store costs $49.95 per month. For the largest and most successful stores, the monthly cost isn't significant, but for smaller-scale sellers it can be. Try to estimate the profit you might make each month, and review your success on a regular basis to make sure your store is worth the cost. You can also consider opening a store only for the period of time that you are holding a major fundraising auction.*

Opening Your Store

It's hard to open a physical, brick-and-mortar storefront. You have to make the purchase, obtain licenses, possibly do renovation … the list goes on, and it quickly gets expensive. In comparison, it's a snap to create an eBay Store.

First, you need to have an eBay seller's account credit card on file with eBay. After that, you need to meet one of the following three requirements:

- You need to have a minimum feedback rating of 20

- You need to have your identity verified through eBay's ID Verify program (verification carries a $5 fee)

- You have to have an account with eBay's payment service, PayPal (**www.paypal.com**)

Once you've got the preliminaries covered, go to the eBay Stores home page (**http://stores.ebay.com**, shown in Figure 9-1), and click the conspicuous Open a Store button.

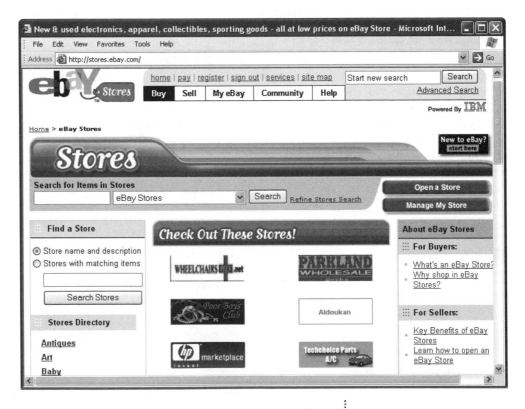

FIGURE 9-1 Come to this page to create or manage your eBay Store.

tip *You can always change your store's categories or description by clicking the Manage My Store link on your store's home page.*

Building Your Own eBay Store

Log in with your eBay password, if you aren't logged in already, and click Sign In. Read the statement that says you are subject to the same User Agreement that governs your auction sales. Then click I Accept the eBay User Agreement to connect to the first Build Your Store page, where you begin to create your store.

You begin with graphics: The Build Your Store: Select Theme page presents you with options for your store's layout and color scheme. Keep in mind that you don't *have* to select one of the predesigned themes for your store; you can also copy graphics from your group's existing web site so you can make your store's design consistent with your other online venues. Here are the steps to follow:

1. Scan the Most Popular set of themes, which are shown on the page you view initially, shown here. If you don't like the way these pages are designed, click one of the other layout options under themes: Left Navigation, Top Navigation, or Easily Customizable. If you want to use your own preexisting graphics, choose Easily Customizable, then click Custom Header Only in Step 2.

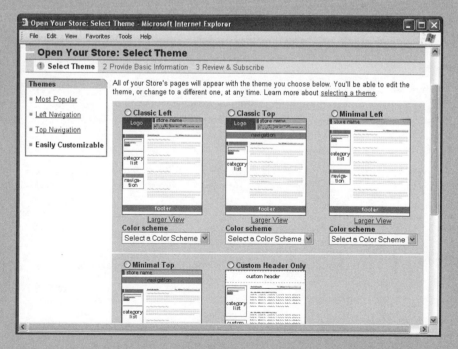

(continued)

2. Click a radio button or choose a drop-down menu option to select the color scheme you want. When you've chosen the "look" you want, click the Continue button at the bottom of the page.

3. When the Build Your Store: Provide Basic Information page appears, type your store's "brand name" in the Store name box.

4. Write a short (300 characters or less) description of your store in the Store description area. (You add more information later on if you run out of space.) Make sure your store's description contains keywords that will turn up in searches. You'll get better results if you say, "We provide medical care, education, clothing, and meals for boys and girls around the world," rather than "We raise funds for kids of all ages."

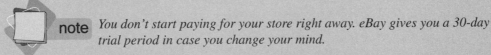

tip *You don't get much room to sell your store—each field in the Store Content page is limited to a small number of characters. If you really want as many words as you need to create your own store, opt for your own web site instead. Otherwise, type your content in any text editor and count the number of characters using the program's Word Count feature (it's under the Tools menu).*

5. Next, you choose graphics for your store. If you already have an About Me page or a web page, you can simply choose one of your existing image files for your store. Otherwise, you have two choices: create a logo for your store, or use a predesigned eBay graphic. The predesigned images are overused and don't distinguish your store in any way. We strongly suggest that you create a logo as we describe Chapter 6. When you're done, click Continue.

6. When the Build Your Store: Review & Subscribe page appears, select the type of store you want to open. It makes sense, if you're just starting out, to choose Basic Store. You can always upgrade later on. When you're done, click Start My Subscription Now.

note *You don't start paying for your store right away. eBay gives you a 30-day trial period in case you change your mind.*

7. Next, you select 1 of 14 main categories for your store. Pick the category you use most for your auctions—or choose Everything Else.

8. Fill out some additional information about what makes your store unique in the Store/About Me page.

9. In the Custom store categories area, enter the types of sales categories your merchandise will be sold under. Supposedly, these choices are optional. However, when you want to sell an item, you have to list it under one of the categories you've already defined here. Do yourself a favor and come up with some categories your merchandise will be listed under. Make the category names searchable keywords, and you'll get more traffic to your store; for instance, rather than creating an "experiences" category, you should create several more specific and keyword-oriented names, such as "restaurant dinners," "museum tours," "concert tickets," and so on.

10. Specify your payment methods and ship-to locations.

11. In the "Store customer service & return policy" box, type in any money-back guarantee, customer service numbers, return policies, or Square Trade memberships you can boast. You have to enter 90 characters or less here, and the field is required.

12. Optionally, if you haven't created an About Me page, you get the chance to do so after the "Additional store information" box. The advantage of creating an About Me store here is that, when users click on your About Me logo, they'll be taken to your eBay Store, just as they would if they clicked on your Stores logo.

13. Next, you get to choose colors for your eBay Store.

Give yourself a pat on the back: you've created your store and now you can start selling.

> **tip** *You can find out more about setting up and configuring eBay Stores on the eBay Stores discussion board. Check it out at* ***http://forums.ebay.com/db2/ forum.jsp? forum=21***.

Organizing Your Store's Inventory

Once you've made the decisions needed to create your eBay Store, you'll probably find listing items for sale a breeze, especially if you're already adept at putting up items for auction on eBay. The principles we describe in Chapter 7 for creating auction listings and creating good images apply. But there's one big difference: you don't have to worry about setting reserve prices or starting bids. You also don't have to worry about monitoring bids as they're placed. There aren't any bids at all; rather, you set a fixed price and the item is listed at that price for a period of your choice (as we stated earlier, the options range from 30 days to an unlimited period of time).

moneymaker

It's a good idea to divide your eBay Store inventory into multiple categories, and to give some thought to the names of those categories, too. That's because eBay submits the store category names to Google, the Web's most popular search engine. Your store category names should be searchable keywords so they attract attention from searchers who are looking on Google as well as those who are searching eBay.

For example, rather than set up a store category of "jewelry," you'll want to split it out in categories, such as "necklaces," "earrings," "cufflinks," and the like. Using specific keywords ensures that Google indexes your store merchandise in categories. Always try to make your store categories as specific as possible.

Selling on eBay's Half.com

If you have a bunch of books, CDs, videos, or other entertainment or sporting goods items to sell and you don't want to pay the monthly fee to operate an eBay Store, consider selling on Half.com (**http://half.ebay.com**), a part of eBay where sellers can easily offer fixed-price merchandise for sale.

For sellers, Half.com provides a far different experience than selling on eBay. Half.com's sales aren't scheduled to end at a specified time, like eBay's auctions or most eBay Stores sales. Rather than individual listings grouped by time or type of merchandise, Half.com groups all items with the same book title, game title, and DVD title, by different sellers on the same page. Further, sellers have very little opportunity to stand out from the crowd, unless they set a price that's slightly less than the other instances of the same item that are already up for sale. They can also write better descriptions of their items, though only the first few words of those descriptions appear on the sales page.

On the upside, Half.com makes creating listings really fast, and unlike eBay's auctions, functions as an intermediary with regard to payments. Half.com bills the buyer and pays the seller, which means there's no danger that a seller will have to deal with a bounced check. If you're looking for certainty, a bit of extra security, and don't mind having your sales items look like everyone else's, Half.com is for you.

Selling Services and Specialty Items

Usually, the sellers who make dining and travel options or professional services available on eBay are specialists. A restaurant will make its own coupons available; a travel agency will sell packages at a discount. As a nonprofit, you have an advantage: you can solicit donations from the restaurant owners, travel agents, dentists, or other professional service providers in your own constituency. You can then make those services and events available on eBay the same way you'd sell collectibles and consumer goods. To give you suggestions, we describe some events and services that are already commonly sold on eBay.

Restaurant Coupons

eBay's one-day auction option is perfect for restaurant discount coupons, which can usually be redeemed with a special code. In fact, restaurants around the country offer gift certificates through Restaurant.com, which is one of eBay's biggest sellers. (It had a feedback rating of nearly 100,000 when this was written.) This company has an About Me page at **http://stores.ebay.com/Restaurant-com**, where you can click on an interactive map (see Figure 9-2) and search for gift certificates at restaurants in locations around the United States.

When a bidder wins one of the Restaurant.com auctions, he or she receives an e-mail from Restaurants.com. The message contains a link to a secure checkout area, where the buyer pay for the gift certificate with a credit card; the buyer then receives a link to a Web page that contains the actual gift certificate, which he or she can print out. The Restaurant.com system, which has resulted in a feedback rating of more than 125,000, is an example you can follow yourself. Do a search for restaurants in your own city: you might be able to solicit a donation of a gift certificate at a restaurant located in your local area.

> **note** *In order to capture an image of a restaurant coupon that can be downloaded and printed, you'll need to scan it with a flatbed scanner (see Chapter 7) and save it as a Portable Document Format (PDF) file. You can convert a limited number of graphic images to PDF format on the Adobe Systems Incorporated web site (**www.adobe.com**). After your free conversions have been used up, you'll need to purchase Adobe Acrobat Exchange to do the conversions to PDF.*

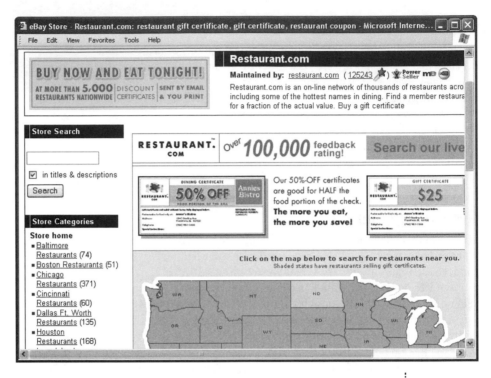

FIGURE 9-2 This eBay seller provides restaurant gift certificates online. You can arrange with restaurants to provide similar discounts to benefit your organization.

Vacation and Travel Deals

Travel experiences are always popular with nonprofits that need to raise funds, and it's not uncommon for nonprofits to see discount airfares or vacation packages on eBay. Figure 9-3 shows one travel package being auctioned on eBay during a spring 2005 fundraiser held by the Kids First Fund. A variety of other airline tickets were donated by ATA, Song Air, and other airlines. The tickets were restricted to certain dates, but the restrictions were clearly stated in the extensive auction descriptions.

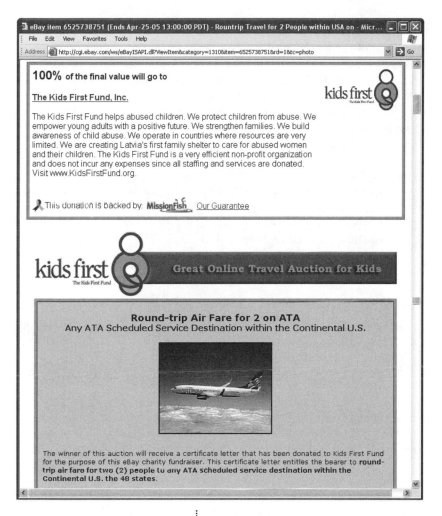

FIGURE 9-3 If you solicit airline ticket donations, you're sure to get bids for them on eBay.

warning *If you're lucky enough to have airline tickets donated to you to sell on eBay, make sure you clearly describe, in the body of the sales description, exactly what the high bidder or buyer needs to do to redeem the tickets. Also, spell out that seats are limited and subject to availability, if that's the case. In fact, you may want to simply retype and publish any of the airline's restrictions on the tickets. The important thing is to prevent disgruntled customers from complaining, asking for refunds, or leaving negative feedback for you.*

One-of-a-Kind Experiences

As a nonprofit seller on eBay, you have access to a special sales category that doesn't exist on the for-profit part of the auction site. Go to the Giving Works home page (**http://givingworks.ebay.com**), scroll toward the bottom of the page, and click the category named Experiences. Scan the list of current sales descriptions so you can get some ideas of the kinds of experiences you can offer on eBay yourself. On a typical day, the Experiences category listed the following:

- A chance for the winner and his or her family to travel round-trip to San Francisco and tour the Gymboree Corporation. The winner's child would also be Gymboree fashion model. The Gymboree Corporation was donating 100 percent of the proceeds to the March of Dimes. The current high bid (of 22 bids) was nearly $15,000.

- A VIP tour of the television show *America's Funniest Home Videos* and dinner for four with the show's host.

- A behind-the-scenes visit to the elephants in the Indianapolis Zoo.

- A chance to drive an Indy racing car for three laps around Indianapolis Motor Speedway.

- Tickets for 15 people to the party suite at the Indianapolis Indians baseball park.

note *The last three items in the preceding list were all part of an online fundraiser to benefit the athletics club at IUPUI (Indiana University-Purdue University Indianapolis), a branch of Indiana University.*

When you receive an experience-related donation, you can create the sales description on Giving Works, as we describe in Chapter 7, and list the item in the Experiences category. (If you're an individual selling on behalf of a nonprofit, you can still list in the Experiences category on the "regular" version (not the Giving Works version) of eBay. But keep in mind that it's a subcategory of the Tickets category, so your listing needs to involve selling tickets to an attraction or event.

Real Estate

It's fairly safe to say that most people don't think of eBay as a place to find homes, lots, and other real estate. But eBay is a perfect venue for individuals who are looking to relocate. If they're able to purchase some property and make a donation to a good cause, it's a win-win situation.

Don't overlook eBay as a venue for offering real estate that's been donated to your group. Keep in mind, though, that there's one very big difference between sales in eBay's Real Estate section and other parts of eBay: many sales are "*nonbinding*." In other words, even if you turn out to be the high bidder, the owner is not always obliged to sell to you. eBay obtains real estate licenses for each state, however, and is able to conduct binding real estate sales. Find out more on the Real Estate category opening page (**http://pages.ebay.com/realestate/index.html**).

Sell Merchandise Bearing Your Group's Logo

When you create an About Me page or an eBay Store, you're able to make links to your web site and other relevant locations on the Internet. One of those locations can be a storefront on the CafePress.com web site (**www.cafepress.com/cp/info/**), a free storefront where you can easily create and sell merchandise bearing your nonprofit group's logo.

CafePress.com is an ideal place to turn if you want to spread the word about your group but you don't have the time or resources to do the selling yourself. Ordinarily, you have to take your logo to a printer, order a certain number of mugs, T-shirts, or other items, monitor the printing process, store the boxes of merchandise once they're delivered, and haul the boxes to various events so you can sell them to interested individuals. Hopefully, you'll sell enough to make back your printing costs and generate some much-needed income for your nonprofit.

CafePress.com dramatically alters the process of printing and selling your own branded merchandise. The biggest change: the site enables you to have items printed on demand. You don't pay for anything until someone purchases it; the object purchased doesn't exist until a order is placed. Then, only the number actually ordered is manufactured and sent to the customer. You don't have boxes of inventory waiting around to be sold.

You also choose what you want to have printed, and you only pay a fee to CafePress .com when something sells. You can either set up a store for free or create a Premium level storefront for $6.95 per month. Each item you decide to sell has a base price (a T-shirt might cost $8.99, for example). The base price is the charge that goes to CafePress.com. You put the item for sale for more than the base price, and the difference is your profit. For its fee, CafePress.com hosts your storefront online and applies the electronic file of your logo to the item you've sold.

(continued)

The Disabled Online Users Association (DOUA), a nonprofit organization that helps disabled individuals sell on eBay, has its own storefront on CafePress.com (**www.cafepress.com/doua**, shown here), as well as its own eBay Store. It derives its operating income, in part, from such sales.

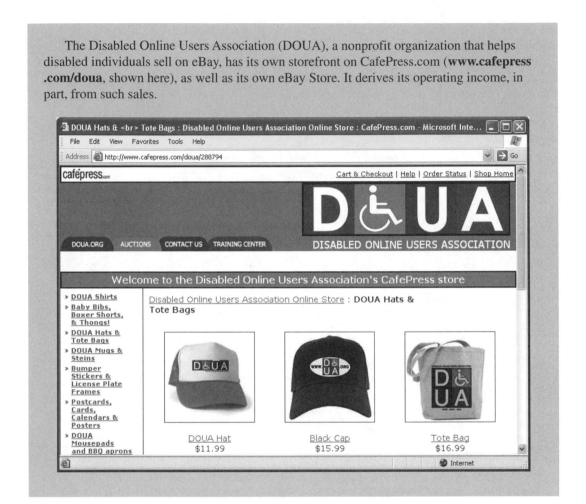

Selling at Live Auctions

If you work for a nonprofit organization and that organization has held fundraising events, you're already familiar with the concept of a *live auction*—an event where bidders gather at the same time and place and bid on items. Occasionally, bidders in the location where the auction is being held compete with people who have placed absentee bids beforehand, as well as others who place bids either by phone or on the Internet.

The same sort of live auction event is available on a part of eBay called (not surprisingly) eBay Live Auctions (**www.ebayliveauctions.com**, shown in Figure 9-4). If your organization wants to hold a live auction event, keep in mind that you can do so on Live Auctions, where you'll potentially gain a far wider audience than if you held your event in a rented hall or school gymnasium. We'll walk you through how to do an eBay Live Auction in Chapter 10, but for now there are a few caveats you should consider.

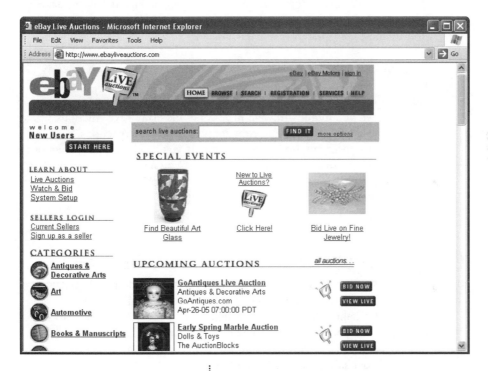

FIGURE 9-4 eBay has its own Live Auctions feature, but charity auctions are rarely seen there.

eBay Live Auctions is easily overlooked in favor of the better known eBay auctions and fixed-price sales. That's just one of several things to consider if you're thinking of holding your own live auction on eBay. For another, conducting a sale on eBay probably isn't something you can do yourself. You have to be a licensed auction house, or you have to have a licensed auction house conduct your sale. Also keep in mind that:

- Buyers not only have to pay the winning bid price but also a "*buyer's premium*" (typically, 10–15 percent of the sale price), which goes to the auction house.

- Buyers have to register for a sale beforehand rather than being able to bid on the spur of the moment.

● Buyers have to wait for long periods of time while the live auction is taking place for their desired item to appear. If their desired item is number 105 in a group (or, as it is called on eBay Live Auctions, *lot*) of 500 items, it will be a while before the customer can actually bid. When the item does come up for auction, buyers have to place split-second bids. (They can, alternatively, place an absentee bid, but there's no guarantee that the absentee bid will place out the live bids.)

In other words, it's more work for a bidder to place a bid on an eBay Live Auction item, whether it's part of a charity auction or not, than on the "regular" eBay system. If you have lots of jewelry and fine art to auction off, however, you might still want to consider the eBay Live Auctions option. These sorts of items are commonly sold on Live Auctions, and customers for them are used to going there. If you do choose Live Auctions, you'll open your sale to more attention than if you only sold to live bidders in your immediate geographic area. And you'll probably get an extra measure of attention, if only because of the novelty factor: charity auctions occur rarely on the Live Auctions site.

Using Special Software to Manage Your Sales

When you're doing the initial groundwork for your fundraiser, it makes sense to create sales listings using eBay's Sell Your Item form, which we describe in Chapter 7. The Sell Your Item form is great for learning to set prices and add photos—at least, when you only have a handful of items to sell. When you're ready to sell lots of items and control the design and timing of your sales, you need to take advantage of software that's designed to streamline selling on eBay.

The Do-It-Yourself Solution: Turbo Lister and My eBay

If you're on a budget or just don't have the desire to install special software for creating and managing your sales, you can make use of the software eBay makes available to all of its members for free. To create and schedule multiple sales, download and install Turbo Lister. The easiest solution for managing your sales and following up with buyers after the final bid has been placed is the My eBay page that's automatically created when you register with eBay and create a User ID.

As the name implies, Turbo Lister speeds up the process of selling on eBay. Its first advantage is that it's free. You go to the program's home page (**http://pages.ebay.com/turbo_lister/index.html**) and click Download Now to download and install the tool.

Once you have Turbo Lister up and running, you're able to create a listing that serves as a *sales template*; that is, the sales description contains standard "boilerplate" information about your preferred shipping method, your preferred method of receiving payment, and a description of your nonprofit organization and your fundraising event. Once you create the template, you can create the sales listing and add photos (see Figure 9-5).

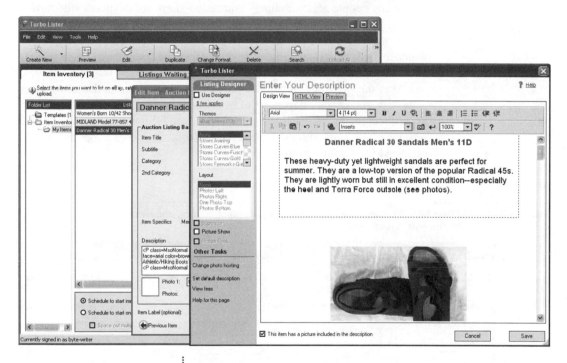

FIGURE 9-5 Turbo Lister lets you create a template so you can reuse standard description elements.

note   *Turbo Lister only works with computers running Windows 98 or later. Because Turbo Lister connects to eBay when you're ready to upload your files, that computer also needs to be connected to the Internet. At minimum, you also need 50MB of free hard disk space, 64MB of RAM for Win 98/ME, or 128MB of RAM for Win 2000/XP/NT to run Turbo Lister.*

One of the best features is the ability to upload all your sales at once so they all begin when you want them. It's beyond the scope of this book to provide detailed instructions on using Turbo Lister; however, you can go to the Turbo Lister page on eBay and click Quick Start Guide or User Guide to follow detailed tutorials describing the program's operation.

Once your sales are online, you can track them in the Items I'm Selling area of the My eBay page. Just click My eBay in the eBay navigation bar that appears at the top of nearly every page on the site. Log in with your User ID and password if required, and scroll down to the Items I'm Selling area. You'll see a list of your items for sale along with numbers indicating how many bids have been received. You'll also see a number that indicates how many people are "watching" your sale—these are members who have marked your sale so that eBay "watches" it and notifies them when the sale is coming to an end. They may or may not bid on your item; the number of watchers isn't always an indication of whether shoppers are truly interested in bidding or not.

After the sale ends, any items that have sold are listed in the Items I've Sold area. A drop-down list next to each item (see Figure 9-6) lets you print an invoice, send a message to the buyer, or even print a shipping label with postage if you ship with the United States Postal Service (the postage is deducted from your PayPal account).

FIGURE 9-6 Your free My eBay page lets you track sales, contact buyers, and even print postage when the sale has ended.

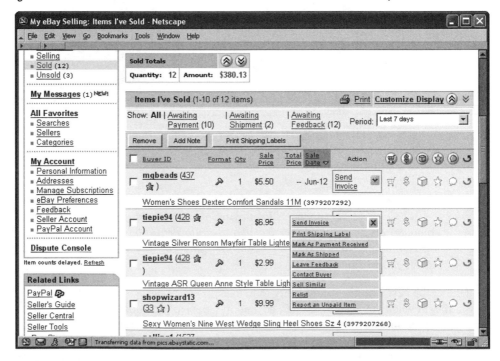

The Outsourcing Solution: Third-Party Auction Software

Turbo Lister is eBay's own solution for creating sales. You may prefer to turn outside of eBay for more sophisticated tools for tracking and creating sales descriptions. Some auction service providers not only provide software for managing sales, but they also give you space for storing auction photos, too.

Suppose you have met with great success in soliciting donations for a fundraising event, and you have 750 separate things to sell. But you only have a week to get all the sales online. And you're the only volunteer capable of creating the listings. What do you do?

Consider using a company such as Marketworks (**www.marketworks .com**), to train you in how to use the company's bulk listing tools, which are popular with many longtime eBay sellers. You also get access to Marketworks' photo hosting services as well as other software that lets you track auctions, relist sales automatically, and automatically leave feedback. Zoovy (**www.zoovy.com**), Andale (**www.andale.com**), and SpareDollar (**www.sparedollar.com**) are all popular with longtime eBay sellers, and they all provide user-friendly software or services for creating and tracking sales on eBay.

Collaborating to Boost Your Cause and Your Sales

Networking has always played a big role in the process of selling on eBay. When nonprofit sellers band together, they can gain more attention than they would working in isolation. How do you collaborate with other nonprofits? We offer two suggestions in the sections that follow.

 See Chapter 12 for more about marketing your cause and your fundraising event on eBay and the rest of the Web.

Start a Group

California artist Laura Iverson, profiled in Chapter 2, is listed among the Giving Works "success stories" (**http://pages.ebay.com/sell/givingworks/ success_stories.html**). Along with conducting her own sales, which typically earmark a percentage of the final eBay sales price to charity through her eBay Store, Iverson has helped create a group of artists called the Worldwide Women Artists (WWAO)—women who want to promote their work while benefiting charitable causes as well. Any prospective buyer who does a keyword search for "WWAO" on eBay finds charity auctions by all of the group's members, and each of the WWAO members' sales descriptions publicizes the group. In this way, the sellers help gain more attention for each others' work.

Exchange Links

Exchanging links is one of the oldest and best ways to get publicity on the Web. The idea goes like this: 1) You create a banner ad (a small graphic image, usually rectangular in shape, that's linked to a web page or web site) or textual link; 2) You find a web site that sells products or services that are complementary to yours (in other words, that don't compete directly with yours); 3) You send a message to the other web site asking to exchange links with you: "You put a link to my site on your site, and I'll put a link to your site on mine."

The same idea works on eBay. Laura Iverson, in fact, also has an invitation to other groups to put her banner ad on their web site, as well as a textual link. If someone wants to copy a link and put it on his site, she'll do the same for him. Look around for a nonprofit that represents a constituency similar to your own, and ask for a link exchange in the hope that you'll both attract more potential donors to your eBay sales.

must have

- Sell items at a fixed price in an eBay Store

- Organize store merchandise by category

- Make full use of keywords so categories and items can be found more easily

- Solicit airline tickets and other travel bargains

- Consider restaurant coupons, one-of-a-kind experiences, and real estate donations to add variety to your auctions and bring in more dollars

- Be aware of eBay Live Auctions as an alternative to a conventional live auction

- Take advantage of special software to streamline your sales activities

- Collaborate with other nonprofits to gain more attention for your sales

Part III
Leveraging eBay for the Biggest Bang

Chapter 10
Making Your Charitable Auction a Major Event

The eBay auction helped generate over 415 million impressions,
a value of over four million dollars.

—Matthew Pye, Just Born, Inc.

What We'll Cover in This Chapter:

- Expanding your fundraising effort by soliciting more or higher priced items and experiences

- Understanding how the workload changes when running a high profile auction

- Considering authentication, insurance, and escrow options

- Outsourcing part of the work to an auction management company

- Using Live Auctions to increase proceeds from "real world" auctions

You may be planning a major event to rally support and awareness for your cause, or you may be in the process of planning a small event when fortune smiles upon you and you find yourself unexpectedly entertaining a unique celebrity opportunity or valuable donation. Suddenly what was going to be an ordinary charity fundraiser now has the potential to garner much wider public attention. One of the many wonderful things about eBay is its role as a great equalizer. It allows smaller nonprofits to run events just like their larger counterparts. Organizations that are creative and come up with great events will be rewarded regardless of the number of people their nonprofits employ.

What does creating a major fundraising event mean for you as its organizer? Along with increased public attention, you get the opportunity to raise more money and field more inquiries about your group or cause. On the other hand, you also increase the chances that something could go wrong. Let's explore the opportunities and issues that accompany a big event in order to maximize its rewards and minimize the risks.

What Is a "Major" Event?

A major charity auction has the same basic goals and involves the same activities as a regular charity auction, but the scale is bigger and you're called on to coordinate a few more "moving parts." Consider the factors that have the potential to increase the size and reach of a fundraising effort. A major event will incorporate some of the following elements:

- **Quantity of items for sale**   The sheer scale of your endeavor can make it noteworthy. A nonprofit that can motivate a community of hundreds of individuals to each donate one or two items per person could mean over a thousand items for sale.

- **Value of items for sale**   If you're auctioning off a valuable antique or work of art, the price will make people sit up and take notice. When you're soliciting items for your auction centerpiece, think beyond "expensive" items to "priceless" items—things such as experiences people can not attain in any other way.

- **Timely or unique items**   Sometimes the novelty of an item will catch the public's imagination and the media's attention. Incorporate unique items, devise an unusual media hook, or time your auction to either piggyback on holidays or events that the media will already be covering, or to provide an interesting news story when little else is going on.

- **Celebrity involvement**   Involving someone famous is a sure-fire way to get the attention of his or her avid fan base and a curious public. Whether they're giving donations, signing items, or supporting your cause by publicly promoting your auction, celebrities can increase the scope of your event.

- **Corporate partners**   With a corporate partner, you may increase awareness for the event with the help of the company's PR department. This department has many marketing tools at its disposal and may be willing to help with press releases, mentions on its web site, and other outreach efforts such as e-mail newsletters. Keep in mind that part of the partner's goal will be publicity and recognition for their nonprofit support and/or their products, so look for ways to incorporate and showcase their products into the auction offerings.

How to Build a Major Event

Some say heroes are not born, they are made. This is certainly true of fundraising events. There is no reason you cannot make your event bigger and more exciting with a little effort. What can you do to take your event to the next level? The preceding section discussed a number of factors that help elevate an auction to a major event. The sections that follow examine strategies for increasing the proceeds and size of your nonprofit event. This is not an exhaustive list, but rather a set of suggestions for getting your creativity flowing so you can brainstorm your own unique ways to captivate buyers and inspire donor participation.

Build Off Annual Events

Adding an Internet auction to your annual fundraising event can help build the buzz for the event and give your auction items advance viewing opportunities. Equally important, online exposure allows you to leverage marketing already budgeted for the event to promote your auction. Since people know about and are anticipating this event, it makes the publicity for the online auction portion of the event easier to execute and more successful (see Figure 10-1).

FIGURE 10-1 Mercedes-Benz Fashion Week added an online component to its week of festivities benefiting the City of Hope.

If you have a black tie event that culminates in a live charity auction with a professional auctioneer, you may be interested in holding a sale on eBay Live Auctions (**http://ebayliveauctions.com**). This part of eBay enables sellers to integrate online and live auctions. The program combines the best of both worlds by letting people preview and bid on auction items before the event while retaining the excitement of a real world live auction. It expands the reach of normal live auctions by allowing bidders around the world to participate in real time and place bids remotely during the Live Auction itself. See "Create a Live Auction with Online Component" later in this chapter.

Create a Media Hook

The media is always looking for a new or local angle for events, stories, and holidays. For example, if your organization helps needy families, then raising funds around Thanksgiving or the holidays with an online auction could earn your event some extra PR as an interesting sideline to the traditional seasonal story.

warning *While adding a new twist to a story the media is looking to tell can provide you with an opportunity, the converse can also be true. If there is a lot going on in the news, it will be hard to get a feature article because the auction will seem less newsworthy in comparison. To the greatest extent possible, try not to run your auction during major events such as heated political races, unless you have a tie-in to the news.*

Sell Donations in Your Store

As long as you are attracting many people to look at your auction items, you should give buyers the chance to "buy" a donation as well. You can list donations in the "Buy It Now" format or the fixed price format in the eBay Store. By listing donations for sale at a fixed price, some buyers will add $25 or more onto their purchase as a donation. eBay makes this easy for everyone by allowing a buyer to make one payment for all items purchased from the same seller.

The best way to list donations is to show people specifically what the donation will accomplish. One organization that does this especially well is Global Giving (**http://stores.ebay.com/GlobalGiving**). On their eBay Store, buyers not only see specifically how their donation will be used, but if they check the Global Giving web site in the future, they will see the progress that has been made on that project. Global Giving constantly modifies

(continued)

its project descriptions with new photos and updates. This makes donors feel great about giving because they can see the results immediately, and may encourage them to donate again.

Leverage Special Occasions

Holidays are an obvious time to promote gift giving, but there are other occasions that present logical opportunities to promote giving. Finding and leveraging these events can open doors to partnerships and collaborative marketing. Take, for example, National Breast Cancer Awareness Month in October. For organizations fighting breast cancer this can be an opportunity to join with other

similar organizations to cross promote fundraising efforts. eBay also creates a special page to showcase all the nonprofit auctions benefiting breast cancer research and survivors, so it's a great time to run your charity event for that cause.

Similarly if your organization helps the environment, is there a way you can collaborate with the organizers of a large Earth Day event to promote your auctions? If you're a museum, consider timing your auction to correspond with a new exhibit opening and auctioning off a private tour before it opens to the public, or selling the chance to meet the artist or scientist behind the work. Libraries might time their events to coincide with the National Literacy Day, July 2, or may even wish to fundraise at the same time they're promoting a ballot measure to support the library system, thereby helping to raise awareness for both issues (see Figure 10-2).

Fuel Friendly Competition with One of Your Rivals

Combining forces with organizations that you normally consider your rivals can boost attention for fundraisers that benefit both institutions. For instance, if you're raising money for a college or university, consider a fundraising contest with a rival campus, timing the auctions to end around the date that the two schools' football teams are scheduled to meet each other. Imagine UC Berkeley's Cal Bear alumni trying to raise more money online than their Stanford rivals, the Cardinal, during Big Game Week and both creating slogans such as "Keep Cal out of the Red" or "Keep the Tree in the Green." Also keep in mind that many wealthy alumni would welcome an opportunity to upgrade their seats, so fervent Homecoming game weeks are great times to auction off some premium seats on the 50 yard line or the opportunity to have the team mascot visit a pregame party.

Take Advantage of Hot Events and Trends

Take some time to review current events and hot trends; you may be able to work those into your fundraising efforts to make the event even bigger, more memorable, and more profitable. Remember when Beanie Babies were a huge craze and the little critters could capture more than ten times their retail value on eBay? The Ty company leveraged the Beanie Babies' popularity when founder Ty Warner signed an American Bear Beanie Baby and it sold on eBay on October 5, 2001 for $24,000 as part of the Auction for America.

You can ride a trend if you can anticipate a spike in demand, solicit these kinds of donations (or even request special "charity edition" versions of products), or simply buy products cheaply in advance and sell them high on eBay. Trends can be a bit risky because you never know when they may end,

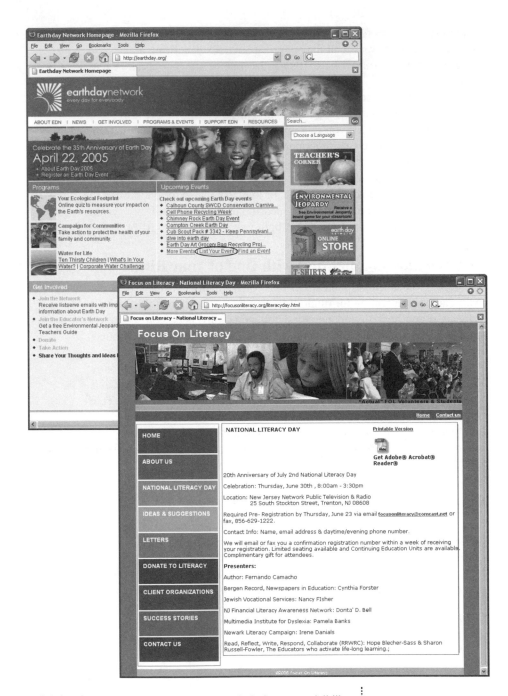

FIGURE 10-2 Joining forces on a common cause can help increase visibility for your own event.

but guessing that NASCAR (National Association for Stock Car Auto Racing) memorabilia will be hot around February when the Daytona 500 happens or that Olympic pins and memorabilia will see a spike every four years is not difficult to anticipate.

Find a Champion

Another way you can expand your online auction is to solicit corporate or celebrity participation in the form of sponsorships, item donations, and PR assistance. Celebrities Ellen DeGeneres, Oprah Winfrey, and Jay Leno have all championed eBay charity auctions on TV.

Partners can use their resources and web site to promote charity auctions they're supporting, such as Mattel did when it hosted eBay auctions for toys from the movie *Robots* to benefit Save the Children. They featured the charity auction on the Mattel home page, **www.mattel.com**, and collaborated on a press release, all of which helped increase awareness for the movie, related toys, and the nonprofit. We'll look at reaching out for partner participation in more detail in Chapter 11, but anytime you can work a high-profile partner into the event, you will not only increase bids and interest, but you will also be able to leverage the partner's resources and staff to help turn the wheels of the PR machine.

Offer Exclusive Experiences

People love the opportunity to tap into the expertise and experience of successful individuals, and a person doesn't need to be a movie star to have a huge following. One very high-priced charity item that sold on eBay in July 2003 was a lunch date with Warren Buffett, the world's second richest man, which sold for more than a quarter of a million dollars in an eBay auction and benefited Glide, a San Francisco charity for the homeless (see Figure 10-3). The winner and seven of his friends bought the chance to pick the brain of the legendary financial guru and helped hundreds of homeless folks at the same time. In contrast to the quarter million raised on eBay, the prior two years a lunch with Buffett had been auctioned off in Glide's own Silent Auction and sold for $27,000 the first year and $35,000 the second year. The lunch date was offered on eBay again in 2004 and sold for $200,000; however, the buyer in Singapore actually increased his donation to match the $250,000 raised the year earlier. In 2005, the auction reached $351,000!

Warren Buffett
Power Lunch

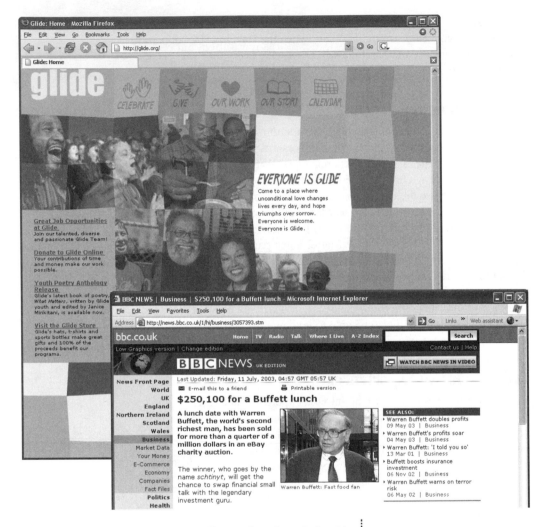

FIGURE 10-3 You're sure to attract bids if you offer a knowledgeable person's expertise.

tip *Keep in mind when developing your auction offerings, that companies, as well as individuals, can be bidders. In the lunch with Warren Buffet example, a large company might welcome the opportunity to consult with a financial leader. The opportunity to name a building is appealing to companies. Some businesses will consider buying large pieces of artwork for their corporate headquarters. So be creative not only in your auction offerings, but also in your publicity for the event.*

Leverage Local Talent

You may not have access to Oprah, Mattel, or Warren Buffett, but people in your community would love the chance to meet a local newspaper columnist or radio host, spend a day with the mayor, have a lesson with a popular tennis instructor, or eat a meal prepared by a local chef. The reality is the champion for your auction can be anyone who can help you increase excitement, awareness, and support for your fundraiser. You don't need a world-renowned celebrity to anchor your auction. There are people in your organization and community who have much to offer.

Ask yourself and your colleagues: Are there people on your board or from your community who have succeeded in politics, business, entertainment, or sports? Can you possibly arrange a drive with a NASCAR driver, a soccer clinic with a member of the US Olympic team, an answering machine recording done by a popular NPR (National Public Radio) radio host, an art lesson with a renowned local artist? Communities in Schools' "Lunch with a Leader" program (**www.lunchwithaleader.com**, shown in Figure 10-4) has auctioned off the opportunity to dine with senators, CEOs, chefs, coaches, journalists, and many other influential people. This has opened doors for many people aspiring to enter those careers and, at the same time, raised many thousands of needed dollars for schools.

Increase the Number of Your Items

Another way to increase the size of your auction is to increase the number of items you're selling by seeking out sources with excess or out-of-season inventory. When Diana Fryer of the Holy Family Institute realized that funding sources weren't keeping pace with the growing expenses of the Institute's residential programs for children and the programs it offers families, she proposed a number of ways to bring in new revenue to the organization before deciding to try eBay. The Institute began soliciting its supporters for donations and promoting its new eBay venture in its newsletter. Holy Family Institute scheduled its eBay drive to coincide in part with an annual Tag Sale. This way it could cherry-pick the donations for the best inventory to sell on eBay and then allocate the rest of the items for the annual Tag Sale. The nonprofit took a longer view with an eye toward sustainability and began to identify sources with excess inventory, such as clothing companies headquartered nearby, in order to supplement its donations with larger in-kind donations from manufacturers.

Points of Light Foundation is successfully leveraging excess inventory for ongoing sales. According to its case study on MissionFish, the Points of Light Foundation has averaged $10,000 a month from sales through its eBay Store. Its stock has included new merchandise donated by Lands' End,

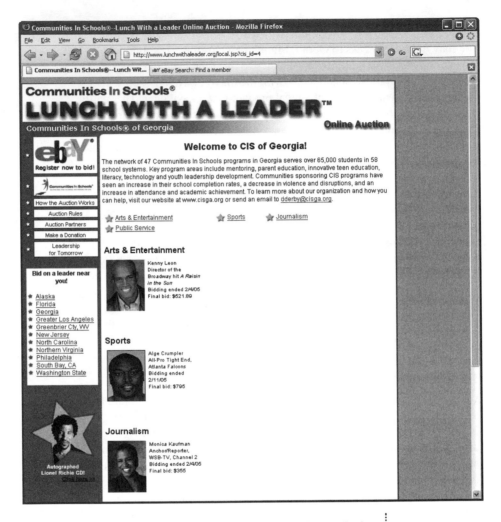

FIGURE 10-4 The "Lunch with a Leader" program has raised money by auctioning off lunch with many influential people.

Hallmark, and Slavic Treasures, as well as over stock and out of season merchandise from Noritake, Ethan Allen, and Lenox. It also offers some high-profile items like signed celebrity memorabilia and items from reality TV series, but its ongoing day-to-day auctions are the result of its staff's in-kind proposal requests to corporations. And, by the way, the Foundation runs the whole operation from an office with one computer and a big closet (which sometimes overflows into neighboring cubicles when it receives a big shipment).

Increase the Value of Your Items

To both increase your inventory levels and to expand the range of items available you'll have for sale, you may want to try to improve your solicitation letters or even hire help to solicit items for sale. Organized nonprofit donation solicitation services may bring an extensive database of companies and individuals to solicit, and may offer services to help you personalize and craft your own custom solicitation letter.

One such company is Silent Partners, an organization that spans every phase of a charity auction management, from procuring items and listing items, to managing both online and offline auction events. Scott Merrin, the CEO of Silent Partners, worked for American Airlines for 17 years and was the person who received all the solicitation letters for the company from hundreds and hundreds of nonprofits. Many were poorly written and more than 60 percent were addressed to "Dear Sir or Madam" rather than him specifically. Most failed to understand the criteria companies use to evaluate sponsorship opportunities, and consequently, very few elicited a favorable response. The majority were fated to receive the "Due to budget reasons, we regret we are unable to participate" letter. Merrin's experience led him to form Silent Partners to help nonprofits be more successful in their fundraising solicitation and auction efforts.

Today, Silent Partners has a database of 30,000 contacts worldwide—including the actual names and correct titles for the folks who receive and evaluate solicitations. Depending on the focus for your event, the company can help nonprofits narrow down their solicitation lists to a recommended 4,000 contacts—contacts that may be selected based on specific areas (wine, golf, travel, men's products, etc.). Silent Partners also helps nonprofits write effective solicitation letters, produce them on their own letterhead, and send them out. The cost for Silent Partners' procurement and eBay listing services is $6,000 plus 30 percent of proceeds and the company guarantees that it will bring in at least enough incremental donations to cover its fees.

Creating Effective Solicitation Letters

For those of you finding potential donors and writing solicitations on your own, Scott Merrin of Silent Partners has the following recommendations for what to include in an effective solicitation letter:

- *Make it one page—no longer.* Do not enclose attachments or flyers.

- *Personalize.* Know who you are writing to and put his or her name and title in the letter.

- *In the first paragraph, clearly state the reason for your letter.* For example, "During the month of June we will be launching four waves of online auctions to benefit charity X."

- *In the second and third paragraphs, briefly explain your cause.* Make your explanation simple and tell a concise story.

- *In the fourth paragraph, appeal to the donor to donate* specific *items.* "We would like to request a donation from you of (bold and italicize the specific items you are seeking such as two tickets, lunch with the CEO, etc.)."

- *In the fifth and last paragraph, explain why this person should donate.* Spell out the positive exposure your event can provide him or her. Here are some factors that may be of interest to a sponsor:

  - An event on eBay will provide brand exposure to a marketplace of more than 150 million people around the world.

  - The person's donation will be in good company (mention any celebrity or other prominent items already donated).

  - The event will help the person reach a desirable demographic (describe your supporters/donor base).

  - You, as the nonprofit, will provide this person with promotion and exposure by including photos and descriptions of the branded donated items, the company logo, and the company web site URL on your item listings, About Me page, and web site, as well as mentions in press releases and media outreach.

- *Include a deadline and all your contact information—contact name, address, e-mail, phone, and fax numbers.* For high ticket requests, considering following up by phone one or two months prior to the event.

What Has to Happen to Make a Major Event Successful?

By now, you realize that there are many ways to enhance your event and add a new level of excitement by sprucing up your product and experience offerings, involving partners, expanding media appeal through unique hooks, and tying into holidays, anniversaries, and shared occasions. With those efforts you have what you need for a big, successful event. Now take a few moments to think about how to best turn these raw materials into a phenomenal fundraiser.

Fundamentally, the basic auction responsibilities are the same. A few things do change, though, as you scale up your event. First of all, you'll need to do the basics steps very well because if something is missing or there's an error, more people will see it, so the potential ramifications are greater. The amount of that work increases so it may be helpful to automate or outsource more of the work. You may need to take precautions to ensure the auctions run smoothly and the bidders are legitimate. Beyond ensuring the auctions run smoothly, you can make a major event more successful by involving partners in the marketing aspects and event promotion. With such a great event, you'll want to make a greater marketing effort to ensure everyone hears about it and that your items reach or exceed the goal amount. Here are some keys to help you reach lofty goals.

Do the Basics Better

With hundreds, or perhaps thousands, of people viewing high-profile auctions, it will be important that you list the items for sale carefully. First, the listing is a very public reflection of your organization. The goal is to convey credibility and get people excited about the items so they have the confidence to bid high. Secondly, it's important to do things right or you will hear about it many times. Third, for the sheer saving of sanity, it's necessary to be extremely clear in the item descriptions to keep the number of e-mail questions you have to address down to the minimum. Here are some quick tips to help you make better listings on eBay:

- **Make listings attractive** Your nonprofit letterhead and web site are designed to look appealing and reflect the colors and style of your organization and so should your eBay listings. For tips, see the upcoming sidebar, "Creating Designer Listings." Also, consider using or creating a listing template to create a uniform look for all your listings (see Chapter 7).

- **Make descriptions complete** For every one e-mail question you'd receive with an average auction, you can expect to receive ten or more with a widely promoted auction. Avoid problems by describing your item completely and posting replies to questions as part of the item listing to reduce the incoming e-mails asking the same questions. Reiterate shipping costs and return policies in the description, even though you'll have already included that information elsewhere in the listing.

Answering Questions and Posting Replies

A great time-saving tip when managing your auctions is to post answers to questions into the listings themselves. Let's face it: if one person took the time to e-mail you a question, several other people had the same question but didn't bother to e-mail you. To get to the questions, you can either:

- View your listing, while signed in, and it will show you how many questions you have waiting. You can then click the link provided to view and answer those questions.

- Click My eBay, while signed in, and then click the Selling link on the left-hand side. You can see the number of questions waiting for each listing. There will be a column that says "# of Questions." (If you don't see that column on that page, you may have to click the "Customize Display" link in the upper right-hand corner of that page and then add the "# of Questions" column to the display—but it is a default column, so unless you removed it, you shouldn't have to add it.) Just click the number of questions to view them and respond to them.

You will have a checkbox when you reply that you can use to post the answer to your listing as long as there are more than 12 hours left for your listing. You can choose which answers you want to post and which ones you don't. Generally speaking, most questions and answers are worth posting unless they're really only relevant to that buyer (How much would it cost to mail the item to me in Japan?) or include personal information (such as phone numbers) in the question.

Once you post a reply, eBay will tack the question and answer into the bottom of your listing. They will appear near the payment details of your listing. Keep in mind that if you choose to post the question and answer, there's no way to remove them once they've been added. An alternative way to add information to your listing without posting the question is to revise your item listing (you will need to know the item number(s) you wish to revise). From the Site Map, simply select the Revise My Item link from the Buying and Selling section.

- **Simplify and streamline shipping**   Rather than putting in a shipping calculator or asking for people's zip codes when the auction ends, it's a good idea to put in a reasonable flat rate cost for shipping to reduce questions and expedite end-of-auction payment. Generally, you can do this by calculating the cost to the farthest U.S. address, adding in the cost of shipping materials, and rounding up a dollar or so to cover handling. Alternatively, see what other sellers with comparable items are charging for shipping and select a similar amount. If you wish to offer international shipping, this still needs to be calculated on a case-by-case basis because the costs vary so widely based on the destination.

- **Proofread and spell check**   You wouldn't send a solicitation letter out with a *missppppelling* and the same should be true for your presence on eBay: Each listing is a reflection on your organization and the quality of service you provide. Take time to pay attention to those small details and your organization will look good.

- **Include more pictures**   While one picture may be fine for a $25 item, it's not enough for a $2,500 item. When people are considering bidding a large amount of money, they expect to see the item from more angles and have close-ups of details. Think about what you would want to see before buying, and provide a number of clear pictures to get people excited about bidding on the item. It's particularly important if the item you're selling is antique or unusual. For commodity items and items new in box, pictures will be less important because people know what they're getting. Take a look at other similar items for sale on eBay to get an idea of what's important to show in the photographs (as well as what buzz words should be used in the title).

- **Consider upgrades**   While for lower-priced items, investing in feature fees for enhancements such as bold text, featured placement, subtitles, etc. may not pay off, this is not necessarily the case for higher-priced items. In addition to drawing eyes toward your items and other listings, eBay has a number of statistics showing that you can make back the investment in fees with increased final value prices, especially for items that are more than $50. Take a look at the stats on the eBay page at **http://pages.ebay.com/sellercentral/ tools.html**.

warning   *Subtitles are a nifty place to talk about the fact that proceeds benefit charity. However subtitles are* not *searchable in basic search (only in "title and description" advanced searches).* Do not *put critical information in the subtitle. Anything that people are likely to search on—all essential item information and organization name—should also be in the title, not only in the subtitle.*

- **Include a FAQ**   Anticipate frequently asked questions (FAQs) and spell out policies to ensure the event runs smoothly. Avoid misunderstandings with people over the return policy or shipping insurance requirements by explaining everything ahead of time.

- **Showcase credentials**   If your organization is registered with MissionFish, GuideStar, or SquareTrade, make sure people can see that on all your listings. Provide links to your nonprofit site from your About Me page and, even better, have the nonprofit web site promote and link back to the auctions as well.

- **Run test listings**   Work through any unexpected kinks in the process by selling a few smaller items before you start selling your important ones. There is a category on eBay specifically for test listings, category number 14111, found under: Everything Else | Test Auctions | General. Work out listing and timing questions so your carefully timed event doesn't end up starting late.

- **Build your reputation**   Equally important, selling builds up your credibility as a seller on eBay by increasing your feedback. Not only are people more willing to bid when a seller's feedback is not zero, but also to use certain listing upgrade features on eBay, you'll need a feedback rating of 10 or 25. Another way to build up feedback is to buy items. Buyers receive feedback in every transaction and it's quicker and easier to buy items, such as office supplies like paper or printer ink cartridges, than it is to list and sell items. Your feedback will go up and you may even save some money on products you would buy anyway. Keep in mind feedback is public and eBay users will be able to see what you bought and whether feedback is from buying or selling so only buying will not fully establish your credibility.

Creating Designer Listings

If you don't have the resources to create custom graphics or a template for your listings, eBay offers a Listing Designer, shown here, in the Sell Your Item Form.

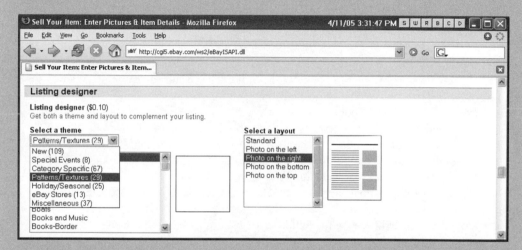

This quick and easy design format costs $0.10 per listing and allows you to select from a number of themes, including special events (weddings, baby, birthdays), category specific items (art, toys, and so forth), holidays/seasons, and patterns. Once you've selected a theme, scroll back down and you're able to select a specific template; for example, you might choose Autumn Leaves if you're doing a fall auction. Now choose the layout you prefer, placing the picture on the left, right, top, or bottom, and preview the listing. If you're satisfied, continue filling out the form; if not, go back and choose other options and preview them until you find one you're happy with.

If you just want to make some simple formatting modifications, you can use the eBay HyperText Markup Language (HTML) text editor or click the Enter Your Own HTML tab. eBay provides some HTML short cuts, shown here, to help you spiff up your listing, such as ones to make fonts bold or larger. For more eBay HTML tips, visit **http://pages .ebay.com/help/sell/html_tips.html**.

(continued)

warning *If things aren't looking the way you expect them to in the Sell Your Item form, it might be your browser. eBay recommends that when you're using eBay, you use Netscape or Internet Explorer (**http://pages.ebay.com/ help/newtoebay/browser-recommendations.html**). So if you're using popular browsers like Mozilla or Safari, you may not be able to toggle between using the HTML text editor and entering your own HTML.*

If you have a web designer or are working with a service such as Kompolt (**www .kompolt.com**), the service can create a custom page for you using specific colors and logos. Remember, if you are not the nonprofit yourself, do not to use the nonprofit's logo without its express written permission to do so. The designer can create the border, background, and standard headline that will go above the unique item description, as well as include a standard policies paragraph (regarding your return policy, shipping instructions, etc.) that goes below the item descriptions. This item listing template should tie into the look of your About Me page as well. If you decide to create a custom template, copy and paste the HTML text the designer provides into the item description space on the "Enter Your Own HTML" tab on the Sell Your Item Form. Then you can add the specific item description, usually in a particular place the designer indicates.

Authenticate and Insure

When it comes to selling expensive items of the sort you might offer at a high-profile event, no matter how credible you are as a seller and how high your feedback is, your buyers will feel more comfortable bidding if you offer a few assurances. Here are some ways you can help your buyers bid with confidence and protect yourself as a seller at the same time.

Authenticate Your Items

Consider what independent source or company might validate high-value items. For sports cards, stamps, and coins there are established standards and organizations that give ratings and authenticate items. Use these whenever possible to establish your item's credentials. Where that is not possible, consider what provenance can be provided. Is there a signed letter from the previous owner or the donor? Do you know the origin and history of the items? Do you have some way of helping to establish the item's genuine status? Autographs can be particularly challenging because they're relatively simple to fraudulently create, so knowing the history of your items will help them sell for their true value.

Services range from the Professional Coin Grading Service (PCGS) for coins to the International Gemological Institute for jewelry, to even more targeted companies that provide authentication services for signed sports collectibles, Native American artifacts—even Ty Beanie Babies! For eBay's complete listing of authentication and grading services go to: **http://pages .ebay.com/help/community/auth-overview.html**.

Use an Escrow Service

To help both the buyer and seller rest easy, you might consider using an escrow service such as Escrow.com (**www.escrow.com**; see Figure 10-5) or eBay's payment service PayPal (**www.paypal.com**) to mediate the purchase. The escrow company acts as middle person until both parties are satisfied. Payment for the item is sent by the buyer to the escrow company, who then notifies the seller to ship the item. Payment is held by the escrow company until the buyer receives and inspects the item. When the item arrives as described, the buyer notifies the escrow company that he has accepted the item and the money is then released to the seller. If the buyer feels the item isn't what he was expecting, he may return the item to the seller, and assuming it's returned in the condition it was sent in, the buyer's money is returned to him.

FIGURE 10-5 Escrow services can be useful for very valuable items.

The fees for this service can be paid by the buyer or seller or split between them. Typically the amount of the fees depends on the purchase price and the level of service. For example, Escrow.com charges between 3.25 percent and 6.3 percent of item price with a minimum charge of $25.

Require Insurance

When shipping high-priced, fragile, or time-sensitive (tickets) and perishable items, it's recommended that you require shipping insurance. Usually the buyers pay for the insurance, but you can specify who pays for the insurance in your listing. You may also recommend insurance but make it optional for the buyer. Specify in the listing that you will pack the item carefully but that the buyer assumes risk for damage or loss if they decline insurance. Usually they'll opt for the insurance if they have any concerns. Keep in mind that if you make insurance optional and something does go wrong, you'll likely decide to refund part or all of the payment to the buyer anyway to maintain good customer relations and positive feedback. For those reasons it may be better to require insurance for high-priced or breakable items.

Most shippers will provide insurance on items up to $100.00 for free and after that you pay a fee for additional insurance of approximately $0.40–$0.50 per $100.00 for declared values more than $100.00. For more information you can visit these shipper sites and search for "insurance" on United States Postal Service (USPS) or "declared value" on FedEx and United Parcel Service (UPS):

- **USPS** www.usps.com/all/insuranceandextraservices/welcome.htm
- **USPS Insurance Purchased Online** www.usps.com/insurance/online.htm
- **FedEx** http://fedex.com
- **UPS** http://www.ups.com/content/us/en/resources/select/receiving/options/insurance.html

Provide Package Tracking

You have several options when it comes to being notified that the item you shipped has safely arrived at its destination. The USPS offers Delivery Confirmation and Certified Mail; both allow you to go online to find out the date and time a shipped item was delivered. Delivery confirmation is cheaper, but it doesn't require a signature at the time of delivery opposed to Certified Mail. If you want a physical copy of the signature, you may add a Return Receipt to either option for an additional fee so you'll be notified of receipt by postcard. UPS and FedEx generally provide this information routinely as well as a package's status in transit.

Some buyers will want to know where their packages are every minute and their estimated times of arrival; using a shipping service with detailed tracking will answer these questions. You can save time answering questions by sending buyers e-mails with their package tracking numbers. This way, they can track packages themselves. To see tracking options, visit:

- **USPS**   http://usps.com/shipping/trackandconfirm.htm?from=home &page=0035trackandconfirm

- **UPS**   www.ups.com/WebTracking/track?loc=en_US

- **FedEx**   www.fedex.com/us/pckgenvlp/track/index.html

Preserve Auction Integrity

Did you know that a Chunnel drill used to build the Channel Tunnel that connects Britain and France sold for nearly £40,000 (approximately $80,000) on eBay and benefited a local hospice? That's a whopping sum of money, but a few days into the auction, the bidding had gone as high as ten million pounds! What happened? Some people retracted their bids. Why? When there's a novel item for sale or bidding begins to climb briskly on a celebrity item, some people get caught up in the excitement or look for a chance at a brief moment of fame. Why not bid one million dollars if someone will outbid you in a matter of minutes? The potential for frivolous bids probably increases in proportion to the attention the item receives. But there are things you can do to prevent such problems, even in auctions of a much smaller scale.

Set Up "Buyer Blocks"

The first and simplest thing you can do is set up "*buyer blocks*." eBay offers a simple way to prevent bidders with negative feedback and nonpaying bidders (people who bought an item but failed to pay) from placing a bid on your items. To set your buyer block preferences, visit the Buyer Requirements page (**http://offer.ebay.com/ws/eBayISAPI.dll?BuyerBlockPreferences**, shown in Figure 10-6) or go to your My eBay page. Under My Account on the left-hand side, choose Preferences; under your Selling Preferences you'll be able to specify your Buyer requirements, including which buyers to block. (You will need to have set up your eBay Sellers Account before you'll see your selling preferences.)

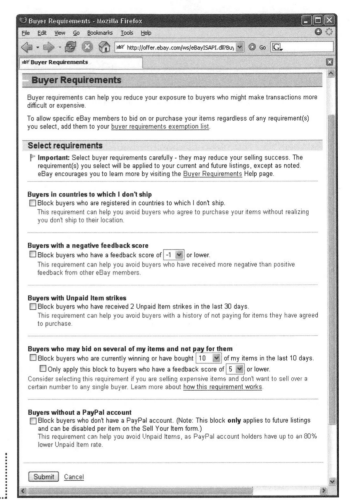

FIGURE 10-6 For high-profile auctions, you may want to block bids from members you don't trust.

Contact Bidders During the Sale

A good way to address the seriousness of your potential bidders is to advise them up front that you'll contact bidders to verify their bids once the bidding hits a certain level. eBay makes it simple for sellers to e-mail their bidders and also makes it possible to request their phone numbers once they've placed a bid on the item (click the bidder's feedback number, then simply click the Contact Member button). For example, you could say in the listing that for bids that are more than $500, bidders will be asked to respond to an e-mail request for their phone numbers to verify their bids within 24 hours or you may remove their bids. Just the notion that they might be contacted will discourage most from spuriously bidding. One nonprofit chose to verify bidders over $500 and then only allowed people who had been bidding to place bids in the last 24 hours before the end of the auction. Keep in mind, many people wait until the last five minutes to place their first bids so if you choose this option, you'll want to create a list of preapproved bidders.

Create a Preapproved Buyer's List

Another way to approach bidder verification is to create a preapproved bidder/buyer list (**http://pages.ebay.com/help/sell/preapprove_bidders .html**). With this tool, only people on a predefined list can bid on the items. This way you can prescreen bidders and only allow bids from individuals serious enough to e-mail you to request that they be added to the bidder list. The list can also be a way to have a relatively "private event" on eBay because you make some auction items available only to members who submit their eBay user names to you ahead of time. Normally you wouldn't do this because typically the more bidders you have, the more money you raise, but there might be times when it is an appealing option for some of your auctions. For example, a board member may be willing to auction off a week at her vacation house but stipulate that it only go to another member of the organization and not the public at large.

Use a Service to Attain More Thorough Verification

Prequalification can take other forms as well. The company Kompolt provides services to more thoroughly verify a bidder, from validating the bidder's identity, to confirming sufficient funds are available, to requesting a deposit, which is held and kept as a payment toward the item if the bidder wins or is returned if the bidder is not the high bidder. If you feel you need this level of verification, you may need to enlist the help of a third party with the experience and qualifications to prequalify bidders to this extent.

Announce You Will Verify Bids

For most auctions, including a simple paragraph in your auction description will deter frivolous bidding and set bidders' expectations appropriately. Describe at what bid amount you will require bidder verification, how potential bidders can be added to the prequalified bidder list or how you will contact the bidders to verify their bids, and how much time they have to respond before their bids may be cancelled if they cannot be reached to verify the bid amounts. Here's a sample paragraph:

> "To help ensure a smooth auction process for all participants we require user's identities be verified on bids of $1,000 or greater. We suggest that interested bidders become preverified. To do so, please send us an e-mail to name@nonprofit.org or call 123-456-7890 and leave a message with a phone number where you can be reached between 8 A.M. and 6 P.M. PST. Members who wish to place first bids during the last 24 hours of the auction are asked to notify us before the last 24 hours of the auction so that we may preverify them. Bidders who are not preverified will be contacted by an agent of the seller via telephone at the number associated with their user IDs. If we are unable to contact a user, this user's bid may be removed."

Manage Workloads and Staffing

Even with the best possible listing, if you have a high-profile auction, it's reasonable to expect more questions from bidders and from the media. So when you're planning your event, timing and staffing should be a consideration. It's a good idea to have one person designated as the PR person to centralize and control information given out to the media. That also takes the pressure off other volunteers.

Keep in mind most questions arrive as the closing time of auction approaches. If you've selected a Sunday evening as the close of the auction (which is reasonable because that's when many buyers are on eBay and, therefore, it's typically a good time to have your auction end), then you'll need to have staff or volunteers available to answer questions at that time as well.

Do your auctions require precise end times to coincide with an advertised real-world date and time? It's probably worth paying the extra fee on eBay or using a listing tool to schedule your listings. If your auction has a large number of items, it can be a good idea to stagger the ending times or spread the auctions out over a number of days (saving the best items for last) to spread out the packing and shipping workload.

Also consider when you might have most volunteers available and try to schedule the event when people aren't traveling or have too many other demands (start of school, holidays). It's equally important to consider the demands on your donor base. Have you held another event or asked for support recently? To avoid donor fatigue and increase participation in your donation drive, avoid holding fundraising events too close together.

Automate with Tools

With more items and more on the line, it may save time to have help. There are tools and services to help things go smoothly, gain higher bids, and leverage others' selling experience. eBay provides many of its own selling tools on its Seller Tools page (**http://pages.ebay.com/sell/tools.html**, shown in Figure 10-7). With a major event, you'll want to save time and improve auction management, so it's a good idea to visit this page and consider the options open to you for listing multiple sales quickly, and for managing sales once they're online.

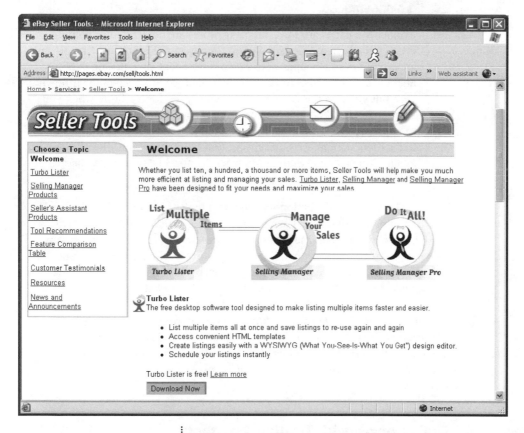

FIGURE 10-7 Consider using special software to help you create and manage auctions.

Software Tools

Many tools help expedite the listing process by allowing you to upload your listings to eBay in bulk and to schedule your auctions. As we detailed in Chapter 9, one of the most popular (not to mention free) programs is called Turbo Lister (**http://pages.ebay.com/turbo_lister**). Other programs, such as Selling Manager (**http://pages.ebay.com/selling_manager**) and Selling Manager Pro (**http://pages.ebay.com/selling_manager_pro**), go beyond that and can help you automate the e-mail communication with your buyers to expedite payment.

About Me pages are free, but eBay Stores are not. If you're holding an event, you may consider signing up for a free trial Store (the first 30 days are usually free) a couple weeks before the event, and closing the Store after the auction ends. You can always open the Store again the following year, but you don't have to pay the monthly fee for the Store when you aren't using it. The same may be true for auction management tools. For example, eBay's Turbo Lister is free, but you can often use a trial version of the more comprehensive subscription-based programs like eBay's Selling Manager and Selling Manager Pro for 30 days free of charge.

There are many auction management tools to choose from. Some of the companies that have been around a while include Andale, Auctiva, ChannelAdvisor, and Marketworks. If you plan to run ongoing auctions or even hold annual events, it might be worth exploring these options. Some have a steep learning curve, but once you learn them you'll save countless hours of repetitive and time-consuming listing tasks.

note   *eBay offers a Solutions Directory (**http://cgi6.ebay.com/ws/eBayISAPI .dll?SolutionsDirectory**) with links to companies, offering services from auction management to sourcing inventory, that can help you run your eBay auctions. This resource also includes a rating system so you can see how others feel about the companies' services.*

Outsource with Trading Assistants

Rather than learning how to sell on your own from scratch, Trading Assistants or Trading Posts (brick-and-mortar stores like AuctionDrop that will sell on eBay for you) can get you up to speed fast since they have experience with eBay. Beyond the technical knowledge of how to sell on eBay, they understand some of the artistry and analysis behind what works and what doesn't on eBay. Their experience and established reputations can result in higher prices than you might attain on your own; so, their fee (typically 10–30 percent) may be partially, or entirely, offset and justified because they bring you increased prices and save you time.

Before hiring a Trading Assistant, be sure to do your due diligence to make sure you're working with a reputable and experienced eBay seller. Besides looking at her recent listings, feedback rating and comments, take the time to talk to some of her references and ask about the specific tasks you'll be delegating to her. See if she is flexible on commission, especially since you're a nonprofit—no one should be charging 40 percent any more these days. In general, how flexible is this person, because you know that nonprofit priorities can shift. How is she on the phone and how responsive is she to your e-mails? Remember this person will be representing your organization to the world so you want someone with a good, patient, customer service–oriented, philanthropic demeanor. You want someone who is in this for the right reasons, not just to make money.

Take for example, Mark Silver (User ID **daddymade**), who helps schools hold online auction fundraisers. Silver has been selling on eBay more than eight years, has a feedback rating in excess of 1,000, and has been helping out schools since before MissionFish came about. Silver points out that with schools struggling and parents feeling nickeled and dimed, it's often easier to ask for donated items than it is for cash. Not only is it easier to ask for a donation, but also it's easier to delegate orchestrating the fundraiser to a professional. "Sometimes schools tell me they have a parent volunteer who could list the items, but in the end, they look to me," Silver says. "Even when volunteers have the know-how, they usually don't have the time to manage the listings and provide the customer support people expect on eBay."

Outsource with Auction Management Companies

Usually Trading Assistants are proficient and efficient with your listings, but they may not be able to help with all the other aspects of an auction featuring famous people or expensive items. Enter companies that provide complete Charity Auction Management Services. Kompolt Online Auction Agency is a premier company favored by the movie studios, celebrities, nonprofits, agencies, and big businesses for their soup-to-nuts execution on eBay charity fundraisers. Its services include design, public relations, on and off eBay marketing, managing listing and fulfillment at an operational level, and auction analysis and reporting. Kompolt also conducts bidder prequalification to ensure fair bidding and successful payment at the close of the auction.

A Passion for Helping Nonprofits: Kompolt

Kompolt is an online event agency incorporating strategy, design, operational support, bidder prequalification, and fulfillment for a seemingly effortless production of major charity events on eBay. Jenny Kompolt, a former eBay employee, started the business after assisting numerous companies and nonprofits hold events on eBay. She realized that some organizations needed to be able to outsource the project in order to streamline the process and deliver greater results. Kompolt boasts a success rate of 96 percent of the items and 100 percent of the vehicles it has listed for sale. In total, the company has helped clients generate more than $4.8 million in revenue, the overwhelming majority of which has gone to nonprofit causes.

"Nonprofits need to think of themselves as a 'brand' just like Coca-Cola does," says Jenny. "Think about how you can use the eBay platform to market yourself. Can you showcase your mission or a new service? Can you educate people about your cause? It is important to think about how you are visually representing your 'brand' and convey a polished, professional image." She also encourages nonprofits to, "Take a look at what you have to sell and see what layers you can add to make them more interesting." Going from good to better to best by adding to your offering can significantly increase returns. For example, a signed Sting CD, Sting's signed bass, and a meet-and-greet with Sting.

"I think that one of the most rewarding parts of our job, is that a great percentage of what we do benefits a charity," comments Jenny. "People who bid on one charity auction often turn and start bidding on other charity items because they like to help a good cause." For Jenny, the most memorable charity auctions are the ones where the buyer's story is as interesting as the item for sale. She recalled how the buyer of Ellen DeGeneres' Swiss Army watch, which sold for $11,100 for the Susan G. Komen Foundation, was herself battling breast cancer. The Jay Leno–signed Harley auction run by Kompolt resulted in the highest priced motorcycle ever sold on eBay ($800,100) and benefited the American Red Cross. The winning bidder was David Steiner, CEO of Waste Management, who displayed the bike in the lobby of his main office building and is touring the bike around to continue raising more donations for tsunami victims.

Kompolt's Five Keys to Success

Jenny Kompolt has a particular passion for helping nonprofits use eBay to raise funds. She offers nonprofits these five key strategies for auction success:

- **Establish a Clear Direction**   Before you start to plan an auction, determine what your top priorities are. Are you looking to drive brand awareness or raise money? If you don't establish your goals up front, you can't really develop a plan. If you don't have a plan, you're planning to fail.

- **Create a Plan for Driving Traffic**   The ability to reach out to millions of bidders is a major advantage of online auctions versus traditional live or silent auctions. You won't capitalize on this, however, unless you make people aware of the opportunity. Be sure to leverage media partnerships, participation or donations from celebrities sympathetic to your cause, and outreach to your own cause supporters.

- **Manage Your Merchandise Mix**   Offering a big item (a yacht, a celebrity's watch, etc.) is great, but in most cases, it makes sense to offer merchandise at low-, mid-, and high-price levels. This enables a wider spectrum of consumers to participate in supporting your cause. The yacht might bring curious bidders to your auctions, but most of those visitors will only be able to afford lower priced items.

- **Provide Good Customer Service and Manage Bids**   There is nothing more potentially damaging to your cause's public image than poor customer service or discovering that the highly publicized winning bid on your auction's signature item was bogus. Ensure potential bidders receive excellent customer service and use bidder prequalification on high-profile, high-revenue items.

- **Assemble a Strong Auction Team**   Depending on your resources and the level of publicity you expect to generate, make sure you involve someone with auction expertise, such as a volunteer or in-house expert (someone with experience selling on eBay), an experienced and trusted trading assistant, or an auction management company such as Kompolt.

Kompolt fees vary and depend on the extent of services and customization desired, but they're most often called upon for auctions involving merchandise that's either high profile (involving famous people or things) or mid to high end (expensive items, experiences, or vehicles). Kompolt ensures the event runs smoothly and is well coordinated, showcasing the participating organizations in the best light possible. The company has run a huge number of auction events, knows what to anticipate, how to prevent problems before they happen, and how to respond quickly to the inevitable new surprises that can crop up.

In addition to Kompolt and Silent Partners (mentioned earlier in this chapter in "Increase the Number of Your Items"), there are a growing number of charity auction management companies that manage both online and off-line auctions for nonprofits.

Mindshare is an agency that assists organizations with their communications and fundraising challenges, including online auctions. They offer a variety of services from strategy and planning, procurement, promotion, logistics, fulfillment, and reporting. The costs for their services vary depending on the number of items, how much of the work you wish to offload onto them, and the potential for a future and ongoing relationship. But generally speaking, your event needs to be raising at least $15–20,000 to make an investment in their services worthwhile.

Fundraising practice manager for Mindshare Interactive Campaigns Shayna Englin has some great tips for nonprofits kicking the tires on online auction fundraising for the first time. She says, "Plan ahead and look at where online auctions fit into your goals. Many nonprofits think it is a great idea to piggyback online auctions with their gala, but that does not have to be the case. Online auctions add work when organizers are already stressed, so it may be better to focus on tying in auctions with your direct mail schedule instead." It is important to set timelines and make sure items are procured by the deadlines you set forth.

"Keep in mind that people will want their items as soon as they pay for them," Englin explains, "so set buyer expectations by being clear in your listings that items will ship between this date and that date. This allows you to gang up shipping for items that may close over several days." The most common mistake nonprofits make when planning for an auction, according to Englin, is "trying to procure high-value items like jewelry rather than focusing on local or national experiences. It can be hard to get the full value for a necklace and if it sells for a lower price, the donor may be disappointed. Experiences are often easier to sell and have the potential to bring in big dollars."

Auction Cause, one of the newer entrants into the field of nonprofit auction management companies, offers the full slate of services, including procurement and execution with an emphasis on creating effective media events. It was started by Eric Gazin, who had been selling on eBay for seven years before launching Auction Cause. For the nonprofits he works with, Gazin's priorities are helping them acquire really great items to sell, investing in good design for the nonprofits online "face," and really promoting the donors of the items so that they'll want to donate to that nonprofit again and again as part of a cause marketing strategy.

"Do your research and then let the market dictate price," Gazin advises new online auction sellers. For high-priced items, he also recommends making the auction "*private*"—or hiding the bidders' names from public view. (There is a check box for this on the Sell Your Item form next to the Auction Duration options.) Not only does this make some bidders more comfortable, but it also has a practical side effect of preventing ne'er-do-wells from "harvesting" your underbidders (contacting your bidders and offering them a similar item for less money off eBay).

Gazin has some concerns about the practice of requiring stringent bidder prequalifications because they may discourage bids and take away from the traditionally "open to all" underlying premise of eBay. Instead, Auction Cause prefers to use the more open approach by simply telling bidders in the item listing that he may be contacting them to verify their bids. He uses the bidder management tools to automatically block those with negative feedback and then looks at the bid history of the top bidders to see if that raises any red flags (for example, a bidder who has never bought anything for more than a dollar now bids $500 on your item could be a red flag). He relies on hands-on customer service to call and verify bids only for those he has concerns about.

Portero provides nonprofits and luxury brands with another interesting option. It provides the services of an online auction management company, listing the items for sale on eBay, but it is also willing to come out to your event and present a computerized version of the traditional "*silent auction.*"

More Information: Auction Management Companies

Company	Web Site	Phone
Kompolt	http://kompolt.com	805-786-0150
Silent Partners	http://silentpartnersinc.com	818-222-3525
Mindshare Interactive Campaigns	www.mindshare.net	202-654-0800
Auction Cause	www.auctioncause.com	323-655-0554
Portero	http://portero.com	877-307-3767
LiveAuctioneers	http://liveauctioneers.com	888-600-BIDS
iCollector	http://icollector.com	866-313-0123

It lists the items for sale on eBay and schedules the auctions to close during a specific time when a real-world event is held. At the real-world event, the company displays the items up for auction, sets up five–six computers so that people can bid and uses projectors to show the auctions on a big screen so people can watch the action.

Portero even provides "*proxy bidders*" standing by so those without eBay or PayPal accounts can still bid at the last minute. The proxy bidders take the bidder's credit card information and then bid on this person's behalf. Portero handles all the payment processing and shipping for all items. According to Portero's vice president of sales Jeff Nortman, the auctions Portero has been involved in deliver 25–35 percent more dollars. Nortman's tip for nonprofits looking to bring their silent auctions online is to focus on premium brands. Portero's focus on top brand items has resulted in average selling prices of $200–$400 per item.

Create a Live Auction with Online Component

If an online silent auction sounds good but you miss the excitement of the falling gavel, there is another type of company that helps nonprofits run online *and* real offline auctions. This way you can have your cake and eat it too. That's right—you can keep your popular real-world auction event right down to the gavel while also engaging the online community. And there are some very compelling reasons to add online bidding to a live auction. Julian Ellison, president of eBay certified live auction company LiveAuctioneers, explains that adding eBay to the auction mix results in "25–35 thousand unique visitors seeing the items before the auction and is followed by incremental participation in the live auction by Internet bidders (17–30 percent of bids come in online). The bottom line, using eBay Live Auctions for a nonprofit event adds a 15–35 percent increase in dollars raised for the cause."

tip *A source of experienced auctioneers to run your live event is the National Auctioneers Association (**www.auctioneers.org**).*

eBay has offered Live Auctions since 2000 and has seen tremendous growth over the past couple of years. It now hosts more than ten live events per day on average. The platform has been used by Sotheby's, Heritage Rare Coin Galleries, Collector Universe, and many other well-known sellers. According to eBay, the price range for items sold has extended from $1 up to $1,000,000, but overall, it has found items listed through Live Auction have an average price five to ten times higher than comparable items on eBay not through Live Auctions. Live Auctions listings have a blue auction paddle icon next to the title, which gives them added promotion for people searching or browsing items on eBay. A fun way to get familiar with Live Auctions is to watch one live and even register to bid on one so you can have the full experience.

To get a sense of how this works, let's look at eBay Live Auctions from the average Internet bidder's perspective.

1. *Before the auction*—Bidders will come across items in the auction on **www.ebayliveauctions.com** and **www.ebay.com**. Any eBay member may register for an auction by selecting "register" or "place bid" on any eBay lot page. Bidders will be asked to agree to the auction terms and conditions and confirm that their contact details are correct. Those who are not eBay members will need to register with eBay, read the Live Auctions agreement (typically, just once—the first time they use the system), submit user identification (either a credit card or via the Equifax ID Verify program), then click the "Sign Up" button that they see next to the catalog title to participate in the auction.

2. *During the auction preview and online bidding*—Before the live bidding, buyers can browse the catalog of *lots* (in other words, items) up for auction and place absentee bids or prepare for real-time bidding by identifying the lots they will be interested in bidding on. The lots are usually available for viewing 30–60 days before the auction and bids can be taken during the 10 days leading up to the live auction.

3. *During the live auction*—Bidding for each lot will start at the amount of the bid of the current high bidder on eBay. Online bidders can watch the action on their home computers; when the lot they're interested in comes up on their computers, they can bid against other Internet bidders and auction floor bidders. They'll see the current price real time as the bids come in. To bid, they simply click the Bid button on the screen, which is continually updated with the current high bid. (See Figure 10-8.) The auctioneer will call a Final Warning before closing the auction.

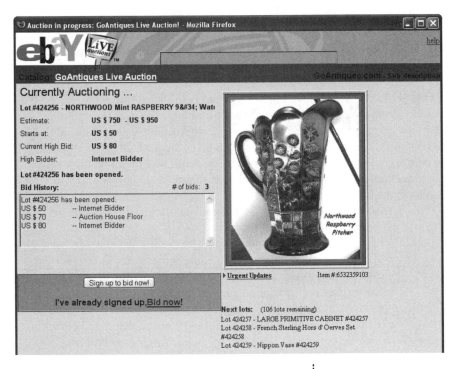

FIGURE 10-8 Viewing a live auction in progress is fun and a great first step if you're considering using eBay Live Auctions at your real world auction.

4. *After the auction*—If the reserve was met and a buyer's bid via the Internet was higher than any other bids placed, that person is the winner. And like every other eBay auction, the winner and the seller will need to contact each other, exchange payment for the item, arrange for shipping, and leave feedback. The only other twist with live auctions is there may be a *Buyer's Premium* (often waived for nonprofit auctions)—a percentage of the selling price of the item that the buyer must also pay to the auction house.

> note *It's not as easy to put items up for sale on eBay Live Auctions as it is on the "regular" part of eBay. In order to use eBay Live Auctions, you need to be a licensed auctioneer yourself, or contract with a licensed auctioneer for the event.*

From the seller's perspective, here's how to do a live auction on eBay:

1. *Know the costs.* There are two fees to sell on eBay Live Auctions: a $1,500 Insertion Fee associated with listing your catalog of items for sale (you can list up to 10,000 lots in each catalog!) and a Final Value Fee of 5 percent of the final selling price due only on successful lots sold to Internet bidders. At the time of this writing, Live Auctions participants receive ten free Featured Plus! items and one free Homepage Featured item, a value of more than $200. These are the online costs and are in addition to the costs of running the live auction (hiring the licensed auctioneer, etc.). Keep in mind many online auction companies quote increases in bottom line dollars raised of 10–35 percent, which should more than offset the investment.

2. *Secure items for the auction and get familiar with the Live Auctions process.* **http://pages.ebay.com/liveauctions/help/ forsellers/forsellers.html**

3. *Register on eBay as a seller.* If you are, or work with, a licensed auctioneer or auction house to run the bidding at your event, you can apply to become an eBay Live Auctions seller (**http://v2.liveauctions.ebay.com/aw-cgi/eBayISAPI .dll?LAApplicationForm**).

   Those who work with a licensed auctioneer can then enlist the help of companies such as LiveAuctioneers and iCollector to put the auctions online at no additional cost. The advantages they bring to the table are experience and efficiency. Their fees are included in the eBay fees (they receive a cut of the eBay fees) so there really is no reason not to take advantage of them, especially if you have never held a live auction on eBay before. Alternatively if you do not have an auction house or licensed auctioneer selected, you can hire LiveAuctioneers to run a turn-key event for you for a fee.

note *If you only wish to sell your items in eBay Live Auctions (and not host a live event), you can instead simply consign your items to Live Auctioneers Discovery Sales (LADS), www.liveauctioneers.com, or a Live Auctions Trading Assistant such as www.goantiques.com and http://live.universal-collectibles.com. Contact them for more information on their processes and fees.*

4. *Create the catalog of lots that will be up for sale.* Similar to the Sell Your Item form we discussed in the earlier chapters, the Live Auction listing form will ask you for title, description, category, and so forth. You can use bulk uploading tools such as Turbo Lister to upload existing catalog information and pictures quickly. The catalog can go up months before the event so bidders can preview the items.

5. *Set bidder requirements.* There are a few tiers of bidder registration requirements available. To get the highest number of registered bidders for the least amount of work, eBay recommends that you require bidders to be ID-verified or to simply have a credit card on file with eBay. (eBay doesn't provide the credit card information to the seller, rather it's used for verifying identities. The seller will still need to arrange for payment at the conclusion of the auction.)

6. *Get training on eBay's Live Auction technology used to accept Internet and floor bids.* No special software is required, only a PC that's Java-enabled and a high-speed Internet connection. eBay Customer Support will train you how to use the seller interface before the live event via phone. If you're using a service such as LiveAuctioneers, you can also receive training from the company and run test auctions until you're comfortable with the process. If you still have any concerns, you can hire LiveAuctioneers to come out and run it for you.

7. *Once your catalog is online, you can watch as buyers place absentee bids before the live auction begins.* Just before the live auction begins, you'll be notified of the current high bid.

8. *Use eBay's Live Auction technology to accept Internet and floor bids.* At the conclusion of the event, contact the high bidder to receive payment. If the winner is an Internet bidder, also arrange shipping and insurance as needed.

tip *Some types of items, because of their very specific audience appeal (such as celebrity-signed items, scripts, and experiences) typically perform tremendously better online than in offline-only auctions. Items like these can often go for amazing bargains in live auction because of the limited number of attendees and the lack of enthusiasts, which may be nice for the bidders, but doesn't help the nonprofit hit its fundraising goals. On the other hand, items like time-shares may sell better in a live auction, and the donors may be more comfortable selling to communities they're more familiar with. Consider this when allocating your items to live or online auctions to optimize the dollars raised.*

"It's like sticking a Ferrari engine onto your scooter . . . and we make sure you can handle that kind of power." –*Julian Ellison, president of LiveAuctioneers, referring to the advantages of adding eBay Live Auctions to your real-world auction.*

To get the best results, Ellison recommends that you promote your catalog of merchandise up for auction on your own web site. He also recommends that nonprofits maximize lead time (at least 30 days) to ensure exposure and prepublicity for items, and that they use selling tools to decrease the amount of staffing time needed to list items for auction. Companies like LiveAuctioneers can save you time and worry since they have been through the process and provide photo hosting. They also have handy editing, invoicing, and post sale tools, and can even help index auction items in Google and other search engines (even incorporating live links to your items once your 10-day auction begins on eBay). Their clients have included numerous companies and organizations, such as Sotheby's New York, Phillips de Pury, Brunk Auctions, Julien's Auctions, Noel Barrett Vintage Toy Auctions, and fashion designer Marc Ecko, who held his own fundraising live auction on eBay (see Chapter 2).

live auctioneers
www.liveauctioneers.com

888.600.BIDS
info@liveauctioneers.com

The Worldwide Leader in eBay Live Auction Events

must have

As you've learned in this chapter, companies and celebrities are finding eBay auctions an attractive way to raise money for causes they champion. It's not exclusively philanthropy, though, as corporations find that getting behind causes can be good for business, too. In the next two chapters we'll look at how to partner with others to build your event and then at how to leverage the power of the Internet to make your auction a success. In this chapter, you learned that:

- A major fundraising event has the same goals as a smaller auction, but the number and variety of items is increased, and celebrities may be involved.

- Conventional brick-and-mortar fundraising events can be combined with live auctions on eBay to increase exposure and produce higher bids.

- Creating a media "hook" for your event can increase attention dramatically.

- Take advantage of holidays or special occasions, as well as hot trends, and create tie-ins to your fundraiser.

- Contact local celebrities and solicit lunches or other "experiences" you can auction off to interested parties.

- Personalize any solicitation letters you send to organizations or individuals.

- Make sure you authenticate bidders participating in your high-profile event; consider blocking bidders you don't trust, or contacting bidders after bids reach a specified amount.

Chapter 11
Partnerships: Good for Bidders, Good for Partners, Great for Nonprofits

The designers were thrilled to participate and the readers had the chance to be the first to own some of the hottest new fashion trends from top designers while helping a good cause at the same time.

—Jenny Barnett, *Harper's Bazaar* magazine

What We'll Cover in This Chapter:
- What partners bring to the auction table
- How to find partners who share an interest in your cause
- Why corporations are embracing cause-related marketing
- How to think like a company and quantify results
- How to work with a partner to set goals and assign tasks

Imagine having great products, great marketing, and raising lots of money without having to do everything yourself. An impossible dream? No! Not only is it possible, but it is a win for all involved. Companies are seeking new ways to make their products stand out and to make their brand attractive to consumers. When faced with a choice of two comparable products, consumers opt for products from socially responsible companies, especially when a portion of the proceeds goes to charity. Corporations are finding this scenario to be true across the board, and have discovered that demonstrating to their community that they're good corporate citizens not only feels right, but it also makes money.

The first step to successful partnerships is identifying which companies are a good fit for your nonprofit. The next step is identifying the needs and goals of the partner companies and determining which of those goals you can help them achieve. Some benefits are universally applicable across partners, including gaining goodwill from social responsibility, building brand awareness, and differentiating products, but there are many other ways you can help your partners while they help you.

How Can You Work with Partners?

What are your goals for the partnership? If you're working on a small-scale event, you may be happy with a sponsor, in-kind donations, or logistical support. If you're working on a large-scale event, you need to find partners who can bring in valuable donations, increase the media reach and public relations (PR) value of the event, and provide resources to help you bring in more buyers.

There are as many different types of partnerships as there are partners. Don't limit your idea of a partner to a large company. Small companies, media partners, celebrities, politicians, clubs, and associations can also be very influential and helpful allies. As you put your event together, look for synergies and multiple ways to work with partners to ensure you both get the most out of the relationship. The following are some of the ways you might work with a partner.

tip *Long-standing nonprofit relationships are favored over short-term efforts. People are looking for stable commitment rather than a company that chooses to help various nonprofits here and there. As a nonprofit, it's good to develop a long-term relationship with a corporate partner for both of you to gain the greatest results.*

In-Kind Support

Wouldn't it be nice if you could shave some of the expenses of running a charity auction by partnering with companies that help you carry out the online auction? It's particularly helpful to find companies who will provide their services to you gratis, or at a discount, in exchange for recognition and their logos in your press materials. To run your event in a frugal manner, seek out companies that can assist you with tasks that are within their areas of expertise and a part of their daily business—they can often help you out at very little cost to themselves. Not only that, but if they treat their services as marketing expenses, the companies may well find the recognition for their support provides a good advertising value and great customer relations. Here are some suggestions of local businesses that have the resources to help you facilitate running your auction on eBay:

- A local printer/copier to reproduce donation drive flyers, solicitation letters, etc.

- A storage facility to store donations until they're sold

- A delivery service or drivers to help collect and transport donations

- A shipping service to help ensure sold items are packaged and shipped promptly

- A media partner to help increase awareness for the event on air and in print

- Companies to provide incentives for people to donate (for example, they might offer a discount or free item with a purchase for those who donate or volunteer)

- Restaurants and grocery stores to chip in refreshments for volunteers

- Computer stores to loan or donate computers so more people can enter products simultaneously

- An Internet service provider to provide high-speed access for the duration of the auction

- A camera store that's willing to loan or donate a digital camera

Public Relations and Marketing Support

Companies often have dedicated PR departments with expertise, media lists, and established contacts. Their knowledge and resources can help you create an effective release to get information about your event widely disseminated. Additionally, a partner company's brand appeal may help your press release get more attention and coverage than your standalone announcement. The more involved in the event that your partner becomes, the more opportunities you'll have to leverage its resources and experience, with everything from branding and design to promotion for the event from company web sites, e-mail blasts, and newsletters to the company's constituencies and the public. (See the upcoming section "Cause-Related Marketing" for more suggestions on branding and marketing your event.)

Strategic Philanthropy: Cash Donations and Sponsorships

Some companies don't have the bandwidth to get involved but, out of interest in supporting the cause or reaching your community, are willing to provide cash to help sponsor your event. Consider putting together sponsorship packages ranging from recognition online and banner ads to mentions in your newsletters. Typically sponsors are interested in reaching your donor demographic or they're interested in supporting your cause because it matches their corporate nonprofit objectives. Specifically, companies look to associate themselves with causes important to their target market. If supporting prostate cancer research is important to the predominantly male customers of a razor company, then supporting that cause may be a good fit for the company.

Whether your event is large or small, be sure to recognize your sponsor, as the charity auction by Michael Douglas and the Motion Picture and Television Fund did for their sponsor Lexus (see Figure 11-1).

Auction Item Donations

Companies that don't offer needed services and aren't willing to donate cash may be amenable to being approached for contributing auction items instead. We're talking primarily about asking for:

- Inventory (in-kind, high-value items)
- Celebrity signed items or experiences
- Hard-to-get or exclusive items

FIGURE 11-1 This auction's organizers showcased their sponsors in the logo and listing descriptions.

For a small-scale event, local stores may be able to donate one or two items. For a large-scale auction, there might be an opportunity for a major manufacturer (perhaps one that's based in your nonprofit's service area) to ship you a pallet of overstock products. This is often a relatively painless way in which a company can help. In fact, a company might be able to convert "problem" inventory that's been gathering dust and taking up space into a tax deduction.

Problem inventory includes excess stock, discontinued or remainder products, opened box items, returns, out-of-season merchandise, and refurbished or old versions of products (particularly in the fast-changing world of computers and electronics). Often it costs the company money to store these items, and they're taking up space that could be better used for new and faster-moving inventory. This situation presents an opportunity for you to solve a company's problem by taking troublesome inventory off its hands. The tax deduction the company receives for the donation may be worth more than selling the items for pennies on the dollar to a liquidator.

Another simple way to involve companies as partners is to solicit desirable items, such as tickets from airlines, accommodations from hotels, tee times from a popular golf course, gift certificates from a winery, and so forth, for the auction. Companies will want to know what they are receiving in the way of recognition and reach in exchange for their donations. If they can justify their donation as an advertising expense, and if there's a corporate commitment or personal connection to the cause, this type of solicitation effort can pay off.

The less obvious, but potentially more valuable, donations that partners bring to the table are their relationships with influential people and celebrities and their access to hard to get items. From celebrity autographed items to lunch with powerful CEOs, and from first off-the-line items to prototypes of products that collectors crave but rarely have the chance to bid on, partners can help you expand the scope of your auction offerings.

tip *Don't be afraid to ask for big ticket items or experiences, but don't lose touch with reality. Make sure it's something they can reasonably provide without a huge investment of time and give them specific ideas. It's better to ask for "lunch with the CEO for four" than for "anything you would be willing to donate," so brainstorm before you sit down to write your solicitation letter.*

Special Edition/Limited Edition Cobranded Products

eBay produced limited edition eBay Pez Dispensers and just 500 eBay Lionel train cars, and then auctioned off a number of them for charity. Ty produced a Beanie Baby bear with the trademark pink ribbon for the Susan G. Komen Breast Cancer Foundation; Marklin produced a UNICEF train car. These are just a few examples where companies have foregone a portion of their profits on a special edition version of a product in order to help raise money and awareness for a cause. For nonprofits, these items raise funds and provide a unique item to sell in their online stores; for collectors, it provides a desirable addition to their collections; and for companies, it's a way to serve both collectors and nonprofits, enhancing their reputations and sales in the process.

© 2003 Ty Inc.

A participating company will consider a cobranded item as long as the nonprofit is a good fit for the company's consumers, and as long as the partner company is able to cover its costs and make a small profit. This can be a profitable venture for both the for-profit company and nonprofit. Keeping production to a limited edition increases the appeal and prices people are willing to pay in auction. The key to either of these—but especially the latter—is to have a brand that collectors covet and, preferably, to have a relatively small edition size. Capitalize on collector interest by having a few items autographed or by issuing items with numbered certificates and holding special auctions for the first and last items in the edition.

Other than getting the buy-in to create a cobranded product, the process is not much different than creating a baseball cap with your logo upon it. The biggest risk and challenge with such an effort is determining who's responsible for the upfront costs to create the items. You also need to know what steps to take to ensure that the items will sell so that you're confident that you'll recoup those costs and bring in incremental revenues and donations. While this can be a straightforward business deal, it can also be a nice marketing tool for the company, which leads us to a related topic—cause-related marketing.

Cause-Related Marketing

Cause-related marketing is the current big craze in the fundraising world. As more and more companies seek to build their brands, and differentiate their products in the minds of consumers, *cause-related marketing*—the partnership between businesses and nonprofits to conduct activities that are mutually beneficial—is becoming both an essential marketing tool for businesses and a prime fundraising tool for nonprofits. These projects can be initiated by either the company or the nonprofit and may be part of an ongoing relationship, a one-time event, or a response to a crisis or natural disaster. Regardless of who initiates the relationship, it's important to align fundraising efforts with the business needs. At the end of the day, both the company and the nonprofit will want measurable results, such as mentions in the media and articles, and statistics on the number of people reached, total dollars raised, and number of products tried or sold.

note *For more information on the benefits of cause-related marketing and how to structure relationships with corporations, take a look at the articles available on sites such as The Corporate Social Responsibility Newswire (**www.csrwire.com**), Cone/ Roper Reports (**http://coneinc.com/Pages/research.html**), Business in the Community (**http://www.bitc.org.uk/index.html**), OnPhilanthropy (**www.onphilanthropy.com**), Business for Social Responsibility (**www.bsr.org**), and About (**www.about.com**; search for cause-related marketing).*

Cause-Related Marketing Works

According to the IEG Sponsorship Report, American companies are expected to spend nearly $1 billion on cause-related marketing campaigns. When you invite corporations to join you in a cause-related marketing effort, it's important to drive home not only the obvious goodwill and benefits of giving, but also to convey the bottom-line business reasons for adopting cause-related marketing into their marketing mix. Here are some key factors on why cause-related marketing is an economic must have, not just a moral responsibility.

Corporate Philanthropy Affects Consumer Buying Decisions

Both intuitively and through a number of studies, it's been found that consumers trust and prefer companies that take part in nonprofit giving. The company reputation and nonprofit track record are factors in the purchase decision, with people preferring, and sometimes willing, to pay more for products affiliated with a good cause. A company that has earned the trust of the community, and is considered socially responsible, often has an easier time when it wants to open a new store. Neighbors are much more open to the new store if they feel the company will give something back to the community.

According to a survey released in 2004 by Deloitte & Touche USA LLP, "Ninety-two percent of Americans think that it is important for companies to make charitable contributions or donate products and/or services to nonprofit organizations in the community."[1] A two-part study entitled "Brand Benefits (2003/2004)" found that 83 percent of consumers have taken part in at least one cause-related marketing program, and 48 percent of consumers "showed an actual change in behavior, saying that they switched brands, increased usage, or tried or enquired about new products" because of a cause-related marketing campaign.[2]

---

[1] "Deloitte Survey Reaveals that 72 Percent of Americans Want to Work for Companies that Support Charitable Causes." Deloitte & Touche USA LLP. October 6, 2004.

[2] "Brand Benefits (2003/2004)." Business in the Community, 2003/2004.

Corporate Philanthropy Helps Recruit and Retain Employees

People prefer to work for companies that are good corporate citizens. Employees are more motivated, which results in increased productivity, greater employee loyalty, and decreased costs in employee recruitment and turnover. The same Deloitte & Touche survey mentioned previously also found that "72% of Americans want to work for companies that support charitable causes," and that charitable giving both positively affects employee morale and can be the deciding factor for individuals choosing an employer.[3]

---

[3] "Deloitte Survey Reaveals that 72 Percent of Americans Want to Work for Companies that Support Charitable Causes." Deloitte & Touche USA LLP. October 6, 2004.

Investors Are Increasingly Seeking Socially Responsible Investments

Not only is there a backlash when companies are participating in unethical behaviors, but there is also a growing number of investors who are putting their money into companies that are committed to goals beyond simply making money. According to "The Business Case for Corporate Citizenship" by Arthur D. Little, Inc., "An increasing number of funds are now managed according to the Principles of Socially Responsible Investment (SRI), with portfolio managers either screening out businesses that do not meet high environmental or social standards or using their influence to improve the ethical performance of these companies."[4]

[4] "The Business Case for Corporate Citizenship." Arthur D. Little Global Management Consulting, Cambridge, UK.

The Media Is Watching Corporate Ethical Standards

Trusted companies are more likely to be given a second chance in the event of problems. The corporate costs and time spent responding to and recovering from mistakes can be reduced if a company has a reputation for honesty and track record of social responsibility. The Brand Benefits survey, mentioned earlier, found that when people were aware of the cause-related marketing activities of a given company, they "consistently rated the company more highly in the categories of trust, endorsement, bonding, and innovation."[5]

[5] "Brand Benefits (2003/2004)." Business in the Community, 2003/2004.

Matching Gifts from Employers

Matching gift programs are already an integral part of the way nonprofits conduct fundraising, and eBay auctions leverage this resource as well. When an item sells on eBay, the nonprofit receiving the proceeds has instant documentation to show what the value of the donated item is. With this information, the nonprofit can acknowledge the actual cash value of the donation and the donor of the item may request a matching dollar gift for their in-kind donation.

It's worthwhile to remind your charity auction buyers to check with their employers to see if their entire donations, or the amount they've paid above the value of the items they've purchased, are eligible for matching. It's an easy, low-cost way to increase your auction proceeds.

Matching Gifts from Challenge Grants

Your nonprofit may have used *challenge grants* before to give people in your community an incentive to donate. The promise that if the group as a whole hits their goal, then a company or individual will match funds raised can be very motivating. A partner who's willing to support such a goal could also help your donation drive. You might suggest the partner offer to match the amount raised or, to increase the number of actual donations, tie the matching donation to each item donated or sold. To be successful, you have to get people excited and engaged in achieving the fundraising goal; many organizations use a "thermometer" tracking progress toward the goal amount. Be sure to prominently display such a gauge not just in the office but online as well.

note *If you can use your eBay fundraising efforts to also provide job skills, teach entrepreneurship, or provide training (or job retraining) for your constituency, you may find partners who are willing to help you do that. Individuals who are out of work, students completing high school, or those challenged by disabilities or needing flexible hours to take care of children will find eBay and online selling a productive work experience that may even lead them to start new businesses, supplement their income, or earn enough to get off federally or state funded support. Tying your eBay fundraising into your philanthropic mission is an added bonus and you may find that you're able to get grants for developing training programs and funding computer equipment.*

Who Are Your Potential Partners?

The question goes both ways—who might have an interest in your cause, and which companies do you have an interest in working with? Start with the businesses who are a natural fit or with celebrities who have already expressed support for your organization or cause.

Look for Supporters Who Care about Your Cause

You're looking for long-time supporters, celebrities with a personal connection to your cause, and companies with specific nonprofit goals or interests. Fundamentally, partners are going to help you out because they believe in what you're doing and because they want to help make a difference. Even if the corporation is large, or the auctions could help its bottom line, the primary driving force and deciding factor for the partnership will be the fit between your cause and the partner's philanthropic interest and goals.

You can't be everything to everyone, so most companies have put together guidelines or priorities for the types of nonprofit causes they will support. It usually reflects their customers' and employees' interests, and is often regionally based or limited to the areas where the company has a physical presence, so starting your search for a partner locally makes a lot of sense. The Foundation Center (**http://fdncenter.org/learn/faqs/html/corporate_giving.html**) offers numerous resources to help you do a little detective work about the types of causes that companies (and their foundation counterparts) are willing to fund. From a database on CD-ROM to a subscription-based online directory, they offer tools that can help you search corporate giving programs to find those that might potentially be interested in partnering with you.

"Ellenthropy" Benefits Many Personal Causes

Ellen DeGeneres has a lengthy eBay track record of benefiting those causes in which she has a personal concern. Her site even asks the trivia question, "What has Ellen *not* auctioned off for charity?" One might well also ask, "Who has Ellen not helped," as her eclectic mix of charitable efforts on eBay have benefited numerous causes, from those organizations near and dear to her, to those aiding recovery from local and global tragedies. Here are some examples of "Ellenthropy" on eBay:

Amount	Item	Nonprofit Beneficiary
$1,025	Spice rack signed by James Spader and Ellen	Los Angeles Regional Food Bank
$4,050	Tennis racket signed by Serena Williams	Susan G. Komen Breast Cancer Foundation
$7,600	Cabbage Patch Kid in Ellen's image	American Red Cross and Noah's Wish
$14,015	Celebrity Tag Sale	Los Angeles Regional Food Bank
$18,500	Sheets with Ellen's likeness	ASPCA (The American Society for the Prevention of Cruelty to Animals)
$25,100	Customized Vespa designed by Coach	Peace Games
$36,800	Toyota Prius for tsunami relief	U.S. Fund for UNICEF

Ellen has also participated in a quilt for the Big Sister League; joined many other celebrities in signing Jay Leno's Bartels' Harley-Davidson motorcycle, which raised a record $800,100 for the American Red Cross International Disaster Relief efforts for

(continued)

tsunami victims; contributed autographed items to the "Wear Red" celebrity auction benefiting the American Heart Association; and even gave her Adidas sneakers to VH1, which sold them on eBay to benefit the Save The Music Foundation. By her example, Ellen encourages others to "Give a Little."

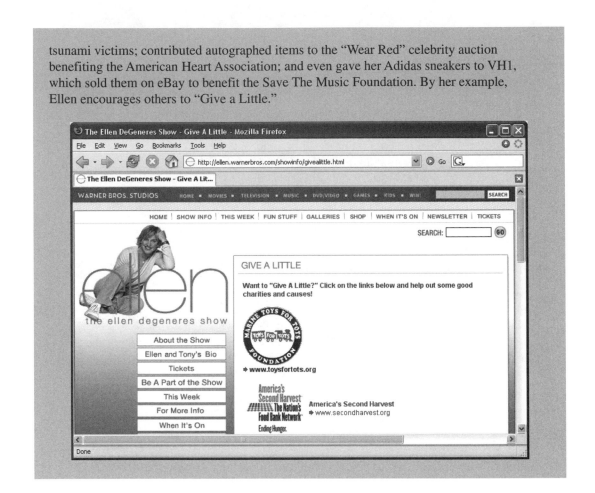

Consider Partners That Can Benefit from Working with You

Who's launching a movie or new product? Is there a product anniversary coming up that might tie into your cause? On the local scale, who could benefit from advertising to your constituency or from your success (for example, businesses near a new or refurbished library might see more traffic)? On the large scale, who could benefit by being associated with your cause or positive PR with your constituency?

How do you find potential partners? Once you brainstorm and come up with prospective companies that might be a good fit, it's time to network, network, network. Do you, or a friend, or a friend of a friend, know anyone who works at those companies? The Internet can be a useful tool for finding the right contacts at the companies you wish to approach. If you don't have any leads, start with the company web site and look at its press releases to identify the PR or media contact. This is often one of the few places you can find a phone number for the company that doesn't drop you into a customer-support telephone queue. And the PR division is the right place to start because cause-related marketing is all about the positive press the company will receive. The folks in PR will often know, or can find out, the right person in business development for you to work with if they think your program will afford them some good PR opportunities.

The Internet also has some great sites and tools to help you network. Find peer support and advice on the chat boards on the eBay Giving Works board (**http://forums.ebay.com/db2/forum.jspa?forumID=4001**) and on other nonprofit resource sites such as TechSoup (**www.techsoup.org**), Charity Navigator (**www.charitynavigator.org**), or GuideStar (**www .guidestar.org**). Learn how to leverage social networking using sites such as LinkedIn (**www.linkedin.com**; see Figure 11-2), Plaxo (**www.plaxo .com**), and Orkut (**www.orkut.com**). It's all about who you know—or rather, who you know within six degrees of separation. If there's a chain of connections to an individual at a company you'd like to contact, you can establish a personal connection rather than simply place a cold call to the company reception desk. Register with one or more of these sites and invite all the folks you've e-mailed in the past several months to link to you. You'll be amazed at how quickly your network of contacts grows.

Sometimes partners find you. When *Harper's Bazaar* magazine wanted to assist with tsunami relief fundraising, they contacted UNICEF USA. This is not at all uncommon; there have been many cases where the company approaches the nonprofit with its fundraising idea.

So how does one "get found" by these philanthropic-minded companies? For one thing, try to recruit volunteers from the companies. Like eBay, many companies and their related foundations give preferential considerations to nonprofits championed by their own employees. Build awareness for your cause and make it easy for corporations to find you on the Internet through web-site and search optimization and possibly even keyword advertising. Once they get to your site, you should have links on your home page inviting companies to work with you on cause-related marketing. Mention prior successful collaborations and include contact information for them to reach you if they have an idea.

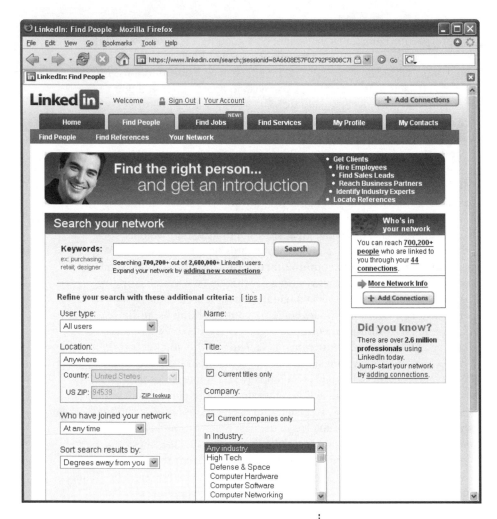

FIGURE 11-2 LinkedIn and other networking sites may help you get in touch with the right people at potential partner companies.

note *Before you send your letter, take a look at "Increase the Value of Your Items" in Chapter 10 for tips on how to write a good solicitation letter. Those tips apply here. You want to sell yourself and your qualifications (prior successful events, etc.) and clearly show how the relationship will be a great marketing opportunity for them.*

Think Like Your Partner

You've identified some prospective partners and have figured out whom to contact. Before you pick up the phone or send a letter, pretend you're in their shoes. What would *your* goals be in working with a nonprofit, and how would you know if you achieved them?

Businesses are typically looking for four main things: goodwill, brand exposure, product differentiation, and the chance to sell more products. How can you help them achieve these goals and measure the success? Think about ways your organization can help a for-profit partner move the dial via a relationship with your nonprofit. It may be through the media, visits to a web site, activity on the web site (sign ups for a newsletter, new site registrations, amount of time spent on site, coupon or promotion code redemption, etc), new sources of buyers, access to a target demographic, positive feedback from their constituencies, and increases in sales. Here are a few of the reasons partners will consider participating in your event:

- *They care about the cause and want to help.* This could be in response to a crisis that has impacted their community or an ongoing commitment to a specific cause. Success would simply be measured in dollars donated and the recognition received for their corporate social responsibility.

- *They wish to introduce new products and create buzz.* The goal is to find a unique way to grab media and public attention for the products. A for-profit company would be looking to your partnership to create excitement about the new product. Success would primarily be measured in media mentions and an uptick in inquiries or sales.

- *They wish to celebrate a product anniversary.* Celebrating a product milestone builds off nostalgia while breathing renewed life and "trendiness" into classic products. Anniversaries are also used to give loyal supporters a reason to go out and buy more and to build community and media excitement. Did you know Hello Kitty is 50, Lionel has celebrated its 100th birthday, and so on? These events are opportunities. Companies want to see their collector community or loyal fans rewarded for their patronage, and they want to celebrate and publicize the brand. Philanthropy helps them do this. Success would be measured in the prestige and recognition achieved, the amount of community involvement, media mentions, and sales.

- *They want a newsworthy event and a call to action.* What message do they want to get out there, when do they want to get it out there, why do they want to get it out there, and can you help them convey that message? Can your event help drive consumer action? For example, if you encourage people to support your sponsors—can you provide specific incentives to visit their web site or store? Perhaps the partners could host a reception or display some of the auction items at their location. If real-world logistics are too challenging, could your celebrity participate in a webinar (a seminar over the Web) or online chat that's accessible from the partner's web site? Understanding the partner's needs will help you come up with a creative proposal that will get them excited.

- *They need a timely or seasonal marketing hook.* Every company has its high and low seasons. Both provide opportunities for you to help. Consider how you might help create a story during a critical time of year for marketing. In spring 2004, the Easter Seals organization partnered with Just Born, Inc., the maker of those popular fluffy marshmallow chicks and bunnies that populate Easter baskets. This is a great example of both seasonal timing and partnering with a corporation whose products fit with your name or cause. The result was a fun PR element that added an online dimension to the larger PEEPS campaign. The event helped generate awareness and donations for the charity and brought in great PR for the company during their peak business season. According to Matthew Pye at Just Born, "The eBay auction helped generate over 415 million impressions, a value of over four million dollars."

PEEPS®, Just Born, Inc.© 2005

- *They want to add a charity component to a larger marketing campaign.* Charity can add a nice dimension to a planned marketing program. For example, in the Just Born/Easter Seals collaboration we just mentioned, the online auction was an extension of a real-world tour and marketing event. The online auction extended the PEEPS tour's promotional reach beyond those on their world tour route and added an interactive, philanthropic, and fun component to their overall campaign.

The other factors that can influence a partner's decision to participate in fundraising with you include:

- How well-known your organization is.

- How creative and fitting your idea is.

- The audience, contacts, auction items, or other partners you bring to the table.

- How easy you can make it for the partner to participate. (The less time and costs involved for them, the more likely they are to help out.)

- How flexible you are and whether or not you have your own budget for the event. (Some companies will be willing to participate only if they can recoup their project costs and have the net proceeds go to charity rather than 100 percent of proceeds go to charity.)

Fundamentally, you want to show a for-profit company why partnering with you makes sense, how your program will fit into, complement, and extend what it is already doing in marketing, and how you can help integrate and provide measurable results to justify the effort of its participation.

How Chivas Made Cause-Related Marketing a Regal Affair

When Chivas Regal turned 200 in September 2001, it wanted to celebrate the birthday in grand style. Taking cause-related marketing to an unprecedented new level, it raised more than £500,000 for charity by auctioning off a number of incredible experiences that "Money Can't Buy." Entitled "CHIVAS 200, The Online Charity Auction," it celebrated its 200 years of excellence by placing more than 200 donated items and experiences up for auction, including:

- MiG-25 and MiG-29 flights, which sold for £16,000

- An audience with Pope John Paul II, which sold for £10,100

- Ballooning with Sir Richard Branson, which went for £8,500

This is not to mention original art, dinner with celebrities, a private Pilates session with Elle Macpherson, and a full Harry Potter collection of books signed by J.K. Rowling.

Perhaps the most impressive part of this endeavor was Chivas' tremendous success in tapping into a truly worldwide audience, leveraging and listing items on multiple eBay global sites, to raise £500,000 to assist hundreds of nonprofits and benefit millions of people.

How Does Cause-Related Marketing Work?

As we discussed earlier, there are many ways to work with partners, but to get a better sense of the possibilities, we've highlighted some of the events that have been held on eBay, the unique items a variety of companies and media outlets that have sold, and what other sellers, corporations, and celebrities have brought to the auction table and have attained by participating. These concrete examples are often the best way to inspire ideas that might fit with your goals.

Creating One-of-a-Kind Items and Experiences: Mattel Pays Attention to the Collector

When it comes to helping you offer exciting items in a charity auction, partners are often in the unique position to provide something no one else can—for example, a tour of the factory, a chance to go behind the scenes, a chance to meet a leader, etc. Often partners can put together fabulous experiences at a relatively low cost to them and a very high perceived value for collectors and customers.

Consider the priceless items Mattel's Boys/Entertainment division has brought to the eBay auction block. The division really understands its collector community and how to put together a package that raises a lot of money for charity, drums up excitement for their collectors, and provides great brand exposure for the company. Here's a look at some of Mattel's early eBay highlights:

- In 1999, Mattel built the "World's Longest Hot Wheels Track," measuring 2,863 feet long, then auctioned off small sections of the nostalgic bright orange track signed by celebrities such as Paul Newman, Michael Keaton, Jackie Joyner-Kersee, Willie Nelson, and NASCAR drivers Jeff Gordon, Richard Petty, and Kyle Petty. A portion of the proceeds were donated to various children's charities and the Winston Cup Racing Wives Auxiliary.

- In 2001, Mattel auctioned off the chance to be a Hot Wheels "Designer for the Day" complete with the chance to meet with famed 30-year veteran Hot Wheels designer Larry Wood. Proceeds from this chance to experience a dream job for the day benefited nonprofits aiding the victims of the 9/11 tragedy.

- In 2002, Mattel commemorated the Matchbox 50th Anniversary with The Matchbox "Ultimate Collectible," a one-of-a-kind, miniature Seagrave "Meanstick" fire engine, crafted entirely in gold and precious gems. It sold for $27,450—at the time, and perhaps still, the highest price ever paid for a single toy sold on eBay. The auction close coincided with the Matchbox National Convention, where the item was displayed for collectors to view. According to a Mattel press release, the winning bidder, Arthur Thomas, said, "The Matchbox 'Ultimate Collectible' truly piqued my collecting interest. I really got wrapped up in the nostalgia of the item and its connection to the 50th anniversary of Matchbox. . . . Knowing that the money was going to an excellent cause like the Ronald McDonald House Charities made the purchase even more satisfying."

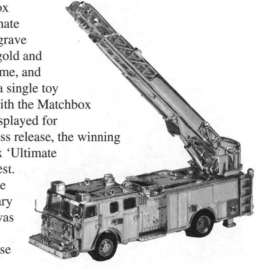

MATCHBOX® is a trademark owned by and used with permission from Mattel, Inc. ©2005 Mattel, Inc. All Rights Reserved.

Using Expertise to Make a Difference: *Harper's Bazaar* Helps Open Purses

In the aftermath of the December 2004 tsunami, *Harper's Bazaar* magazine wanted to help. But what could a fashion magazine do to provide relief to the tens of thousands who had lost everything? It used what it knew and leveraged its magazine and web site to get the word out. *Harper's Bazaar* decided to help UNICEF by auctioning off the fashion that it knows so well. It called upon all the designers who had handbags featured in its March 2005 issue and asked them, as well as a number of celebrities, to donate handbags for a special charity auction.

The response was excellent; upon receiving 70 donated designer handbags (see Figure 11-3), *Harper's Bazaar* enlisted the third-party service Portero, (**www.portero.com**) to list the items on eBay for them. According to *Harper's Bazaar* executive editor in chief Jenny Barnett, "The designers were thrilled to participate and the readers had the chance to be the first to own some of the hottest new fashion trends from top designers while helping a good cause at the same time. The fact that the items had been featured in the magazine made them even more collectible and desirable."

FIGURE 11-3 Partnering with a magazine like *Harper's Bazaar* may offer opportunities for acquiring unique items, as well as expanding the reach of both pre and post publicity for the auction and charity beneficiary.

To further add to the provenance, *Harper's Bazaar* enclosed a letter from editor in chief Glenda Bailey, thanking the buyer for participating in the fundraiser; and some of the designers handwrote notes to the accompany their bags. *Harper's Bazaar* pitched its charity auction to its readers in the March issue and then also followed up in the May issue to let readers know how the event turned out. The auction was a tremendous success, netting $37,000 for UNICEF and providing a unique outlet for *Harper's Bazaar* to engage with its readership and provide relief to those suffering halfway around the world.

In addition to promoting the auctions, if you ask, partners will often put a link to your nonprofit web site or a link to how to donate online on their sites as well.

Pairing with a Purpose: Marc Ecko Gets an Apple for the Fashion Teachers

When Marc Ecko, who we profiled in Chapter 2, became the newest member of the Council of Fashion Designers of America Board of Directors, he was challenged to find a new way to involve fashion in charity giving, and that was when he came up with A Case for a Cause, a fundraising initiative for the Fashion Targets Breast Cancer (FTBC). What made his effort unique was that he deliberately sought out partners that would help him achieve his personal and business goals of "bringing new energy to the organization using art, music, and youth culture." Ecko's pairing of Apple iPods, one-of-a-kind carrying cases created by fashion designers, and playlists customized by celebrities created great buzz for the designers and Apple as well as the cause.

Ecko took it one step further by introducing a mass-produced iPod case he designed as part of A Case For a Cause (a light-blue leather case featuring FTBC's signature bull's-eye logo) and packaging it with literature on breast cancer awareness. The case, shown here, was initially available only at Apple stores. By doing this, he extended the reach of the event, increased education on breast cancer, promoted his Marc Ecko brand to the Apple audience, and provided Apple with an exclusive item to offer in their stores.

Finding the Right Cultural Fit: Montblanc Uses the Pen to Battle Illiteracy

According to its eBay About Me page Montblanc is "Founded on one of the oldest forms of human culture, writing, the company feels it has a moral and cultural duty to confront the global problem of illiteracy." Playing to its corporate image of premier writing implements, Montblanc joined with UNICEF to fight illiteracy by auctioning of a number of its pens (see Figure 11-4).

Beyond the cause to further literacy, UNICEF was also a good fit for Montblanc as a global company. The company wanted a nonprofit that served all its major markets: France, Germany, and so on, as well as English-speaking countries.

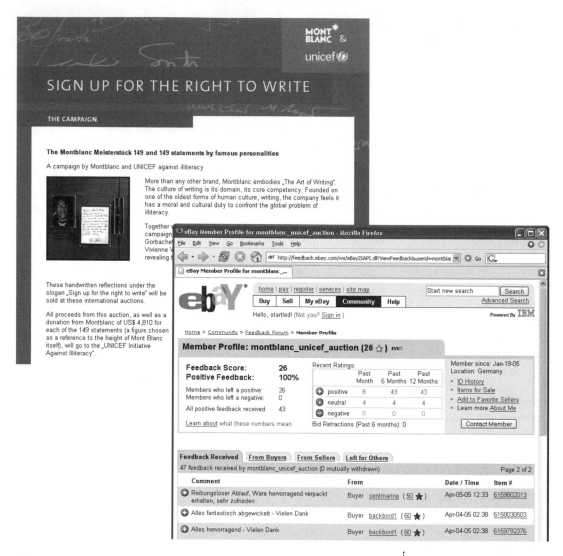

FIGURE 11-4   Montblanc made its listings available in multiple languages to reach buyers around the world.

tip   *If you have the bilingual resources, consider writing your item descriptions in multiple languages and listing them on other eBay country-specific sites such as eBay.de (Germany). This increases the number of people bidding on your items as well as awareness for your cause in other countries.*

Launching New Lines: BMW Is First off the Line

You don't have to create an event to produce a hard-to-get experience. Sometimes you can make an event out of something that's happening already. Take, for example, when BMW auctioned the chance to purchase the first BMW X5 Sports Activity Vehicle, complete with the opportunity to be there as it rolled off the line. BMW not only gave one person the chance to purchase a car *before* it was available to the public, but it also turned the event into a once-in-a-lifetime experience by adding in a factory tour and specialized driving instruction on the Performance Center's driving skills course. One hundred percent of the top bid of $159,100, as compared the suggested retail price of $57,105, was donated to the Susan G. Komen Breast Cancer Foundation. BMW also used the auction to promote its Ultimate Drive program, which encourages people to test-drive BMWs by donating $1 to the Komen Foundation for every mile that's test-driven during these events.

It is not just cars that hold the "first" appeal. When PDAs (personal data assistants) were first all the rage, Handspring gave bidders the chance to be the first on their block to own the very first Handspring Treo 180 communicator with a built-in keyboard. Starbucks offered bidders the chance to be among the first to own the Starbucks Barista Utopia vacuum coffee brewer, as well as three Once-in-a-Lifetime trips to Seattle, the home of Starbucks, featuring coffee with the then-Starbucks chairman and a tour of the roasting plant. That experience may not excite everyone but to the true Starbucks aficionado, you can imagine he was hearing a chorus of angels singing when he saw that auction. If you can partner with a company that's willing to provide you with the prototype or to prerelease a limited quantity for your cause, you can often raise significant donations because people are willing to pay a premium far over retail just to be the first to own the latest, greatest creations (even if they're the first only by a week or two!).

Launching a Ride and Park Attendance: Six Flags Takes Bidders to New Heights

A new roller coaster is news but being the first to ride a new roller coaster is radical. For fans of roller coasters, in the past the only way to be the first was be lucky and to stand in line for a long, long time. Six Flags used the opening of a new roller coaster as an opportunity to help both those who really wanted to be first onboard and a charity at the same time. It auctioned off the seats on the roller coaster's maiden voyage.

Bidding was hot (see Figure 11-5), and participation great—getting Six Flag free mentions in the media, which saved advertising dollars and extended publicity for the new ride. Bottom line, the auction contributed to the company's overall goal of increasing attendance to the park. If you hear about a hot new attraction or exhibit being added to an amusement park or a museum, there's often an opportunity to piggyback on the marketing strategies while helping the organization make the event more exciting by auctioning off premier experiences before the general public is allowed in. The nonprofit component makes it especially appealing to consumers and media.

FIGURE 11-5 Unusual experiences get a lot of bids and help reach a niche audience—in this case, roller coaster enthusiasts.

Engaging Celebrities: Julien's Auctions
Serves Up Stars' Guitars

Bringing together Gibson Guitar and Hard Rock Café corporations was just the first step for Darren Julien of Julien's Auctions. He wanted to come up with something unique to auction off—not just a celebrity autographed guitar but a one-of-a-kind work of art. To make it happen, he needed guitars, and musicians willing to expand their definition of recording "artist." Gibson came through with the guitars, friend Téa Leoni and Hard Rock Café helped find the musicians, and thirty musicians-turned-artists came through with amazing embellished guitars of all descriptions to benefit the Expedition Inspiration Fund for Breast Cancer Research.

The key to Julien's success was coming up with unique works, and using eBay Live Auctions to combine bidding with a real-world auction to get the best of both worlds. According to Julien, "Online auctions get things moving more quickly. Normally in a live auction, if a person is interested they will wait until the end and bidding gets off to a slow start. With the online element, they know they need to get in there or miss out, so it really generates excitement." In fact, although the guitar (shown here) from U2 guitarist The Edge sold to Gary Shandling at the live auction for $25,000, the Joe Perry guitar had no bids from the auction floor but still sold for $18,000 to a gentleman in Japan through online bidding.

Now that other people are jumping on board with celebrity art, Julien is looking for his next big idea. Taking what he learned from this event, he plans to create a benefit for Amnesty International—"Time Is Running Out." He plans to engage celebrities by having them donate watches they have worn, together with a picture of them sporting the actual auction item on their wrist.

To get a great event off the ground, Julien says, "All it takes is a fresh idea and someone with clout . . . that, and a lot of hard work." So once you have those elements, now the work really begins.

How Do You Work with a Partner?

Working with a partner gives you more resources, but it also requires more resources. As a team player, you have an obligation to look after your partner's image and brand as if it were your own. It will be important to set your partner's expectations appropriately upfront and manage those expectations through good communication and updates as needed. Remember the person you're working with will have to report results and answer questions about the event; make sure she can.

Set Goals for Your Event

Every partner will have different processes and expectations. But once you have more cooks involved, you need to make sure everyone is looking at the same recipe. As with any recipe, you'll need to understand what the ingredients for your charity auction are, who's providing the ingredients, and when and how the ingredients will be combined.

- Clearly determine goals (short-term and long-term opportunities)
- Identify the scope and timing of the event
- Agree upon the measurable results for both parties
- Assign tasks and resource contributions for both parties
- Put together a written agreement such as a Letter of Agreement

It's important to spell out who will have the lead on different tasks and which tasks will need partner review or approval. As you've seen, the components of a successful online auction include product solicitation, product listings, listing and web design, auction management and customer support, payment and shipping, and marketing and branding, including pre and post publicity. List out what resources each partner is bringing to the table.

Give Yourself Enough Time

Allow plenty of time to work with a partner and to get into his planning processes. The more advance time he has, typically, the more integrated the auction can be with other programs. Try to understand when and how you can tie in with partner events, schedules, and existing marketing. If you're an adjunct to a larger campaign, get an overview of the program and how you fit in. If you're the main focus, figure out the timing and results the company seeks and take steps ahead of time so that you'll be able to receive feedback and measure results.

Remember that partners will have their own review processes, often including legal, public relations, and brand reviews and approvals. Check to make sure you have copies of their brand guidelines for the design, colors, and use of the logo. For example, often different versions of a logo are available depending on the background color the logo is placed against. Try to ensure that partner trademarks and brands are handled carefully and that they're properly acknowledged in the *mouse print*, the legal text in small print at the bottom of all printed and online pages that contain partner logos.

Observe the "Four Cs"

Make sure you have the four C's for a successful partnership: Communication, Coordination, Collaboration, and Commitment for the event:

- *Communicate* formally, ideally at a weekly touch-base phone meeting, as well as through ongoing e-mails.

- *Coordinate* to make sure schedules are in-sync and deliverables are received in a timely manner (from both sides!).

- *Collaborate* to make sure both parties are reaching their goals and leveraging the tools available. Pooling ideas and resources such as e-mail, newsletters, web sites, and press releases is an essential part of successfully marketing and promoting the auctions.

- *Commit* not just physical resources but also staff resources—both sides need a primary contact at the partner company to help get things done, navigate the reviews and approvals process, and champion the program and the cause internally as well as to the public.

Let's add a fifth C—*Congratulations*. Don't forget to congratulate and thank each other to close the loop with your partner after the event. Share your "after auction" analysis to showcase the results and determine what worked well, as well as what you can build upon to create an even more successful event next time.

must have

In this chapter we explored how companies and celebrities are adding a new dimension to nonprofit fundraising. Much more than charity, cause-related marketing is good business. And the key to both the nonprofit and the company having a successful experience almost always comes down to marketing, so in the next chapter we'll look at ways you can tell people about your event—not just to get them to bid, but also to cultivate new donors for the nonprofit and new customers for the corporate partners.

In this chapter, you learned that:

- Participating in a charity auction is more than goodwill; it's good for businesses.

- Think like a business and look for synergies to figure out who can benefit most from a relationship with your nonprofit.

- Businesses need measurable results, so find out what they're trying to achieve and make sure you set up ways to track those activities in advance. When the businesses are successful, they're more willing to support your event again in the future.

- Working with a partner opens the door to resources and a variety of new auction items.

- Working with a partner takes more time, planning, reviews, and approvals.

Chapter 12
Marketing to Make the Most of Your Event

We were on every TV station in town, in the daily newspapers, on radio stations, and event got coverage in The New York Times *and* The Washington Post.

—Thom Karmik, Illinois
Institute of Technology

What We'll Cover in This Chapter:

- Using the power of grassroots marketing

- Creating effective press releases

- Promoting your event online

- Leveraging search engines and e-mail to drive traffic to your auctions

- Discovering "buzz" marketing

- Remembering post-event marketing opportunities and benefits

The refrain "If you build it, they will come," which originated in the baseball movie *Field of Dreams* in 1989, is now part of the public lexicon. However, that message doesn't always hold true online, especially where fundraising events on eBay are concerned. As Maria Hermann, of the Points of Light Foundation, explains in her case study posted on the web site of MissionFish, eBay's charitable arm: "The fact that our proceeds support a nonprofit makes people feel good when they buy, but we still have to help them find us in the first place." In other words, you can build the best store, have the best items to auction off, and the most meaningful cause on the planet, but unless you market it, "they" will not come. Marketing, my friends, is why you get paid the big bucks (ha ha, a little nonprofit humor there).

Effective marketing can make the difference between a resounding success and a small-scale, low-key fundraiser. We're not saying if you list a few regular items each day that they will not sell. One of the great things about eBay is that those items do, in fact, sell on a regular basis, for market prices and without much fanfare. But for nonprofits, the stakes are too high. In order for you to take full advantage of your donations and to make major charity events successful you'll need to invest some time and energy into marketing, following the suggestions we present in this chapter.

Combining Offline and Online Marketing Opportunities

Just because your event is online, don't make the mistake of assuming that going online is the only way people will find your event. Think of your fundraiser in the same terms that you think about a real-world event. If you were having a black-tie ball or a bake sale, you would let people know the event was happening. You would give them a deadline to donate or sign up, and have a place where they could get more information. The same holds true for your online event; make sure you convey that information and have a place for prospective donors to go to find out more. Get the word out on the real and virtual streets.

Taking It to the Streets

Start with your bread and butter. Make sure your loyal supporters know what's going on, how to bid, and when to bid. Even though your goal may be to bring in funds from outside your community, it's important not to skip or ignore your constituency. You have access to your constituents through e-mail and solicitation letters, as well as other communications, so this means you don't have to outlay funds for promoting this event. Rather, you can piggyback on mailings that were already going to happen as part of your routine campaigns. Your current donors already feel positive about you and will try to support you any way they can. Not only that, but if you follow the tips for product selection that we present in Chapter 4, you're probably offering some experiences and items they won't want to miss out on, especially if there are some great local connections. Consider these old-school, tried-and-true vehicles to get the word out:

- **Letters and newsletters**   Leverage newsletters and solicitation letters that you've already budgeted for and are scheduled to be mailed by promoting the charity auction. Be sure to tell recipients how to participate (donate and bid). You may even wish to time your auctions to coincide with these mailings.

> **tip**   *eBay and MissionFish have collected sample newsletter articles and letters that are a great resource as you draft your materials. You will need to sign in first to reach the Tips and Tools page: www.missionfish.org/include/toolstips/tools.jsp*

- **Word of mouth**   Don't underestimate the power of people. eBay's huge success is built in large part to grassroots growth as a direct result of collectors telling other collectors about the company. Make sure influential people in your community promote the event and solicit items at meetings they attend. Ask each person to tell five more people and so on. Leverage clubs and associations to create peer pressure (only in the best way) and a base of support.

- **Flyers**   Put flyers up in retail shops, coffee houses, college campuses, and libraries. Anywhere there is a community bulletin board, you should be there. Not only does this help you reach new people, but also this type of outreach provides reminders to both donate and bid for those who've already heard about the event. Flyers can also be a great PR vehicle for your donors. Along with your web site and other outreach vehicles, be sure to incorporate your sponsors' logos on flyers with the message "Please support our sponsors and tell them we sent you!" This gains you brownie points for helping your sponsors. It also helps sponsors quantify the value that they receive for their generosity, and helps them rationalize their participation as more than goodwill: it's, in fact, good business as well.

● **Press releases to local papers and TV** You can disseminate press releases the old-fashioned way, through the mail or fax to local media, or you can easily and cheaply release them through online wire services. The neat thing here is that at an age where information travels at Internet speed, local articles may be picked up and syndicated by wire services and information portals such as Yahoo!, etc., without any extra work on your part. Be sure to include links in your releases; it both drives traffic and helps your pages show up in search engines—more on this later. For local media (radio, TV, and local papers), it may be most effective to simply fax your press release to the news desk.

One of the samples eBay showcases is this postcard for MS (Multiple Sclerosis), which encourages its supporters to sell on its behalf (see Figure 12-1). You could create a similar postcard to solicit donations or publicize a "save the date" for your auction event.

FIGURE 12-1 Postcards and flyers help you connect with donors who are already on your mailing lists.

To get attention for your event, make your press release as effective as possible. Observe the dos and don'ts summarized in Table 12-1.

Also be sure to include:

- A link directly to your eBay listings or eBay About Me page (or a page on your own web site if you have a link to your items there). Don't muddy the water with more than one link. (Consider using a trackable link so you know where your leads come from.)

- A compelling picture.

- A strong headline (no more than approximately 8–10 words).

- Contact information, including a phone number.

Do	Don't
Be concise and to the point. No more that 400 words is recommended. No one wants to read a ten-page release.	Write in first or second person. In other words, avoid using "we" do this, or "you" can do this. Write in the third person, such as: "Through various efforts, Important Foundation provides services for children ages 8–18."
Focus on urgency. Not who you are, but why the event is interesting now. To get started, complete the sentence "People need to know about this today because …"	Tell a story. Instead, convey the goal that you want to accomplish clearly (and what action you want people to take).
Emphasize the novelty or uniqueness of the items offered for sale, or the unusual aspects of the event. Leverage celebrity involvement prominently. If the items are not unique, focus on the volume of items (selling 1,000 items to help 1,000 kids) or theme (selling red items on Valentine's Day to fight heart disease).	Spend a lot of time talking about you. Beyond saying that proceeds will benefit your nonprofit, save the more detailed organization information for the end, where you can include who you are, what you do, and who you serve.
Convey a local angle for local media. Why do people in your community want to know about this event, and how are local people and organizations involved as sponsors, donors, or beneficiaries.	
Tie into current events. Is there a local headline news item related to your organization? For example, during a story on reported increases in homelessness and hunger, a fundraiser for one of the nonprofits serving this community might merit an on-air mention or a sidebar article in the newspaper next to the lead story.	
Be there to answer the phone the day the press release goes out.	

TABLE 12-1 Dos and Don'ts for Marketing Your Fundraising Event

How to Put a Press Release on the Wire Services

While you may want to contact local media personally, there are some great advantages to putting a press release out on the wire services. Once a release is online, it may be picked up by multiple venues as well as search engines increasing exposure for the event and awareness for your cause. You have a few options. Depending on the newsworthy nature of your event, you could try submitting a release in the following ways:

- *Submit your press release directly to the Associated Press (AP) (**www.ap.org**) or Reuters (**www.reuters.com**) news services.* You can e-mail submissions with national or international significance to AP info@ap.org. To submit press releases in the U.S. to Reuters, you can e-mail press releases to editor@reuters.com.

> **note** *Do not send attachments in e-mail messages—either paste the release into the body of your e-mail or include a return address on your envelope and mail your press release to AP's General/National Desk or International Desk at Associated Press, 450 W. 33rd St., New York, NY 10001.*

- *Go local.* If you have a story of regional significance, you can send your release directly to a local AP bureau (there is one in every state) or you can send press releases to specific departments by consulting AP's list of Beats, AP editors, and Writers (**www.ap.org/pages/contact/contact_pr.html**).

- *Pay a major service.* A major service can release your press release to the major news outlets and journalists—the two main ones are the Business Wire and PR Newswire, but there are others. Both offer discounts for registered nonprofits but it will still run you $200–$500 dollars per release depending on the length of your release and the reach (exposure) you want.

  Submit the release by providing the following information in an online form: headline, dateline, contact information, distribution preferences, and then the actual release (using copy and paste or as an attachment). The service will review the release and take care of formatting it to comply with AP Style, grammar, and so forth, as well as adding keywords that will help people and search engines find your release. Releases can go out immediately or be scheduled for a specific day and time.

- *Utilize cheaper or free wire services.* Generally these services' databases of subscribing journalists are smaller than those of the more expensive services, but they may include some interesting outlets such as *blogs* (web logs), which the larger services do not serve. For example, Eworldwire (**http://eworldwire .com**) charges $75–$300, depending on your distribution, less a 10%–1% discount for nonprofits, and includes AP, Reuters, local papers, magazines, and blogs on its distribution lists. Free services are an option for those on a tight budget and include ArriveNet, PR Leap, and PR Web, among others.

- *Take advantage of nonprofit specific wire services.* According to its web site, AScribe newswire (**http://ascribe.org**) "delivers public-interest news releases from more than 600 nonprofit organizations and governmental agencies—including foundations, public-policy advocates, professional associations, think tanks, colleges, universities, medical and scientific research centers, publishers, and public relations agencies." Annual membership is $125, and as a nonprofit you can choose packages including five releases for $425. There are others, some specific to particular causes, so if your nonprofit's focus is on saving the environment, for example, you might choose to use the Environment News Service, (**www.ens-newswire.com**), which breaks stories affecting the environment. So take a look to see if there's a service that will reach editors and magazines specific to your cause.

Internet Marketing: Hitting the Virtual Streets

Internet marketing encompasses everything from web site marketing to keyword advertising, to e-mail marketing and search optimization. There are many new tools in your new marketing arsenal and it's a good idea to get familiar with them so you can pick and choose the ones that work best for you. Don't feel overwhelmed or think that you must do all of these things. Rather, this is a menu and you can pick and choose what you feel like having at this particular event given your staffing, technical know-how, and scope of the event.

Promote Your Event from Your Web Site

There is much you can do to promote your own event on your own web site. If you have your own web site in addition to your eBay About Me or Store page, you need to promote your event from the home page and, ideally, link to a new page specific to the fundraiser. This page should talk about how interested people can participate. Whether you're encouraging people to sell on your behalf or to donate items or bid on items, this is your venue to explain who, what, where, when, why and, equally important, how.

Link to Your eBay Listings from Your Own Web Site

Use eBay and MissionFish link buttons to direct traffic to your listings. Once you're registered with MissionFish, go to **www.missionfish.org** and sign in. Then, click Tools and Tips in the left navigation column. Click Tools to Download and scroll down to the Links library. The site walks you through how to save the graphics you want to your computer, identify the URL for your MissionFish home page, and add them to your home page or auction page on your site (see Figure 12-2). You can also choose to link directly to your eBay Store or About Me page if you prefer.

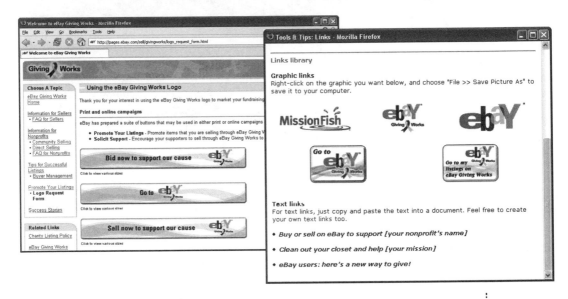

FIGURE 12-2 Choose between promoting community selling on your behalf or linking to the items you're selling—or both.

If you're not using eBay Giving Works and MissionFish (for the reasons we discussed in earlier chapters, such as bulk loading), then you'll need to use the more generic eBay buttons, banners, and logos. From the eBay home page, click the Site Map, then in the center column under Manage My Items for Sale, select Promote your listings with link buttons or search on the page for "buttons" if this link has moved. Or better yet, use the Affiliate links that we'll describe shortly.

Show Your eBay Listings on Your Web Page

Even more compelling than a link, the more advanced and totally optional alternative is to actually showcase your listings on your web site in real-time. People love to see what you're selling and what the current prices are. eBay provides a Merchant Kit to help you do this. It's basically one line of HyperText Markup Language (HTML) code that eBay generates for your eBay User ID and that you or your webmaster can easily add to your web site. For more information, go to **http://pages.ebay.com/api/merchantkit .html**; see Figure 12-3 for an example. For extra kicks you can even embed your premium auction items and current prices into banner ads if you'd like. For more information on that, read up on the eBay Editor Kit (EK) at **http://affiliates.ebay.com/tools/editor-kit/**.

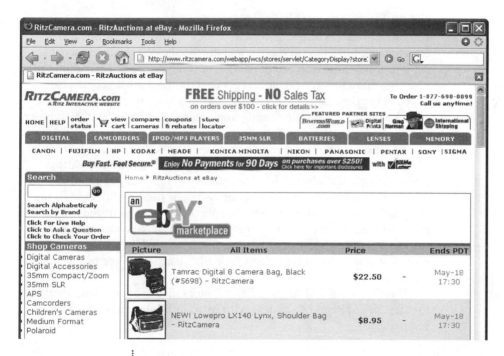

FIGURE 12-3 RitzCamera promotes its eBay auctions on its corporate web site using the Merchant Kit.

Show People How to Use eBay on Your Site

In addition to linking people to your listings or the location where they can begin listing items to sell for you, it can be really helpful to let people know what to expect when they get there. For example, include text such as "Registering on eBay is easy, free, and fast. Once you enter some simple information (name, address, e-mail) and confirm your registration when you get the e-mail from eBay, you can start bidding immediately!"

Or if you're encouraging others to sell for you, you might include links to one of eBay's How to Sell Tutorials or describe the process as being as simple as filling out a form and describing the item that you're selling.

If you really want to encourage selling, you might consider hosting and promoting an information night where a volunteer who's an experienced eBay seller or Trading Assistant walks other newbies through the selling process. It can be a fun community event and a way to kick off a fundraising campaign by encouraging each person to bring one item with them to list (and maybe having a shipping party a week later when the auctions close!).

Get on Board with Affiliate Programs

Hey, what gives? You're sending a lot of new traffic over to eBay and even training folks how to register and use the site. We think you should get something for that and so does eBay. As long as you're adding links to your site, make them trackable and get paid for those great people you're directing to eBay. Enter the eBay Affiliate Program. Here's how it works. eBay keeps track of people coming from your site and whether they register or bid. If they do, eBay pays you.

To get started go to the eBay home page (**www.ebay.com**), click on the tiny word Affiliate at the very bottom of the page or simply go to **http://pages.ebay.com/affiliates/**. It's free and easy to join and you could earn up to $45 per *active registration* (meaning each new person who registers on eBay and bids on or buys an item). Simply follow the instructions on the eBay Affiliates page to join Commission Junction, confirm registration, select the buttons or banners you wish to use, and add them to your site any place that you're driving people to your eBay items or telling people how to register on eBay.

For eBay's army of Affiliate links, buttons, and banners, some specific to categories of items or holidays, visit **http://affiliates.ebay.com/tools/banners/**.

$$$ moneymaker

There are a number of Affiliate Programs out there besides eBay. If you find yourself talking about a book or product that could be helpful to your community, why not link to places where community members buy those items using affiliate programs—you help people find the items they want, it helps other sites sell products, and you make a small amount of revenue that can help fund your nonprofit activities. For example, Amazon.com, Target, and many others offer programs and usually that little affiliate link is a text link at the very bottom of their home pages.

Promote Your Items on eBay

In the earlier chapters, we discussed how to make an effective listing and mentioned some of the upgrades that are available to you to make your listings stand out. You already have the ribbon icon next to your items, which will help draw attention if you have listed the items through eBay Giving Works and MissionFish. But eBay offers many other ways to help you increase traffic.

Submit Your Event to eBay Giving Works

There are a few places on eBay where your item can receive some additional promotion and exposure to drive more bidding on your items. Primarily, the promotion space exists on the Giving Works page under the In the Spotlight section for featured events or in the Shop by Nonprofit area. Due to space limitations, this promotion space is typically reserved for larger events, but it never hurts to submit your event for consideration even if you consider it to be small-scale.

To be considered for this additional promotion, e-mail eBay Giving Works (givingworks@ebay.com) and provide information about your event (eBay User ID, contact information, start and end dates, types of items, your cause, planned media outreach, the URL for your About Me page, and so on). In addition, you need to create and attach small graphics (sometimes called *widgets* or *icons*) that can be used to promote your auction (see Figure 12-4, and visit **http://givingworks.ebay.com/promote/** for more information). Information and the graphics need to be received at least two weeks prior to your event.

The graphics are a standard 100×100 pixel size, but the format varies depending on where you want to receive promotion. It might be worthwhile creating two to four versions of the graphics, one promoting the event or nonprofit, and a few others promoting the specific items being sold to benefit the nonprofit. If it's a major event or high priced item(s), Giving Works may work with the eBay PR and merchandising departments to seek additional promotion for the event elsewhere on the eBay site, but this is by far the exception and not something you should count on—unless your name is Jay, Oprah, or Ellen.

$$$moneymaker

The graphics you create are different sizes depending on where you'd like to be promoted. Providing two to four versions may increase the odds of being seen.

Widgets

FIGURE 12-4 Be sure to send Giving Works some small graphics called *widgets*.

The other way to get involved with eBay is to participate in organized fundraising efforts. When eBay senses that the community wants to respond to a crisis and is looking for ways to help, eBay will help bring together and promote community members, corporations, and nonprofit efforts to raise funds. Some examples are Auction for America, Tsunami Disaster Relief, and Hurricane Katrina Recovery. If your organization is involved in recovery from a disaster, let eBay know so that it can inform the eBay community on how to assist in raising funds for your efforts. Keep in mind that it is helpful to have already registered on MissionFish, and to have a graphic of your logo ready in advance of an emergency. This will allow you to quickly notify eBay and take advantage of this fundraising opportunity with minimal time taken away from the other pressing activities.

eBay has also aided many nonprofits during Breast Cancer Awareness Month in October and has annually sought to support giving during the holidays in November and December. eBay supports these fundraising efforts through the creation of a portal page, an example of which is shown in Figure 12-5, aggregating nonprofits that aid those causes and marketing that page and the nonprofit participants and listings throughout the site using links, banners, and graphics. This creates awareness and drives buyers to the nonprofit listings. It's obviously a huge boon to the nonprofits involved as it helps their auctions rise above the crowds on eBay and causes a spike in bidding and support. Watch for future organized theme fundraising events, such as literacy campaigns coinciding with back-to-school time in September, etc., on the Giving Works portal, where eBay gives advance notice of upcoming events and details about how to get involved.

FIGURE 12-5 Every October eBay promotes and showcases charity auctions that benefit the fight against breast cancer.

Be Sure to Cross-Merchandise

If you have an eBay Store, be sure to take advantage of the powerful cross-promotion tools eBay provides (**http://pages.ebay.com/ merchandisingmanager/**). These tools enable you to determine which of your other items eBay will promote to users in the item listing pages and in the e-mails you send out confirming purchase and payment. The goal, of course, is to up-sell people into buying more than one item from you by showing them other great items or items related to the one they just bought.

Even if you only have an About Me page (and not a store), you can cross-promote your items from there by listing your other items for sale on the page. In the text of the About Me page, you can describe the items that have already been donated so people become aware of the neat items you're offering. You may also use the About Me page to drive interested donors to your web site for more information about your cause or to sign up for your newsletter. This way, even if shoppers don't end up buying, they can still become active donors or supporters.

Stir Up Some Viral Marketing

Every listing on eBay has an Email to a friend link in the top right that allows viewers to tell an acquaintance about the auction item. As a seller, you can encourage people to browse your listings and use the same link to send an e-mail that includes a link to that item. Encourage your supporters to do this and you'll find it's a nice tool for *viral marketing*—the all-important word-of-mouth publicity that has helped many web sites and online events become popular.

Build a Loyal Following

Encourage buyers to bookmark your page (in other words, to use their web browsers to Add a bookmark) and to save you as a favorite seller by clicking on the Add to Favorite Sellers link in the top right Seller Information box that appears on every eBay listing page. The latter will be important later if you have an eBay store and wish to use eBay's e-mail marketing tools to send newsletters and special information to those members who opt in.

From your About Me page, you can also encourage people to sign up for your regular e-mail nonprofit newsletter—which leads naturally to our next topic, e-mail marketing.

E-Mail Marketing

E-mail marketing is a great way to reach out and let people know about your event. It's low cost and generally not a very time-consuming method of communicating with prospective bidders. E-mail marketing, though, isn't without its own learning curve and legal considerations because people are cautious about spamming. If you're just setting up an e-mail marketing effort for the first time, the most important thing is to make sure people opt in to your e-mail and have the opportunity on every e-mail to opt out. The following sections present some ways to leverage e-mail in your own marketing efforts.

Seize the Signature

First of all, for any e-mail message you or your volunteers send out, be sure to include a promotional "signature" that appears at the conclusion of every e-mail. You can either copy and paste the same information onto your messages, or use your e-mail program to automatically append your signature file to each message. Many e-mail programs, including Netscape Navigator and Internet Explorer, include a signature option which will do just that. Everyone in your organization can customize his or her own signature file and help spread the word. Here is a simple sample signature (say that three times fast):

> *Your Name*
> *yourname@nonprofit.org*
> Participate in our auction on eBay to support the *nonprofit foundation*.
> Click here to learn more www.missionfish.org/cgt/nonprofit/np.show
> .home.do?NP_ID=(*fill in your nonprofit number by copying the URL*
> *from your MissionFish page*)

Consider eBay Store E-mail Marketing

eBay Stores offer their proprietors access to e-mail marketing tools to which other eBay sellers don't have access. You'll find them at **http://pages.ebay .com/storefronts/emailmarketing.html**. The tools allow you to create newsletters and send them to eBay users who add you to their favorite sellers and opt in to your newsletters. For most nonprofits, you're better off directing people to sign up for your regular newsletter, but if you don't yet have one, this can be an easy way to get started.

Leverage E-mail Communications

You'll likely have communication with your buyers as you answer questions, confirm shipping details, and receive payment. After you convey the information that pertains to a specific transaction, add an invitation to join your mailing list. Certainly use such outreach efforts to include a link or mention of the charity auction. There are four main times when you'll want to communicate with your supporters:

- When you're soliciting donations
- During prepromotion for the auction, approximately 30 days in advance of the sale to create awareness
- During the auction to drive bidding
- After the event to thank sponsors and share the success and results with your constituency

MissionFish's Giving Mail can help you create and format letters for your direct e-mail campaigns (**http://givingmail.com/ebay/**) but if you need help setting up a robust e-mail marketing program, consider some of the companies that specialize in this, such as Constant Contact (**www .constantcontact.com**) or Return Path (**www.returnpath.com**).

Search Engine Optimization and Search Marketing

How are people going to find your auctions? The first important thing to realize is that you'll need to market the product and not necessarily the event. Sure, if you're the Great Chicago Fire Sale, you want to promote the brand, but that's not what people are buying or searching for as a general rule. While you may think that your event is spectacular, the majority of people on eBay won't know about it, let alone be excited about it. On eBay, and the Internet in general, people are shopping for items and experiences. The cause adds value and can tip the scale in your direction if a shopper is deciding whether to bid on your item or those of competing sellers. It may even increase the amount of money a shopper will spend for the item, but, fundamentally, it doesn't drive the purchase decision. You need to find the people that want your goods or experiences. What does this mean? You need to optimize and market the specific items you're selling.

Optimize Your Site for Search Engines

You don't have to be a web wizard to do a few things to make your web site and your event found more easily by search engines. What search engines typically do is have *bots* crawl from site to site using links. They read and index the keywords you've added to your auction titles and sales description. This information is one of the key elements that helps determine which links show up highest (and for free) when people search the Internet. The easier you are to find, the more people will be able to find and bid on your items, so here are a few tricks of the trade:

- *Register your site directly with Google, Yahoo!, and MSN.* Ninety-five percent of search results come from these top three sites. If people are searching for your organization so they can make a donation, you want to make sure they can find you.

- *Don't use just pictures.* Search engines look for words, so if you show a picture of the items you're selling, be sure to caption the picture with a detailed description of the items and brands beneath the photo.

- *Get links from directories and sites relevant to the items you're selling.* We'll talk about this more in just a moment, but the important thing to understand is that the more sites that link to you, the more credible your site is to the search engines. Links act sort of like votes online and help the search engines prioritize who's valuable or important.

- *Use keywords.* If there is more than one way to describe the items you're selling, use them. Some people might search for cat but not kitten so if you only use one on your site, then some of the people searching won't find you. Embed keywords everywhere, including links—don't just say "click here for more information"; say "click here to bid on back stage passes to the concert."

- *Tell your web savvy volunteers or webmaster that it's recommended to put keywords in the meta tags, file names, and body text.* Also, tell them to avoid using frames and drop down menus, since the search engines have a hard time indexing those. They'll know what that all means.

> **tip** *Be sure people can find your organization online. Register to submit your site to the main search engines and directories: Google (**www.google.com/addurl.html**), Yahoo! (**http://submit.search.yahoo.com**), MSN (**http://search.msn.com/docs/submit.aspx**), and the Open Directory Project (**www.dmoz.org**). Also consider other nonprofit specific directories such as **http://charitynavigator.org** and **http://guidestar.org**. Guidestar will include any 501(c)(3) organization while Charity Navigator is primarily for large nonprofits.*

Get Speedy, Targeted Promotion Using Pay-per-Click

This is a short cut to use so you'll appear at the top of search engine results. What you do is "buy" very specific words on eBay, Google, or Yahoo!

Search so that when buyers search for those items, your listing appears at the top of search results. Sounds great but, of course, you do have to pay for this privilege. The key is to buy selected keywords that are affordable for just your big ticket items, and to buy them just for the duration of the auction and, perhaps, the week or so leading up to the event to increase awareness. Many specific terms are available at a very low cost. Typically, the cost is $0.10 per click but the actual price will vary depending on how many other people are bidding on those terms. Equally important, you can set a daily limit on how much you're willing to pay per day so you don't end up paying a fortune in marketing by mistake.

In the "olden days" of the Internet, people would talk about paying for ads based on the number of impressions or "eyeballs" that saw your advertisement. You would pay a flat fee or cost per 1,000 (CPM) impressions. Pretty soon people got the idea that most of their ads were ignored or reaching the wrong audience. They wanted more results and more accountability. So now you typically pay on a cost per click (CPC) basis, meaning you *only* pay when someone actually clicks on your ad! This is good news because if you can be very clear in your ad, you can encourage only truly potential bidders to click on your link.

Why bother paying at all? If you have a valuable offering, won't people find it? Not necessarily. With so many items available online, your listing may not appear at the top, or even the first few pages, of search results. Search engine optimization may take time and may not be successful or even worthwhile for short-term promotions and events. If you have some marketing budget and want people to find out about your great auction items, careful keyword marketing for select items makes sense. For a small marketing investment, you could literally double or triple the amount of money raised for some items. Why? Because if you have backstage tickets along with the chance to meet a celebrity, you need to make sure that many people—and especially the fans—know this experience is available. Your goal is to find two people who really want the item and let them bid the price of the experience up. Without that, you could be very disappointed when your Behind the Scenes meet and greet with the Blues Brothers sells for less than $1,000 rather than probably more than $5,000 if you'd reached the right fans.

There are three main places to do pay-per-click marketing for your eBay auctions: eBay, Google, and Yahoo! Search Marketing. eBay displays ads on its site only; the latter two both *syndicate* their listings, which means their search results are delivered through other search portals besides their own. For example, Microsoft search results are powered by Yahoo! right now, although it plans to launch its own keyword advertising in 2006. If you can bid enough to be in the top five paid results, you may find your ad appearing all over the Internet.

The first step in creating any keyword, or AdWord, marketing campaign is picking the items to promote and the keywords to use. Begin by reviewing your items to see which ones need the additional exposure and justify the expense or investment. Once you have done so, list the keywords that typically are associated with the celebrity or group name(s), the genre of music or movies, the venue or concert where the experience takes place, and the activity (concert, lecture, lunch, or book signing, for example). Then use the *keyword tools* from eBay, Google, and Yahoo! to evaluate the terms and find new ones (see Figure 12-6). Typically the tools will show you other related terms and phrases that people are searching for, and sometimes the number of times the phrases are searched on.

> note *Yahoo! typically includes plural terms automatically, but with Google, you'll have to add the plural form of your keywords. Later on when you're choosing your bid amount, you'll be able to see the competing bidders and the current cost-per-click to be in the top position for each keyword term.*

You're looking for advertising terms with reasonable impression rates, which are very specific to your event. Ask yourself: If someone was searching on those terms, would she definitely be interested in your item? If the answer is yes, then look at the cost-per-click. If it is more than 50 cents per click, you probably should try to narrow your term down further by combining the keyword with another related keyword. Often you will find two- or three-word phrases are less expensive and more targeted. (See the "Tips for Effective Keyword Ads" sidebar later in this chapter.)

Using Keyword Selection Tools

The most important part of setting up a pay-per-click campaign is selecting the best terms to use. Generally you should be as specific as possible to avoid paying too much, and the keyword suggestion tools will help you discover many combinations of words that will help you get to your target audience.

- To use Google's Keywords tool go to: **https://adwords.google.com/select/ KeywordSandbox**

- To use Yahoo! Keyword Selector tool go to: **http://searchmarketing.yahoo .com/srch/**

- To use eBay Keyword Suggestion Tool go to: **http://ebay.admarketplace.net/ ebay/servlet/ebay/template/KST.vm**

- To actually sign up with Google and start creating your ads, go to: **https:// adwords.google.com**

- Yahoo!: **http://searchmarketing.yahoo.com (formerly www.overture.com)**

- eBay: **http://ebay.admarketplace.net**

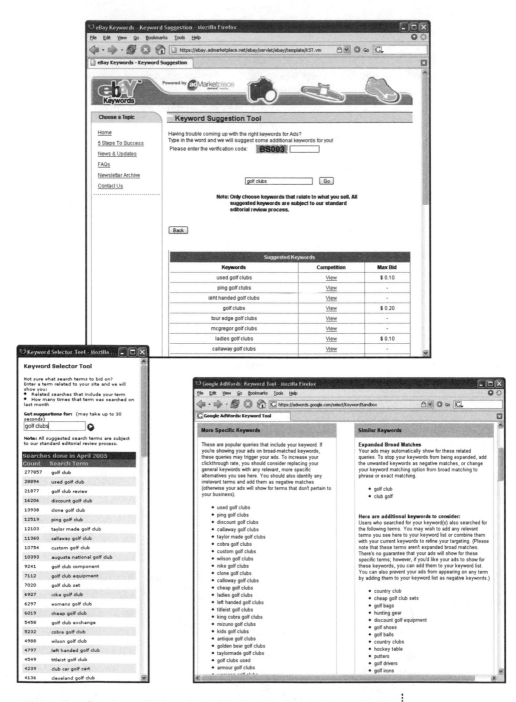

FIGURE 12-6 eBay, Google, and Yahoo! (clockwise from top) have keyword tools to help you choose the best terms for driving traffic to your auction items.

note   *You do* not *need to be in the number one position! In fact, it's probably the least profitable place to be as others come in and try to knock you down and compete by raising their bids. The happy and economical place to be is number three. Positions 3 to 5 are typically still syndicated and are usually much cheaper than top positions.*

Tips for Effective Keyword Ads

In order to write an effective ad:

- *Be clear.* Remember you only want people who are interested in bidding to click.

- *Be concise.* You have only about 95 characters (or letters), including spaces, so make every one count. Use abbreviations as necessary.

- *Use attention grabbing words.* For example: Once in a lifetime chance to meet "Celebrity X."

- *Include call to action.* "Bid now on this charity auction."

- *Mention nonprofit angle secondarily.* "Proceeds benefit 'X' Foundation."

- *Use the keywords in the description.* This has been shown to improve ad performance.

Choose the right *destination URL*, or landing page. This is the page people will see when they click on your ad link; it will usually be your eBay About Me or eBay Store page, or your MissionFish home page. It's not your nonprofit's home page in most cases, unless you're showcasing the listing on that page. Better yet, once the auction begins, link directly to the specific item you're advertising—the idea is you want to take interested people directly to where they can see the item that was described in the ad so they can bid on it with the fewest clicks and without having to search for it (because they won't).

Limit your ad distribution to your target audience. For example, if your listing is in English, you may want to limit the ad to run in the United States, Canada, the United Kingdom, and Australia. If you don't want to ship outside the United States, then don't run your ad outside of the United States.

Choose to limit your keywords to *exact match* to avoid showing up in unrelated searches. If you use *broad match*, you could show up in any search that includes your keywords in combination with any other words. If you're going to be doing charity auctions on an ongoing basis or want to play with the more advanced tools, take a look at using *negative match*, or excluding words that aren't relevant to your items. Similarly, there are ways to track *conversions* from your clicks. If you have a web person, he can look into this because it's nice to have reports summarizing the results of your campaign. But to be honest, that may be more advanced than most nonprofits need, especially for a one-time event.

Once you decide on your terms, you'll need to follow a few simple steps to set up your account and ads. With both Google and Yahoo! Search Marketing (shown in Figure 12-7), you'll need to register, write your ad (you can see a preview of how it will look as you create it), choose the

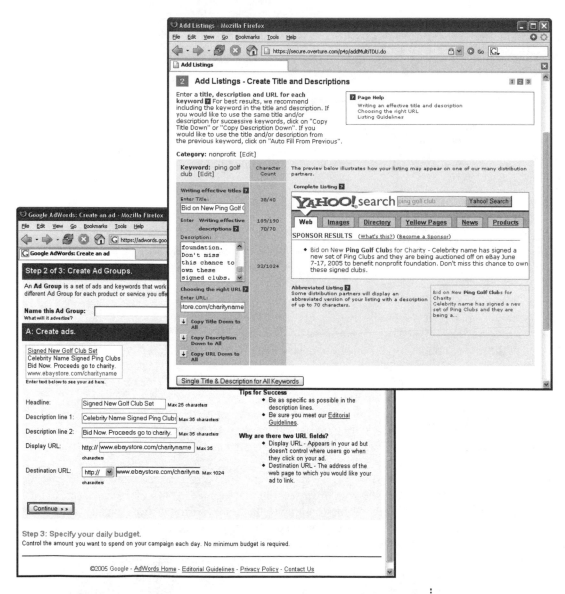

FIGURE 12-7 On Google and Yahoo!, your ad is shown to you real time as you enter the information.

landing page URL that you want people seeing the ad to click over to, associate the ad with your chosen keywords, place a bid for each keyword, set your daily maximum budget, and then submit your ad. Be sure to click the Calculate Estimates on Google and refine your terms before submitting your keyword ads. Google ads will go live almost immediately, while Yahoo! ads will be reviewed usually with 24 hours, before they go live.

eBay's Keyword Program works in a similar manner and will deliver your advertisement when people search on the eBay Marketplace for items. It's a great way to reach targeted shoppers already browsing on eBay. With eBay it's more difficult to do prepromotion for your items because the eBay Keywords Program requires that you must have at least one auction item to promote with more than 24 hours of auction time remaining. It's really designed for leading buyers to the items once they're available for purchase on eBay. You cannot use eBay Keyword ads to link to your web page from eBay nor can you use ads that include or suggest a URL. eBay recommends running two to three keyword phrases specific to the model of the product or the celebrity name, etc., and in combination with a specific ad message, for best results.

Buzz Marketing and Community Marketing

Do you *have* to spend money on pay-per-click ads to reach the right people? Of course not. You can do a little research and go straight to the online Mecca for the fans. This strategy can be very effective as you create "buzz" among the fans, which travels virally to others who share the same interest. The online Mecca for your auction item could be a celebrity fan site, a popular blog (weblog), a movie web site, or any other site where people interested in your item or experience gather to talk. Your goal is to have the webmasters of these sites put up a link to your page or the item listing. Many are happy to help out since they like to be the leading source of information on their subject or celebrity and, typically, love being the first to know and publicize exciting new information.

Here are a couple of key strategies for starting a "buzz":

- *Find the fans*. Find the top five–ten sites relevant to your anchor or high-value auction items and experiences. (See Figure 12-8.)

- *E-mail the webmaster*. Contact the webmaster or blogger, explain your event, and send your graphic or banner ad, a link, and more information about the event. The webmaster may even be willing to post a press release on the site as well.

- *Get on the boards yourself*. Get out there and chat with the fan base. Not only can you answer questions and build excitement for the event, but also you build awareness for your nonprofit cause at the same time.

FIGURE 12-8 Official fan sites and targeted niche news sites are a great way to get free publicity and reach a very enthusiastic group of fans.

- *Prepromote your event.* You can build awareness and schedule your event to be featured on community sites before the auction goes live. If you send information about upcoming events, the sites can let people know to watch for the event. When the auction actually starts, you can e-mail them the auction link as soon as it is live. Since you have already spoken with the webmaster and she understands the event, she can immediately add the information. Some sites even have calendars of upcoming events, which can be another place to promote your event. The alternative is having to explain things after the auctions have begun and the clock is ticking. Just trying to get in touch with the webmaster could take a week and then they will have missed the auctions entirely!

> *tip* *Andy Trilling of the Starlight Starbright Children's Foundation reports that when the foundation was auctioning off signed memorabilia and a visit to the set of the television show* Angel, *buzz marketing to star David Boreanaz's fan sites and other sites where the TV show's fans chatted was key to the items selling for top dollar. According to Trilling, "Doing research for celebrity fan sites doesn't take as much time as you would think and it is a great volunteer or intern project. Not only does your auction get more promotion but your volunteer team gains valuable Internet marketing skills in the process."*

Post-Event Marketing

Whew! The auction is over and everything went great. Time to heave a sigh of relief and bask in the glory of a job well done. Do that, but before too much time has gone by, take a moment to recap the event and summarize the results. You need to follow up with several folks: your sponsors, your volunteers, your buyers, and the media.

The Sponsors

It's a great idea to close the loop with sponsors. Not only does this make them aware of the value of their donations and convey your appreciation for their contributions, but it also opens the door for future donations. If you plan on holding the event again next year, it's not too early to mention your hope that they'll participate again and perhaps even brainstorm on other types of items or experiences they might provide in the future.

The Volunteers

Your event's volunteers will want to share in the success and hear how the funds raised will now be specifically used. More important, just like every other nonprofit endeavor, you want to recognize and give credit to the volunteers for their hard work. Closing the loop with them reminds them that their contribution is valued and has played an integral role in the success of the project.

The Buyers

This is your chance to cultivate new donors and express your appreciation for their support of your cause. By sending your buyers a thank you note or e-mail, you have the opportunity to make them feel like part of the campaign and part of the solution. Share your accomplishments and then invite them to subscribe to your newsletter so they can see how the funds raised will benefit your constituency.

The Media

If you had articles or media interviews before the event, send a follow-up note to those journalists you spoke with. Issue a follow-up press release summarizing the exciting auction highlights and total amount raised. If you can include testimonials from the celebrities or buyers, all the better. Many buyers will say that they were pleased that their purchase goes to benefit a good cause and will encourage others to support the cause as well. Any additional online or offline mentions you can secure extend the exposure for your organization and increase the PR value of your event for yourself and your sponsors.

Post-Event Analysis

If you haven't been doing so, this is a good time to go back and capture some screen shots of your successful auctions, your About Me page, and feedback from buyers. eBay, and many other sites, only keep event information for a limited time and if you try to go back later, you may find the pages are gone. Keep samples of your press releases, e-mails, newsletters, and flyers. Tally and print out all articles and calendar mentions about your event from various newspapers, magazines, and web sites, including blogs and other online mentions. If you used a free counter on your listings, or tracked the number of visitors to your site and total page views during the promotion, or used the keyword conversion tools, summarize these statistics in one place before all is lost and forgotten. Review your auctions to see which items sold for the highest amounts and which ones did not sell at all, even after being relisted. Keep photos of the highest-priced items that sold.

Why bother aggregating all this information you ask? Here are some things to consider:

- You will forget what you did, and the next time you try to do an event, you'll have to start from scratch again, unless you've kept notes.

- Analysis will help you to understand what worked and what didn't so you can refine your marketing efforts next time. It will help you solicit more of the items that sold and less of the ones that did not.

- The pretty articles, screen shots, and flyers will help you solicit future sponsors and donors. With data and samples, it's much easier to convince corporate sponsors and other partners the value of participating.

- Your analysis will help you convey how successful the event was to all involved, including board members and volunteers alike.

- Your analysis will help you set goals for the next event you wish to run.

The Big Picture

Don't try to do it all and don't try to do it alone, or you could easily find yourself overwhelmed and paralyzed by the perceived amount of work "needed" for a successful auction. It is not that complicated. Going back to our discussion at the start of the chapter, this is really about options, and having a menu of marketing methods to choose from. For your event, pick out the one or two methods that you think will have the biggest impact on results and focus on those. This focus will free you up to run a good event. Your marketing doesn't have to be perfect and publicity is on a continuum, not on or off, so whatever efforts you pursue will yield results. Not only that, but you can always test different marketing efforts on future events so don't feel you have to cram everything into your first effort.

must have

There certainly are many ways to promote your auctions. One key to success is to focus on the items you are selling (rather than your cause) when marketing. This will help the right buyers find your items. Once they find your item, you can share how purchasing this item will also benefit a good cause. Since there are a number of options, here are some tips for choosing the best marketing strategies for your auctions:

- *Focus on your strengths*. Do the marketing you know how to do and use the tools at your disposal (newsletters, e-mail, etc.).

- *Leverage your partner's strengths*. If you're working with a corporation, media or government partner that has a PR department, let them handle the press releases and some of the marketing responsibilities.

- *Look for low hanging fruit*. What are the easiest marketing things for you to do that will take the least amount of time? Work with the people who want to help you rather than try to convert those who are less enthusiastic.

(continued)

- *Delegate and coordinate.* It may be easiest if you have a number of people delegated to any given task, but you'll still need to make sure you have a central point person for PR. This way you make sure everyone is communicating the same message and that press inquiries get forwarded to a central location, so you can provide needed information and pictures in a timely manner. (It also enables you to track the coverage you receive.)

- *Make your marketing message clear.* Make sure the same branding and message appears on the About Me page and in the listings so if the media can't reach you, they already have the core information they need to be able to write about your event.

- *Be available for the media.* Especially when you send out your press release, you need to be available by phone and e-mail to answer questions from journalists on a deadline or you'll miss the opportunity.

- *Market your event before, during and after.* Every piece of media coverage after the auction helps ensure you get the biggest bang for your efforts and the most exposure possible for your cause. Follow up also endears you to the media, your sponsors, donors, volunteers, buyers, and general public.

Conclusion

Fundraising on eBay is fun, exciting, and completely doable. Sure, doing something for the first time can seem intimidating. But keep in mind that millions of people have learned how to sell on eBay, and more than 700,000 are making part or all of their living on eBay. Nonprofits need to take advantage of this marketplace, not only because of its sheer size and the opportunity to raise big money, but because it helps them reach new donors and spread the word about their important work. In its essence, using eBay for fundraising is not unlike other fundraisers, except that you don't need to hold an event and you have the upside of increased revenues from donors around the world. eBay has made selling for charity as simple as filling out a form, so give it a try! Start out small and then take advantage of the ideas and best practices in this book to scale your eBay fundraising. Good luck!

Glossary
eBay Terms

About Me   A page that you can create on eBay's web site that provides some brief personal information about you or your organization. You can showcase your current sales on this page as well.

absentee bid   A term used primarily in eBay Live Auctions and in traditional live auctions that refers to a bid placed in advance of the sale by someone who is not present when the sale is actually conducted.

as is   An item that you sell in its advertised condition and with no other warranty, either implied or stated.

auction management company   A company, such as Kompolt, that handles, on your behalf, all the work required to list, promote, and manage items for sale on eBay.

authentication service   A service that authenticates an item (such as a painting, or a piece of jewelry) as legitimate and not a fake. If your nonprofit is holding an auction at which a number of highly valuable items are up for sale, you may want to hire one of these services.

bid increment   A predetermined amount by which bids are increased as they are placed. The increment varies depending on the current high bid.

bid verification   The process of verifying that a bid is legitimate and not a "joke." It ensures the bidder is serious about the bid and will pay for the item if he or she wins.

blocked bidder   A person who has specifically been excluded from bidding on an item, usually because of problems with previous transactions.

bulk listing   The process of listing multiple items at a predetermined time, so the sales all start simultaneously.

buyer blocks   The process of identifying eBay members whose bids you will not accept, because they have zero or negative feedback, for instance. See **blocked bidder**.

Buy It Now   A way to sell your item on eBay for a fixed price. Buy It Now auctions can be conducted in one of two ways. In a Fixed Price auction, you offer an item at a fixed Buy It Now price and the buyer purchases it immediately at that price. In an online auction, the buyer can buy the item at the Buy It Now price only before the first bid is placed; after a bid is placed, the Buy It Now option disappears.

cause-related marketing   The process of holding a sale or fundraiser on behalf of a cause in order to benefit both a nonprofit and for-profit corporation.

community selling   Recruiting eBay members to donate a percentage of their sale's proceeds to benefit your nonprofit institution.

compressing (images)   Reducing the file size of a digital image by applying a formula that deletes some of the information in the image without sacrificing quality. Joint Photographic Experts Group (JPEG) has such a formula.

cropping   Eliminating a part of an image so its physical size is smaller and only the most important features appear when the image is published.

Customer Relationship Management (CRM)   The cultivation of customer relationships in order to build loyalty and encourage future purchases or donations.

direct selling   Selling on eBay by a nonprofit institution in order to benefit its own charitable cause.

eBay Motors   An auction area on the eBay web site where participants can buy and sell motor vehicles, including cars, boats, and planes.

eBay Stores   A feature that enables sellers to sell a group of items at a fixed price on their own web pages.

escrow   A way of completing transactions through the use of an intermediary. The buyer sends payment to the escrow company; the seller ships the item to the buyer; the buyer inspects and approves the item; the escrow company releases funds to the seller.

feedback   A system of communication that enables eBay users who have been involved in transactions with other users to leave comments that describe the level of responsiveness, the quality of the transaction, or related (and sometimes unrelated) issues.

fixed price format   A sales format in which eBay users can purchase an item for a fixed price the seller specifies; an alternative to the variable pricing of an auction.

Giving Board   A discussion board on eBay that has been designated for nonprofits and those who sell on their behalf to raise issues and support for one another.

high-profile event   A fundraising or other event that involves celebrities, media coverage, public relations efforts, and other strategies in order to gain maximum attention and raise the most money for the desired cause.

HTML   The abbreviation for HyperText Markup Language, the set of instructions that is used to present and format text and images on web pages (or on eBay auction descriptions).

ID Verify   A program in which sellers or buyers have their personal information verified against consumer and business databases so others can trust that they are who they say they are.

meta tags   Key words or phrases that describe your site and that are included in your web site HTML for search engines to read and classify your site.

My eBay   A starting page that aggregates all your eBay activities and preferences on one page, including feedback, selling preferences, the items you have sold, and the items you are watching, bidding on, or have purchased recently.

photo host   An organization that provides space on a web server (a computer that is connected 24/7 to the Internet) in which digital image files can be stored so they appear on the Web.

preapproved buyers   A set of eBay members who have been prequalified before the sale so they are allowed to bid. See **prequalification**.

prequalification   The process of verifying a prospective bidder's identity before a bid is allowed to be placed, in order to prevent bid retraction after the sale.

reserve price   An amount specified by a seller as the minimum price the seller is willing to accept in order to sell an item. The reserve price is kept secret until a bidder meets it. The seller is not obligated to sell an item if the reserve price has not been met.

scaling (images)   Reducing the physical size of an image so it takes up less space when it is published on a web page or in print.

second chance offer   If the high bidder or buyer of an item fails to pay, eBay enables sellers to make a second chance offer to an underbidder—giving them a chance to purchase the item because the high bidder backed out.

Trading Assistant (TA)   A person or company that has been certified by eBay and is allowed to list information in the Trading Assistants Directory. Trading Assistants sell on eBay on behalf of other sellers.

underbidders   Bidders who did not bid high enough to win an auction.

vanity URL   A short, easy-to-remember domain name that can be typed quickly when a visitor wants to connect to a particular web site. Instead of a long domain name such as www.myinternetprovider.com/~mywebsite, a vanity URL such as www.mywebsite.com is used.

Index

About the Authors

Greg Holden, an eBay PowerSeller, has been hunting down and reselling collectibles, unusual items, and antiques for much of his adult life. Greg has written more than 30 books, including the best-selling *How to Do Everything with Your eBay Business* (now in its second edition), and *The Collector's Guide to eBay*. He is acknowledged as being one of the top book authors and experts writing about eBay, and is a frequent contributor to the AuctionBytes web site (http://www.auctionbytes.com). Before becoming an author, Greg worked for more than 12 years at a well-known nonprofit institution, the University of Chicago, as an editor and publications manager.

Jill Finlayson has been buying and selling on eBay since 1997, but not content with being only an eBay user, she joined the fledgling startup in 1998 and ran the eBay Toys and Hobbies categories for nearly five years. During this time, she helped numerous companies and nonprofits hold charity auctions on eBay, and she was a member of the first eBay Foundation Governance Committee. Like her coauthor, Jill also worked at a nonprofit institution, her alma mater the University of California at Berkeley, where she coordinated volunteer research projects around the world, fostered intercultural programs at the International House, and devised emergency preparedness and disaster recovery plans for the campus. Now vice president for product development at M Networks, Jill develops books, training, and curriculum materials for seminars, expos, and online courses designed to teach individuals, small businesses, and nonprofits how to use the Internet effectively to start or expand their business.